THE GLORY OF ATHENS
The Popular Tradition as Reflected in the Panathenaicus of Aelius Aristides

By

JOSEPH W. DAY

ARES PUBLISHERS, INC.
CHICAGO   MCMLXXX

Copyright 1980
ARES PUBLISHERS, INC.
7020 N. Western Avenue
Chicago, IL 60645-3416

Printed in the United States of America
International Standard Book Number
0-89005-346-4

THE GLORY OF ATHENS
The Popular Tradition as Reflected in the Panathenaicus of Aelius Aristides

For
My Mother and Father

CONTENTS

Preface ix

List of Abbreviations xi

Introduction xiii

Chapter I   *Oratorical and Historical Concepts of Truth in Historiography* 1

Chapter II   *Triptolemus as an Athenian Political Symbol* 15

Chapter III   *The Departure of the Spartans* 39

Chapter IV   *The Battle of Eurymedon* 75

Chapter V   *The Athenian Intervention in the Revolt of Egypt* 107

Chapter VI   *The Peace of Callias* 140

Chapter VII *Conclusion: The Transmission of The Tradition* 172

Appendix I 181

Appendix II 197

Bibliography 201

Indices 211

PREFACE

Just as today a foreigner visiting Athens might remark with a smile upon the local citizens' fierce pride in their city's past, the tendency of ancient Athenians to glorify the history of Attica struck Tacitus and Lucian as quaint. Theopompus exhibited less patience when he attacked popular versions of Athenian history as tendentious boastfulness, and certain historians of our era have followed his lead by attempting to search out the 'facts' and by discarding the 'glory' as mere political propaganda. In spite of such criticism in ancient and modern scholarship, however, no student of antiquity can ignore the glorification of Athens in literature and art. This leitmotif is naturally almost universal in Attic works of all ages, and various forms of it, particularly the one which represents Periclean Athens as a golden age, have constituted an integral part of the classicizing tradition of the West.

The present monograph, which is a revised version of my doctoral dissertation (Stanford, 1978), began as a hopelessly broad attempt to study the glorification of Athenian history in Attic literature. Under the gentle, able, and much appreciated tutelage of A.E. Raubitschek, it was transformed into an examination of Aristides' *Panathenaicus* which has been intended to serve as a methodological paradigm for the study of the whole Athenian popular tradition as well as a detailed investigation of one segment of that tradition. Insofar as the present work contains anything worthwhile, therefore, it owes very much to Professor Raubitschek's advice and to his own research in this and related fields. I should also like to acknowledge the influence of one of my undergraduate teachers, another student of Professor Raubitschek, F.W. Schlatter, S.J., under whom my interest in Athenian popular history was first aroused in a class and a senior thesis on Isocrates. Where I have exceeded the limits of the evidence, not to mention those of probability, the fault is entirely my own.

A special debt of gratitude is owed to my wife and colleague, Leslie Preston Day, whose scholarly acumen has provided me with many useful suggestions and whose critical reading has led to the correction of numerous errors. I am also most grateful for the unceasing moral and financial support of my parents, to whom this volume is affectionately dedicated. Furthermore, I have the sad duty of recalling the memory of my aunt, Gladys McGregor, who bequeathed to me a sum of money to help defray the cost of publishing this book.

I also wish to thank Messrs. Al. N. Oikonomides and Joseph Breslin of the Ares Press, whose generosity and editorial assistance have proved invaluable throughout the process of publication. Finally, I should like to express my appreciation to the College of Wooster for a generous grant, which has made the publication of this study possible.

The College of Wooster   J.W.D.
April 1980

LIST OF ABBREVIATIONS

ATL	*The Athenian Tribute Lists* by B.D. Meritt, H.T. Wade-Gery, and M.F. McGregor, 4 vols., Cambridge (Mass.), I; Princeton, II-IV, 1939-53.
Beecke, *Historischen Angaben*	E. Beecke, *Die historischen Angaben in Aelius Aristides Panathenaikos auf ihre Quellen untersucht* (Diss. Strassburg, 1905).
Behr, *Sacred Tales*	C.A. Behr, *Aelius Aristides and the Sacred Tales* (Chicago: Argonaut, 1968).
Busolt, *Gr. Gesch.*	G. Busolt, *Griechische Geschichte*² (Gotha: Perthes, vol. II, 1895; vol. III, 1, 1897).
FGrH, or Jacoby, *FGrH*	F. Jacoby, *Die Fragmente der griechischen Historiker* (Berlin and Leiden: 1923-).
Gomme, *HCT*	A.W. Gomme, *A Historical Commentary on Thucydides*, 3 vols. to V. 24 (Oxford, 1945-1956).
IG	*Inscriptiones Graecae consilio et auctoritate Academiae Litterarum Borussicae editae* (Berlin, 1873-).
Lenz, *Aristeidesscholien*	F. Lenz, *Untersuchungen zu den Aristeidesscholien* (Berlin: Weidmann, 1934).
Lenz, *Prolegomena*	F. Lenz, *The Aristeides Prolegomena, Mnemosyne* suppl. 5 (Leiden: Brill, 1959).
Loeb Aristides	Aristides trans. by C.A. Behr, in the Loeb Classical Library, 4 vols., Cambridge (Mass.), I, 1973.
Meiggs, *Athenian Empire*	R. Meiggs, *The Athenian Empire* (Oxford, 1972).
Meyer, *Forschungen*	E. Meyer, *Forschungen zur alten Geschichte*, vol. II (Halle: Niemeyer, 1899).
ML	R. Meiggs and D. Lewis, *A Selection of Greek Historical Inscriptions* (Oxford, 1969).
Oliver, *Civilizing Power*	J.H. Oliver, *The Civilizing Power: A Study of the Panathenaic Discourse of Aelius Aristides* (Philadelphia: American Philosophical Society, 1968) = *Transactions of the American Philosophical Society* 58, 1.
Oliver, *Ruling Power*	J.H. Oliver, *The Ruling Power: A Study of the Roman Empire in the Second Century after Christ through the Roman Oration of Aelius Aristides* (Philadelphia: American Philosophical Society,

	1953) = *Transactions of the American Philosophical Society* 43, 4.
RE	Pauly-Wissowa-Kroll, *Real-Encyclopadie der klassischen Altertumswissenschaft* (Stuttgart, 1894-).
SEG	*Supplementum Epigraphicum Graecum.*
De Ste Croix, *Origins*	G. de Ste. Croix, *The Origins of the Peloponnesian War* (Ithaca: Cornell, 1972).

INTRODUCTION

Athens never regained the political and military independence that Philip had shattered at Chaeronea. Moreover, in spite of the well-known and deserved distinction of her philosophical schools, the status and spirit of the city suffered a gradual eclipse that reached its darkest point when Athens collaborated with Mithridates and endured Sulla's retribution.[1] In time, however, the Athenians learned to reconcile themselves with their foreign masters so well, that from the end of the first century before Christ Athens began to take her proper place in a cosmopolitan world. Under the philhellenic emperor Hadrian and his friend, Herodes Atticus, Athena's city prospered as a major international center. Simultaneously, the entire Greek East was experiencing a classicizing renaissance in art and literature, especially in the genres of history and oratory.[2] A new generation of sophists, men like Dio Chrysostom and Aelius Aristides, discovered a faith in the Hellenism they found embodied in the historical and cultural traditions of classical Athens. They frequently preached their message by telling the story of Athens in historical declamations. Predictably, their inquiries rarely took them beyond Chaeronea and never past the death of Alexander;[3] yet they repeatedly extolled the mythical and classical glories of Athens in orations that could almost have been composed in the fifth or fourth century B.C. An exemplar of this sort of discourse is Aristides' *Panathenaicus*.[4]

When modern students of antiquity attempt to reconstruct fifth-century Athenian history, they give short shrift to the historical oratory of the Second Sophistic in their understandable preference for primary sources.[5] Around a skeleton of more or less incontestable archaeological and epigraphical data, they construct a continuous narrative from the accounts of Herodotus, Thucydides, Xenophon, and Aristotle.[6] The lesser historians of the fourth century are now largely lost, but they exert some influence on modern historiography through later compilers, historians, biographers, scholiasts, and lexicographers, whose works are sifted for fragments of Ephorus, Theopompus, and the Atthidographers. Insofar as the oratorical tradition of the later or, for that matter, the earlier sophists comes into view at all, it is used only to supplement the more 'historical' testimony. Thus, although Aristides' *Panathenaicus* consists primarily of a continuous history of Athens, its lateness and artificiality appear to preclude its use as evidence except in the case of events for which other sources fail the historian.[7] Aristides is correctly perceived as occupying a position in the Isocratean tradition against which Mr. Meiggs levels a serious criticism.

> This sharp decline in critical judgement is in large part due to the influence of rhetoric for which Isocrates must take much of the blame. The fifth century had been more interested in substance than in form.... Rhetoric was more concerned with persuasion than with truth and developed an unhealthy interest in ornament; the historian's function was extended to include that of the moral teacher.[8]

From the viewpoint of a search for the facts about historical events, Meiggs' criticism is well taken and even appears to place him beside Thucydides, who deprecated the historicity of epideictic oratory and the more romantic flights of political rhetoric.[9] Contemporary historians, however, would do well to consider more closely the practice of Herodotus and Thucydides. Both authors believed that the historian ought to investigate people's opinions as well as their actions, a dual commitment that was felt to apply particularly to the study of real or alleged causes of political events. Since a people's image of its own past can profoundly affect present and future policy, the ancient historians found room in their works for the mythical pretensions, patriotic vaunts, outright falsifications, and popular versions of well-known events that were standard fare in oratory. Herodotus' version of the Athenian speech before Plataea exhibits the same boastful commonplaces, the same chauvinistic view of history as one finds in Isocrates and Aristides.[10] Thucydides put the same topics into the speech delivered by Athenian diplomats at Sparta in 432, and he made Pericles develop other patriotic topics in the *Epitaphios*.[11] The great historians of the fifth century accepted the clichés in these speeches as genuine elements of the received tradition and important gauges of popular opinion; yet they reconciled this acceptance with a severely critical attitude towards the accuracy of the popular versions of events.[12] These commonplaces are no less deserving of our attention; they ought to be studied regardless of their compatibility with our understanding of events themselves.

The conclusion of the previous paragraph assumes added significance when we examine the life of the 'popular tradition' itself. The commonplaces noted above antedated the composition of the great fifth-century histories just as they continued to find expression in later literature. In fact, I will contend in the following chapters that the historical topics of Greek oratory went back to an oratorical version of history which represented more than occasional storytelling or blatant propaganda. When taken together with similar references to events in other popular media, this version can be seen to have constituted a continuous tradition of Athenian history rooted in popular stories that originated amongst Athenians very soon after the events themselves. This Athenian popular tradition of fifth-century history was transmitted in the first place by oral media whose influence we can still detect in scolia, epigrams, tragedy, family traditions, and of course extant oratory. Fifth-century monuments, inscriptions, and works of art echoed the oral tradition, and within a generation of Plataea the popular history of the city of Athens acquired its own form of literature with the advent of the *Atthis*. Undoubtedly, the canonical historians presented in their narrative sections a more accurate version of history than this tradition did; yet a study of the popular tradition can tell us something about the way most Athenians viewed their past, expand our knowledge of lost or fragmentary testimonia, and serve as a paradigm for analyzing the mechanics of all popular traditions of history. In addition, the importance of the popular tradition as evidence for purely factual history increases dramatically for the period of the fifth century which lacks its proper historian.[13] Thucydides' Pentecontaetia is a mere summary, and the popular tradition offers an important alternative to his brief account of that period. Moreover, the mere absence of 'historical' evidence does not supply us with the only reason for taking the popular tradition more seriously than heretofore. Fifth- and fourth-century audiences and readers seem to have exhibited a certain critical sense, and, although they may appear to us to have been rather gullible, we cannot completely identify their credulity with naiveté. Speakers in

Herodotus and Thucydides showed a reluctance to rely on purely mythical paradigms, which they felt could not support serious claims of credibility.[14] Instead, they quickly moved on to recent historical events, the authenticity of which was guaranteed by the fact that everyone knew them.[15] When oratory moved from the podium to the pamphlet, writers like Isocrates bolstered their claims upon their readers' critical sense with specific references to the truth and accuracy of their historical allusions.[16] Cicero, a thoroughgoing Isocratean, understood perfectly well the claims of historical oratory and even subsumed history itself under the genre of epideictic oratory: *videtisne quantum munus sit oratoris historia?*[17] The pretensions to historical accuracy reappear in Aristides, who carefully reproduced the vocabulary of previous oratorical historiography. We cannot easily dismiss these claims of truth in speeches which gained such widespread popularity as the encomia of Athens did. Consequently, I propose to examine these claims and their bases in the following chapter, before going on to study Aristides' *Panathenaicus* in relation to the popular tradition.

The *Panathenaicus* contains a more extensive history of Athens than can be found in any extant, popular medium. The work would therefore be of great value for the student of the Athenian tradition, if it could be shown to have reproduced the popular version of history carefully. Thus, in an attempt to lay a foundation for further study of this and similar documents, the present monograph will consist primarily of a demonstration that Aristides faithfully followed the Athenian popular tradition in his account of Athens' continuation of the war against Persia in the first part of the Pentecontaetia. In each of the five main chapters, I will examine in detail one element of the popular tradition and trace the close affinity between the text of the *Panathenaicus* and the consistent view that can be derived from the often fragmentary and usually casual references to the same element in earlier popular media. Although in each case I have used evidence from the fifth century to authenticate particular stories or details as elements of the true popular tradition, it can be inferred that Aristides also reproduced the traditional Athenian version of many events which are beyond the scope of this monograph and for which the earlier evidence has completely disappeared. It is, of course, much harder to pinpoint Aristides' source for any particular statement, and his allusive style betrays a penchant for voluminous research into a wide variety of sources.[18] We can, however, make suggestions about the kinds of sources he used. Most scholars assume that Aristides employed only literary sources, and one can certainly discover the influence of the *Atthis,* Ephorus, Aeschylus' *Persae,* and especially such oratorical works as the *Panegyricus,* the *Epitaphios* in the *Menexenus,* and undoubtedly declamations of the Hellenistic period.[19] We should not, however, ignore the possibility that a living version of the popular tradition survived at Athens in oral media and ceremonial practices down to Aristides' day. This suggestion will receive special attention in the final chapter.

1. Such a statement should be qualified somewhat in the light of the philanthropy of certain Hellenistic monarchs towards Athens and other bright spots in the city's history. Cf. W.S. Ferguson, *Hellenistic Athens* (London: St. Martin's, 1911); M. Rostovtzeff, *The Social and Economic History of the Hellenistic World* (Oxford, 1941); J. Day, *An Economic History of Athens under Roman Domination* (Columbia Univ., 1942).

2. Cf. E. Bowie, "Greeks and their Past in the Second Sophistic," *Past and Present* 46 (1970) 3-41.

3. *Ibid.,* pp. 10-25.

4. The *Panathenaicus* became something of a textbook for those who would praise a city. This was effected by Menander the Rhetorician, who employed the *Panath.* as his chief model in a handbook on discourses in praise of cities. Cf. Oliver, *Civilizing Power,* p. 19; A. Boulanger, *Aelius Aristide et la sophistique dans la province d' Asie au II'siècle de notre ère* (Bibliothèque des Écoles française d' Athènes et de Rome, 126: Paris, 1923), p. 369, n. 2.

5. I use the term primary in its normal sense here: cf. A.E. Raubitschek, "Theophrastus on Ostracism," *Cl Med* 19 (1958) 74f. For alternative definitions, cf. Appendix I.

6. The status of at least the first three authors was recognized in antiquity. They, along with Theopompus, were considered canonical by the author of Treatise B, part of the prolegomena to the Scholia on Aristides: cf. Lenz, *Prolegomena,* p. 115.

7. A conspicuous example appears in G. Hill, *Sources for Greek History*[2], ed. by R. Meiggs and A. Andrewes (Oxford, 1951), p. 342f., where Aristides is cited only for the vexed problem of the First Peloponnesian War, despite the fact that the *Panath.* contains a narration of numerous events from the Pentecontaetia.

8. Meiggs, *Athenian Empire,* p. 8f.

9. Thuc. I. 22. 4, calls the epideictic work an $ἀγώνισμα$, a term which would have been acceptable to Isocrates, who likened his oratorical effort to an athletic $ἀγών$: cf. the prologues of the *Panegyricus* (4) and *Helen* (10). Cf., also, M.I. Finley, *The Use and Abuse of History* (New York: Viking Press, 1975), pp. 13, 29, and 45f., who cites Ranke's famous, *wie es eigentlich gewesen ist.*

10. Hdt. IX. 27. I should point out that Meiggs himself is not insensitive to the importance of popular media: cf. *Athenian Empire,* "Fifth-Century Judgements," pp. 375-396.

11. Thuc. I. 73ff. Cf. A.E. Raubitschek, "The Speech of the Athenians at Sparta," in *The Speeches in Thucydides: A Collection of Original Essays,* ed. by P. Stadter (University of North Carolina, 1973), pp. 32-48. Cf., also, Thuc. II. 36. 4; V. 89; VI. 82f.

12. Thuc. I. 20ff.: cf. *infra,* Chapter II.

13. Cf. Finley, *supra,* n. 9, pp. 22 and 216, n. 19.

14. Cf. the speeches mentioned in nn. 10 and 11, *supra;* Isoc. *Paneg.* (4), 30.

15. Hdt. IX. 27. 4; Thuc. I. 73. 2. For the Attic orators' care in attributing a popularly accepted source to their historical allusions, cf. F.W. Schlatter, S.J., *Salamis and Plataea in the Tradition of the Attic Orators* (Diss. Princeton, 1960), p. 11ff. For an oral society's ability to maintain accurate versions of historic events over a long period of time, cf. Finley, *supra,* n. 9, pp. 24-30; A. Momigliano, *Studies in Historiography* (London: Weidenfeld and Nicolson, 1966), pp. 211-20.

16. Cf. *infra.,* Chapter II.

17. *De or.* II. 62. Cf. *Or.* 37, 66, 207; *De leg.* I. 5.

18. J. Haury, *Quibus fontibus Aristides usus sit in declamatione quae inscribitur* Παναθηναικός (Diss. Augsburg, 1888), attempted to demonstrate that Aristides relied almost exclusively on Ephorus. Beecke, *Historischen Angaben,* and Oliver, *Civilizing Power,* detect a much wider use of sources by Aristides.

19. For the importance of Hellenistic oratory as a link between the fifth-century sophists and the Second Sophistic, cf. G. Kennedy, *The Art of Rhetoric in the Roman World* (Princeton, 1972), p. 560.

CHAPTER I
ORATORICAL AND HISTORICAL CONCEPTS OF TRUTH IN HISTORIOGRAPHY

Aelius Aristides' monumental encomium upon the city of Athens encompasses a continuous narrative of Athenian history from the beginnings to Chaeronea. After the splendors of the Attic countryside have passed before the reader as a series of symbolic manifestations of Athenian philanthropy, the land gives birth to men and so begins the parade of patriotic Athenian mythology. Subsequently, Aristides abandons the world of myth and abruptly enters the historical period with his account of the Persian War.[1] Faced with the proliferation of sources for the relatively well-documented fifth century, Aristides apologizes for his inability to survey all the stories and states the criteria of his eclecticism (I. 194):

> *Now we have to face the equally difficult tasks of determining which stories must be left out and of worthily narrating those which deserve to be told. Even in a simple chronicle, no one has ever fully recounted all the events of Athenian history. People are always writing on the subject of Athens, and in fact she has practically received more encomia than all other cities combined. As a result, it is impossible to go through each and every detail accurately; we have to omit the majority of details in order to concentrate on the greatest.*

When Aristides confronts the prospect of more omissions later in the oration, he recalls the apology cited above and further defines his methodology (I. 260):

> *Moreover, as I have said, I do not intend to relate in full all the events of Athenian history in the manner of a simple chronicle—even that would take me five years to recite. It is my intention to bring up the city's most noble wartime achievements and to do the utmost to avoid omitting any of her recorded excellences. I can accomplish this, not by going through each detail of Athenian history, but by omitting no form of praise.*

Aristides employs a highly selective vocabulary in the two methodological statements quoted above and in other, less detailed passages of the *Panathenaicus*.² He is always most concerned with the Athenian ἦυος,³ and he asserts that his interpretation of Athens' moral worth presents the truth (μετ' ἀληϑείας).⁴ In another passage, he again identifies himself with those who examine each important event accurately (δι' ἀκριβείας), and he calls this activity, ἡ περὶ τὰς ἀποδείξεις σπουδή and ἡ ἐξέτασις.⁵ Aristides aims at the ethical improvement of his hearers, and his method consists in accurately presenting carefully selected events as paradigms of virtue and vice. Thus far, Aristides' words speak for themselves, but a philological analysis of the terms with which he describes his historical method will indicate how he explicitly places himself in a long tradition of historiography.

Aristides' historiographical terminology repeats the equally pregnant and indeed nearly identical vocabulary of certain methodological statements of Isocrates. Ἀκρίβεια and ἁπλότης appear as opposites in the epilogue of Isocrates' *Panathenaicus*, in which the orator and a fictitious critic discuss the literary merits of the main body of the oration. The critic characterizes this as an educational speech, filled with philosophy, artistic expertise, and mythological elements as well as a great quantity of Athenian history; yet he says that these qualities become manifest only to the person who reads the discourse accurately (ἀκριβῶς). To casual readers, the work will appear to be simple (ἁπλοῦν).⁶ The orator himself subsequently expands upon the key requirements of this historical oratory of his (*Panath.* (12), 271):

> Let me just express my admiration for those of my hearers who fully accept this speech. They know that seriousness and philosophy reside, first, in educational and artistically wrought discourses rather than in the kind that are written for show or the courtroom; secondly, in speeches that aim at the truth rather than those that seek to mislead the opinions of the audiences; and, finally, in those that reprove and admonish the sinful.⁷

When Isocrates claims that his form of discourse contains seriousness (σπουδή), philosophy, and truth, he is asserting that it teaches ethical behavior through mythical and historical paradigms. By implication, then, Isocrates would agree with Aristotle's opinion that history of the simple sort⁸ is incapable of functioning as a serious pedagogical tool (*Poet.* 1451b):

> *The historian and the poet.... The difference between their functions is that, while the former records events that have actually happened, the latter records those that might happen. Consequently, philosophy and seriousness reside in poetry rather than history, since poetry is the more universal pursuit and history is confined to a detailed examination of particulars.*

The philosopher and the orator diverge, because Aristotle follows a more traditional line by extolling the educational value of poetry, while Isocrates' remarks illustrate his frequently stated intention of transferring the stewardship of Hellenic education from poetry to his own brand of oratory.[9] In both cases, however, it is the genre of history that suffers by comparison.

In spite of the disparaging remarks of Aristotle and similar criticism of history in the orators, however, the Greek historians had long been voicing their claims upon the attention of serious students of the past.[10] Hecataeus professed a commitment to the truth,[11] and Herodotus' historical method consisted in sifting various accounts of an event in order to state the facts with total accuracy. Nevertheless, although Herodotus' term for accuracy (ἀτρέκεια) was the Ionic equivalent of the Attic ἀκρίβεια, the word always connoted certitude of fact rather than ethical interpretation.[12] The Ionians did not engage in the sort of ethical investigation for educational purposes that Isocrates, Aristotle, and Aristides believed to be the most worthwhile sort of historiographical activity. Ionian historiography was the sort that they would call 'simple,' and it should be noted that, in the context of the passage cited above, Aristotle mentions Herodotus as the historian *par excellence*.

Attic historiography began to deviate from the Ionian tradition with Thucydides, whom Aristotle rather pointedly omitted from his criticism of history. In his most explicit statement of methodology, the historian unambiguously claims to tell the truth with particular exactitude in matters of fact (I. 22. 2):[13]

> *As to the details about the actual events of the war, I did not think it right to base my investigation on any chance source or even my own opinion. Instead, I have limited myself to recording either those events at which I myself was present or those that I have heard from others but have investigated individually with as much accuracy as possible.*

If this passage were to be removed from its context, it would simply repeat the assertions of the Ionians,[14] whom Thucydides criticizes severely elsewhere.[15] However, Thucydides goes on to explain the ultimate aims of his work, and those aims are to some extent practical (I.22.4):[16]

> *I will be satisfied if my history is considered useful by those readers who want to examine a clear record of past events and of the similar and parallel events that will occur again in good time thanks to the consistency of man's nature. My work has been composed as a possession for all time rather than a contest-piece for casual listening.*

To make his work universally valid, Thucydides did not simply report words and deeds: his inquiry required him to delve beneath the surface and distinguish true causes from mere pretexts.[17] He then set forth his interpretations in a manner designed to educate rather than please.[18]

In the following centuries, historians considered the production of ethical paradigms to be their primary function, but this development did not stem from the influence of Thucydides as much as from the expanding authority of Isocrates. The commitment to truth and accuracy remained; yet, in varying degrees, the rhetorical goals of education and pleasure invaded the realm of history.[19] At its worst this tendency fostered the growth of simplistic moralizers and tragical historians, but a tradition of reliable, albeit oratorical, history remained.[20] For example, Theopompus actively burrowed below the surface of events to discover virtue and vice and to assign praise and blame accordingly.[21] It was presumably this practice which earned him the epithet 'lover of truth' (φιλαλήθης).[22] Ephorus, though perhaps less ambitious than Theopompus,[23] wrote history on the model of Isocrates' oratory; he attempted to improve the character of his readers by presenting moral exempla.[24] According to Polybius, history provided the best practical education for men of affairs.[25] Its learned interpretation of facts should inculcate exact understanding (ἐπιστήμην... ἀτρεκῆ) into the student and thereby bring him benefit and pleasure.[26] Polybius could even feel justified in reversing Aristotle's distinction between history and tragedy. The Hellenistic historian maintained that, since poetry was confined to the merely plausible, its sole function was to attract or inspire an audience momentarily.[27] History, on the other hand, dealt with the truth (τἀληθές) and therefore had the power to edify lovers of learning (φιλομαθοῦντας). An examination of Plutarch's *Lives* will indicate how thoroughly these ideals of history were translated into biography. Plutarch rejected any attempt to go through the anecdotes about his subject καθ' ἕκαστον; he selected only those stories that could illustrate ἦϑος.²⁸ Finally, in the tradition of these Greek writers, the best Roman historians never lost sight of Cicero's insistence upon truth being the first law of history, but they consistently maintained that the chief value of history lay in the edification of the reader. Sallust, Livy, and Tacitus consciously practiced Cicero's rule that in history *significari quid probet scriptor*.²⁹ It is no wonder that Cicero repeatedly identified history as a branch of epideictic oratory together with encomia and works such as Isocrates' *Panegyricus*.³⁰

Cicero was a sufficiently astute critic to recognize a real similarity between the aims and methods of oratory and history; yet the two genres clearly produced different results. Scholars have long recognized that historical allusions in the orators were frequently at variance with historians' accounts of the same events. This fact poses a question which is vital for my investigation: who or what caused the divergence between historians and orators in matters of fact? The most obvious answer derives from the essential methodological difference between historiography and rhetoric. A competent historian begins from a mass of particulars: the various details and accounts found in his sources. He judges the sources and sifts the accounts until he produces a narrative which he considers accurate.³¹ This highly personal product provides a foundation for ethically universal conclusions. History, regardless of the bias exhibited in its conclusions, remains committed to the organized presentation of a large body of facts which appear in their proper sequence and context. The starting point for the orator, however, is his immediate rhetorical purpose: persuasion, praise, blame, etc. If he alludes to historical events, it is solely to those which demonstrate the validity of his purpose.³² Moreover, since an allusion to a single important event or individual carries more dramatic weight than a mass of details, orators capitalize on a small number of particularly important events that tend to become commonplaces.³³ Sequence and context too often lose their significance, and a certain cavalier attitude can arise regarding historical facts.

The story of Harmodius and Aristogiton would seem to offer a useful paradigm of the divergence between a historical and an oratorical version of the same event.³⁴ Numerous orators referred to these men as tyrannicides who murdered the Pisistratid tyrant Hipparchus and thus brought freedom to Athens.³⁵ In each case, however, the reference served a rhetorical purpose: normally the orator brought forward the tyrannicides as a standard of patriotism against which he could judge the subject of his discourse for good or ill. Historians, on the other hand, sifted through the sources and, without the bias or exaggeration of the orators, they discovered the true and sobering facts: Hipparchus' brother Hippias was the tyrant, and the former's murder was neither politically motivated nor fatal to the tyranny.[36] The difference between historical and oratorical methodology, then, would nicely explain the difference between history and oratory in this case, were it not for the overwhelming support that the oratorical version receives from other genres and media. Not long after the event itself, the Athenians dedicated to their 'tyrannicides' the first honorary statues ever erected for individuals and apparently adorned the monument with an epigram in praise of the assassination.[37] Subsequently, other statues were erected to these heroes, and imitations appeared in various artistic media.[38] There were also fifth-century scolia honoring Harmodius and Aristogiton as tyrant-slayers, and the oratorical version of the story eventually secured a place in the *Atthis*.[39] The popular story even became embodied in Athenian social practice, since the descendants of Harmodius and Aristogiton received special privileges from the city.[40] The tyrannicides continued to excite the popular imagination at least until Lucian's day.[41]

In the tradition of the tyrant-slayers and in many similar cases, rhetorical expediency cannot explain either the amazing unanimity shown by the popular media or even the consistency amongst the orators themselves. We must posit the existence of some influence stronger than rhetorical methodology in order to explain how orators and artists, poets and local historians could have consistently proclaimed exaggerations and half-truths to hearers who should have known better. This 'influence' need not remain a vague archetype, since certain ancient critics of the oratorical tradition perceived its power and, by attempting to expose it, provoked Isocrates into defending himself against their attacks.

Lucian, despite his late date, used fifth-century terminology and concepts with such familiarity that he might well illuminate the literary controversy of half a millenium before his own age. When he chose to deal with history proper rather than school exercises, he demanded Thucydidean standards and reaffirmed the distinction between history and encomium which his contemporaries had confused. The Ionians would have felt at home with Lucian's description of historiography as, συγγράφειν ἱστορίαν, διεξιέναι πράξεις and τὰ γεγενημένα.⁴² Historical oratory, on the other hand, received scorn from a 'serious' Lucian, who parodied orators' attempts to win fame in Athens by expatiating upon all too familiar topics such as Marathon.⁴³ Apparently the Athenian public in Lucian's time was just as prepared to applaud boastful pretensions about its glorious past as it had been when Theopompus complained about the spurious vaunts and deceptive historiography that were prevalent amongst Athenians.⁴⁴ It was Thucydides, however, who mounted the most consistent attack against general acceptance of inaccurate, popular stories:

1. I. 20. 1: *It is simply in our nature as men to accept from each other accounts of the past on hearsay and without proper checking even when the events happened in our own country.*

2. I. 20. 3: *There are also a good many other traditions, even ones about the present, ones that have not been long forgotten, that the other Greeks completely misconstrue.... This is how carelessly people pursue the search for the truth; they just turn to the most readily available sources.*

3. VI. 54. 1: *I will demonstrate that neither the Athenians nor anyone else speak accurately about their tyrants or any other aspects of their past.*⁴⁵

Interestingly, the first and last of these passages come from Thucydides' criticism of the popular story about the tyrannicides. The implication of Thucydides' remarks is that this and other popular anecdotes became so canonical that any contradiction of them displeased Athenian audiences.⁴⁶ What was worse, the basis of these stories' appeal was nothing more than hearsay or oral tradition (ἀκοάς).⁴⁷

The reaction which the historians' criticisms evoked from Isocrates amounts to a statement of his reliance on the very tradition which the critics deplored (*Panath.* (12), 149):

Perhaps there might be some who would criticize me—there is certainly nothing that prohibits me from interrupting my speech—because I dare to recount, in the manner of someone who has accurate knowledge, events at which I was not present.

This is the orator's perception of the historians' challenge: Isocrates' answer follows (*Panath.* (12), 150):

I could demonstrate that all men obtain more exact understanding from 'hearsay' than from personal observation. We come to know far more great and noble deeds by hearing about them from others than we could ever hope to experience in person.

Isocrates bases his claims of ethical accuracy (ἀκρίβεια) on the 'hearsay' (ἀκοῆς ἀκηκόασιν) which Thucydides condemned. The very popularity of the stories guarantees their authenticity: διὰ γὰρ τὸ πολλοὺς εἰρηκέναι καὶ πάντας ἀκηκοέναι προσήκει μὴ καινὰ μέν, πιστὰ δὲ δοκεῖν εἶναι τὰ λεγόμενα περὶ αὐτῶν.[48] The orator might choose and interpret historical anecdotes for rhetorical purposes, but he would neither invent history nor disturb the essential details of the popular versions (*Paneg.* (4), 9):[49]

Events that have occurred in the past are the common property of us all; yet it is the peculiar task of the well-educated to apply them to the correct circumstance, to construe a properly logical context for each of them, and to set out the whole in a fitting style.

In the criticisms of the historians and the defense of Isocrates, we can recognize the pervasive influence which forced the historical allusions of the orators into a single mold: the influence of a unified popular tradition of Athenian history. As we have seen in the case of Harmodius and Aristogiton, this tradition has come down to us in artistic media, inscriptions, and the works of poets, local historians, logographers, and especially orators; but it survived and flourished in antiquity because the general public saw and heard it constantly and believed in it. Athenian listeners would applaud only those anecdotes which conformed to their versions of the facts, and apparently they all accepted very similar versions. This might seem to imply that the popular tradition was continuous in its entirety as well as consistent in its particulars, since many major events from Athenian myth and history found their way into popular media. Unfortunately, we cannot easily confirm this implication or even study the particulars properly at their roots, since no sufficiently continuous version of the popular tradition remains from the fifth or even fourth centuries. The surviving *Epitaphioi*, especially that of Lysias and the one in the *Menexenus*, and Isocrates' *Panegyricus* and *Panathenaicus* present the most nearly continuous accounts, but they emphasize or ignore anecdotes with a view to demonstrating their theses and consequently do not present the whole tradition as most Athenians would have known it.[50] This is particularly true of the tradition about the relations between Athens and Persia during the Pentecontaetia, which tended to be overshadowed by the achievements of the Persian War in Greece or omitted to make room for the domestic Greek politics of the period. The only oratorical work which seems to give a detailed account of the popular tradition of the Persian conflict during the Pentecontaetia, and indeed for all Athenian history, is Aristides' *Panathenaicus*, to which I now return.

There is no question that Aristides narrated a longer, more detailed, and more continuous history of Athens than any other orator. The problems arise in trying to determine how faithful Aristides' account remained to the classical Athenian tradition and what his particular sources were. The question of sources, that is, the transmission of the tradition to Aristides, will receive brief attention in the final chapter. For a student of the tradition rather than of Aristides, however, the former problem is more pressing and, fortunately, more easily solvable. Ancient and modern commentators agree that Aristides employed a wide variety of literary and possibly monumental sources.[51] His extensive research had familiarized him with all the commonplaces of encomiastic literature and a great many other details of Athenian history (I. 152):

> Some sing the best poems they can create to honor Athens' ancient history and her affinity with the gods; others, in recounting just a part of Athens' war-record, pick as their topic a war against other Greeks or, in different cases, a war against the barbarians; still others go into the details of the constitution; and, finally, there are those who address funeral orations to men who have died.

In the face of such a massive and comprehensive body of tradition, Aristides affected the same insecurity as Isocrates had before him.[52] Isocrates, of course, found his way through the inundation of historical anecdotes by following the lead of the popular tradition.[53] A process of natural selection, as it were, had guaranteed that only those stories became popular which were capable of accurately (ἀκριβῶς) inculcating ethical paradigms. As we saw at the beginning of the chapter, Aristides purported to imitate Isocrates in making ἀκρίβεια his goal and thus in determining to recount fully and truthfully only the most important events. In theory, then, we would expect Aristides' use of the word ἀκρίβεια to be doubly significant. The word clearly denotes correctness in ethical interpretation; yet it should also serve as a signword to alert an Athenian audience that the authenticity of the moral lesson is guaranteed by its place in the popular tradition. The weak spot in this theory is that a bookish dilettante like Aristides might repeat Isocrates' methodological pronouncements without understanding or intending to implement them.

It remains, therefore, to select a continuous and suitably extensive series of anecdotes from Aristides' *Panathenaicus* and to compare it with what we know of the fifth- and fourth-century popular tradition. In this way, I can hope to test my theory that for Aristides, just as for the earlier orators, ἀκρίβεια implied accuracy in following the popular tradition as well as in moral interpretation. I have selected for scrutiny five passages which appear in succession in the first half of Aristides' section on the Pentecontaetia. They are: the myth of Triptolemus as a political symbol, the transfer of the hegemony of the naval alliance from Sparta to Athens, the Battle of Eurymedon, the Athenian expedition to Egypt, and the Peace of Callias.

---

1. The fourth century panegyrics and the *Epitaphioi* exhibit a similarly drastic break between the mythical period and the Persian Wars. This may reflect the origin of the epitaphic tradition in the Persian Wars: cf. K. Walters, "We Fought Alone at Marathon" (unpublished paper delivered at the Spring meeting of the local chapter of the Friends of Ancient History in Los Angeles, 1975). Mr. Walters referred to O. Schroeder, *De laudibus Athenarum a poetis tragicis et ab oratoribus epidicticis excultis* (Diss. Göttingen, 1914), pp. 68-76. Cf. *infra*, Chapter VII, nn. 16 and 21.

2. In this and what follows, I am very much indebted to Professor Oliver's discussion of the technical terms in Aristides and earlier literature: *Civilizing Power*, pp. 25ff. Cf. also, F.W. Walbank, *Polybius*, Sather Classical Lectures, Vol. XLII (Univ. of California, 1972), pp. 32-96.

3. Cf. Oliver, *ibid.*, §§ 109 and 166.

4. I. 238. Oliver, *ibid.*, p. 25, defines μετ'ἀληθείας as, 'in all respects.' Thus it closely resembles the meaning of ἀκρίβεια. For a different use of ἀκρίβεια, cf. K.J. Dover, *Lysias and the Corpus Lysiacum*, Sather Classical Lectures, Vol. XXXIX (Univ. of California, 1968), p. 155.

5. I. 224f.

6. Isoc. *Panath.* (12), 246.

7. Isocrates would call such an oration ἀπηκριβωμένον (*Paneg*. (4), 11). Such oratory involves sacrificing the plurality of events: cf. *Philip*. (5), 59: καθ' ἕκαστον μὲν οὖν τῶν τότε γενομένων εἴ τις λέγειν ἐπιχειρήσειεν, οὔτ' ἂν διελθεῖν ἀκριβῶς. Cf. *infra*, n.14.B.L. Ullman, "History and Tragedy," *TAPA* 73 (1942) 45, sees this desire for unity of subject behind the popularity of the historical monograph.

8. Cf. *Panath.* (12), 246; Oliver, *Civilizing Power*, pp. 27f., and 114, where the term ἱστορία is identified with ἁπλότης.

9. *Antid.* (15), 45-50; *Evag.* (9), 1-11. Cf. D. Stuart, *Epochs in Greek and Roman Biography,* Sather Classical Lectures, Vol. IV (Univ. of California, 1928), Chapter IV; G. Heilbrunn, *An Examination of Isocrates' Rhetoric* (Diss. Univ. of Texas at Austin, 1967), pp. 37 and 127.

10. Cf. F. Jacoby, *Atthis* (Oxford, 1948), p. 202; F. Walbank, "History and Tragedy," *Hist.* 9 (1960) 221f. The historiographer must beware of an oversimplified categorization of genres. History seems to have originated from poetry, and it frequently exhibited epic, tragic, and oratorical traits. Cf. A.W. Gomme, *The Greek Attitude to Poetry and History,* Sather Classical Lectures, Vol. XXVII (Univ. of California, 1954), Chapter III.

11. *FGrH* 1 F 1a: τάδε γράφω ὥς μοι ἀληϑέα δοκέει εἶναι, οἱ γὰρ Ἑλλήνων λόγοι πολλοί τε καὶ γελοῖοι.

12. Liddell and Scott (9th ed., 1953), *s.v.* ἀτρέκεια. Cf. Oliver, *Civilizing Power,* p. 28, 'straight reporting with a minimum of subjective interpretation.' The matter is not simple. Herodotus in his Proemium (I. 1) gives pride of place to the facts but promises to explicate causes and prevent great and wondrous deeds from losing their due glory.

13. For the translation, cf. Gomme, *HCT* I. 142f. Note the obvious implications of ἡ ζήτησις τῆς ἀληϑείας (20.3) and ἀληϑέστερον (21. 1) as well as the claim to represent in speeches the general sense of τῶν ἀληϑῶς λεχϑέντων. Cf. F. Egermann, "Thukydides über die Art seiner Reden ...," *Historia* 21 (1972) 572-602.

14. Note particularly, περὶ ἑκάστου, and cf. the passages cited *supra,* p. 1 and n. 7.

15. I. 21. 1 (logographers in general) and 1.97.2 (Hellanicus).

16. Gomme, *HCT* I. 149, correctly distinguishes Thucydides' 'practicality' from that of later historians, who tended towards simple moralizing.

17. Cf. the classic statement on the causes of the war, I. 23. 6.

18. Thucydides' style was not recommended to historians who sought to please: cf. A.D. Leeman, *Orationis Ratio* (Amsterdam: Hakkert, 1963), p. 172.

19. Ullman, cf. *supra,* n. 7, p. 53. It seems that Xenophon straddles the two worlds of Thucydides and the more oratorical history of the fourth and following centuries. He intended to continue Thucydides' tradition of an eye-witness narration of Athenian history in his *Hellenica;* yet his historical criteria do not always reflect those of Thucydides. Cf. *Hell.* 4.8.1: τῶν πράξεων τὰς μὲν ἀξιομνημονεύτους γράψω, τὰς δὲ μὴ ἀξίας λόγου παρήσω. Although the passage bears some resemblance to Thuc. III. 90. 1, Xenophon never states any objective criteria for deciding which events are of greater significance. E. Soulis, *Xenophon and Thucydides* (Diss. Bristol, 1972), pp. 11-31, points out that Xenophon selects events on the basis of their didactic value or their marvelous nature. Moreover, one must not forget that Xenophon wrote the *Agesilaus* and *Cyropaedia* as well as the *Anabasis* and *Hellenica.*

20. The question of tragical history is both extremely interesting and terribly vexed. Basically two schools of thought exist on the topic. Ullman, cf. *supra,* n. 7, posits the existence of a true genre originating from Isocrates. K. von Fritz, "Die Bedeutung des Aristoteles für die Geschichtsschreibung," *Histoire et historiens dans l'antiquité* (Fondation Hardt, *Entretiens* IV, Geneva, 1956), pp. 85-145, argues for an origin in the Peripatos. Walbank, cf. *supra,* n. 10, examines the matter from a wider perspective and rejects the existence of a specific genre. At any rate, Callisthenes, Clitarchus, Duris, and Phylarchus actually wrote, and Cicero urged Lucceius to write,

histories that read like tragedies: cf. Leeman, *supra,* n. 18, p. 174. Cf. now, R.B. Kebric, *In the Shadow of Macedon: Duris of Samos* (*Historia*-Einzelschriften, Heft 29, 1977).

21. Cf. Dion. Hal. *Epist. ad Pomp.* 7 (*FGrH* 115 T20), where this activity of Theopompus is described as ἐξετάζειν. Aristides identified his historiography as ἐξέτασις (I. 224f.). Cf. Lucian, *Hist. conscr.* 59.

22. Oliver, *Civilizing Power,* p. 27, cites the famous anecdote concerning Theopompus' need of the rein and Ephorus' of the goad (*FGrH* 70 T 28) and suggests that it may well reflect a criticism of their historiography. Cf. W.R. Connor, *Theopompus and Fifth-Century Athens* (Washington: Center for Hellenic Studies and Harvard, 1968), p. 14f.

23. Oliver, *ibid.,* notes that Ephorus is significantly called, τὸ ἦϑος ἁπλοῦς.

24. Ullman, cf. *supra,* n. 7, p. 30f., and G.L. Barber, *The Historian Ephorus* (Cambridge Univ., 1935), p. 103. One is always faced with the problem of identifying Ephorus as the source of Diodorus' statements. Ullman and Barber see Ephorus behind Diodorus' contention that history, εἶναι ταύτην φύλακα μὲν τῆς τῶν ἀξιολόγων ἀρετῆς, μάρτυρα δὲ τῆς τῶν φαύλων κακίας, εὐεργέτιν δὲ τοῦ κοινοῦ γένους τῶν ἀνϑρώπων (I. 2.2). Walbank, cf. *supra,* n. 10, p. 229, n. 58, is not convinced that Ephorus was the source for this passage; he suggests the influence of Posidonius. Still, Leeman, cf. *supra,* n. 18, p. 173, sees Ephorus behind a similar statement at Diod. XV. 1. 1. Certainly Ephorus' teacher, Isocrates, urged Nicocles to study history for just such an ethical purpose: cf. *Ad Nic.* (2), 35.

25. I. 1. 2: ... ἀληϑινωτάτην μὲν εἶναι παιδείαν καὶ γυμνασίαν πρὸς τὰς πολιτικὰς πράξεις τὴν ἐκ τῆς ἱστορίας μάϑησιν.

26. I. 4. 9ff.; cf. Walbank, *supra,* n. 2.

27. II. 56. 11f.

28. Cf. *Alex.* 1, and, for comparison, Nepos, *Pelop.* 1.

29. *De or.* 2. 62-4. Cf. Sall. *Cat.* 4. 3; *Jug.* 4. 5-6; Liv. *Praef.* 10; Plin. *Epist.* 7. 33. 10; Quint. *I.O.* X. 1. 31; Tac. *Ann.* III. 65; Leeman, *supra,* n. 18, pp. 67 and 338.

30. Cic. *Or.* 37, 66, 207; *De or.* 2. 62; *De leg.* 1. 5. Cf. Ullman, *supra,* n. 7, p. 52.

31. Cf. F.W. Schlatter, S.J., *Salamis and Plataea in the Tradition of the Attic Orators* (Diss. Princeton, 1960), pp. 1ff., where attention is called to Jacoby, *RE,* Suppl. vol. II, *s.v.* Herodotos, cols. 392-419, for an analysis of this technique. The conclusions of Fr. Schlatter in this and related matters have been invaluable to me.

32. Cf. Schlatter, *ibid.,* p. 14, who cites the explicit avowal of this technique by Isocrates (*Philip.* (5), 57). Schlatter also calls attention to K. Jost, *Das Beispiel und Vorbild der Vorfahren bei den attischen Rednern und Geschichtschreibern bis Demosthenes* (Paderborn: Schöningh, 1936), pp. 124-26. Cf. Aristot. *Rhet.* 1393a. For a detailed list of such rhetorical uses of historical allusions in Isocrates, cf. C.B. Welles, "Isocrates' View of History," in *The Classical Tradition: Studies in Honor of Harry Caplan,* ed. by L. Wallach (Cornell, 1966), p. 15-21. Cf. *infra,* Chapter VII, n. 21.

33. Cf. *supra,* nn. 7 and 14. Biography occupied a position midway between history and encomiastic oratory, and distinctions between the genres were not absolute.

34. Cf. A.J. Podlecki, "The Political Significance of the Athenian 'Tyrannicide'-Cult," *Hist.* 15 (1966) 129-41; C.W. Fornara (ed. and trans.), *Archaic*

Times to the End of the Peloponnesian War, Vol. I of *Translated Documents of Greece and Rome,* ed. by E. Badian and R.K. Sherk (Baltimore: Johns Hopkins, 1977), p. 39; "The Cult of Harmodius and Aristogiton," *Philologus* 114 (1970) 155-80.

35. Demosth. *Lept.* (20), 18, 70, 127; *De fals. leg.* (19), 280; Din. *Dem.* (1), 101; Hyper. *Phil.* (2), 3; *Ep.* (6), 39f.; Lycurg. *Leoc.* 51; Is. *Dic.* (5), 47; cf. P. Berolini, 13045, Fr. ii, lines 315-8.

36. Hdt. V. 55; Thuc. VI. 54-59; Aristot. *Ath. Pol.* 18. Cf. Pollux, VIII. 91; Theodoretus, *Therapeutica,* VIII. 117. 41.

37. For the testimonia, cf. R.E. Wycherley, *Literary and Epigraphical Testimonia,* Vol. III of *The Athenian Agora* (Princeton: ASCS, 1957), pp. 93-98; the epigram (Agora I 3872) appears as No. 280, p. 97. Cf. A.E. Raubitschek, *Dedications from the Athenian Akropolis* (Cambridge, Mass.: AIA, 1949), p. 513f.; M. Moggi, "In merito alla datazione dei Tirannicidi di Antenor," *ASNP* 1 (1971) 17-63.

38. Raubitscheck, *ibid.* Cf. also J. Frel, "Some Notes on the Elgin Throne," *Ath. Mitt.* 91 (1976) 185-188, pl. 65-67. The "tyrant-slayers" and Theseus, slaying the Amazons, are sculpted on opposite sides of the Elgin Throne.

39. For the scolia, cf. Athenaeus, XV. 50, 695a-b; Schol. Aristoph. *Ach.* 980; Hyper. *Phil.* (2), 3. The *Marmor Parium* (ep. 45) and possibly Diodorus (IX. 1. 4; X. 17) reflect the *Atthis.* Aristotle (*Ath. Pol.* 18. 5) mentions δημοτικοί as a source for a story friendly to Aristogiton. Since the term normally applies to the democratic party, U. von Wilamowitz-Moellendorff, *Aristoteles und Athen,* Vol. I (Repr. Dublin: Weidmann, 1966), p. 276f., recognized in it the influence of the 'democratic' *Atthis.* Jacoby, cf. *supra,* n. 10, pp. 75; 234, n. 36; 290, n. 6, corrects Wilamowitz' impression that all *Atthides* were democratic and believes that the present use of δημοτικοί refers specifically to the democratic Cleidemus.

40. Demosth. *Lept.* (20), 18, 127; *De fals. leg.* (19), 280; Din. *Dem.* (1), 101; Plut. *Aristid.* 27.6; Is. *Dic.* (5), 47.

41. Luc. *Par.* 48; cf. *Philops.* 18; cf. Chr. Habicht, "Zur Geschichte Athens in der Zeit Mithridates VI," *Chiron* 6 (1976) 135-142.

42. *Hist. conscr.* 4 and 9. Thucydides (I. 97. 2) called Hellanicus' work ξυγγράφη. Jacoby, cf. *supra,* n. 10, p. 81f., adduces considerable evidence in support of the view that Thucydides was not citing the title of Hellanicus' book, but rather its genre.

43. Cf. *Rh. pr.* 14, where Lucian delivers a particularly heavy blow by describing historical oratory as easy to write, if the author follows certain absurd rules accurately (ἀκριβῶς). At *Rh. pr.* 18, Lucian gives a list of the commonplaces: Marathon, Cynegeirus, Athos, Hellespont, Thermopylae, Salamis, Artemisium, and Plataea. Plutarch, *Praec. ger. reip.* 17, gives a similar list.

44. *FGrH* 115 F 153, where Theopompus attacks the Athenian vaunts about the Battle of Marathon, the Oath of Plataea, and, apparently, the Peace of Callias. On the significance of the fragment, cf. Connor, *supra,* n. 22, p. 88; Welles, *supra,* n. 32, p. 11f., and n. 69.

45. Cf. R. Vattuone, "L'excursus nel VI libro delle Storie di Tucidide," *RSA* 5 (1975) 173-84.

46. Thuc. I. 21. 1; 22. 4.

47. Cf. however, Gomme, *HCT* I. 136, on the meaning of ἀκοάς.

48. *Paneg.* (4), 30.

49. These are the findings of Schlatter, cf. *supra,* n. 31, p. 6ff.

50. I believe this is true notwithstanding Isocrates' claim to praise Athens merely for the sake of praise, without any rhetorical purpose beyond pure encomium: cf. *Panath.* (12), 35. The degradation of Sparta, the digression on Agamemnon, the critical epilogue, all these reduce the historical elements relating to Athens to a much smaller quantity than one finds in Aristides' *Panathenaicus.*

51. The only dissident voice is that of Haury, cf. *supra,* Introduction, n. 18. The Scholia to the *Panathenaicus,* Beecke, and Oliver all detect a very wide selection of sources. Recent scholarship has discovered a similarly wide use of sources in Plutarch: cf. F. Frost, *The Scholarship of Plutarch* (Diss. UCLA, 1961), pp. 12ff., concerning the influence of an oral tradition on Plutarch; P.A. Stadter, *Plutarch's Historical Method* (Harvard, 1965). For the influence of monuments on Aristides: the Stoa Poikile, Beecke, *Historischen Angaben,* p. 16; the Stoa of Zeus, J.H. Oliver, *Demokratia* (Johns Hopkins, 1960), p. 165f.; the Troizen Decree, M. Jameson, "A Decree of Themistocles from Troizen," *Hesp.* 29 (1960) 202 and 214.

52. Cf. Isoc. *Paneg.* (4), 74; Oliver, *Civilizing Power,* p. 92

53. Cf. *supra,* p. 7f.

CHAPTER II
TRIPTOLEMUS AS AN ATHENIAN POLITICAL SYMBOL

Aristides opens his account of the Pentecontaetia in a manner that reproduces the frenetic pace which characterized the Athenian campaigns against the Persians from 479 to around 475; he hastens through the battles at Mycale, Eion, Sestus, and Byzantium in a single sentence. A triple simile, however, gives Aristides the opportunity to enliven his narrative and expand his description of the Athenians (I. 245):

> A. *They traversed the entire area as if they were expiating an abomination and, in fact, they came to anchor no less frequently than merchantmen on their routes. The Athenians actually imitated the airborne progress of Triptolemus that was mentioned earlier. They surpassed the ancient hero, however, by going about punishing those who deserved it, while he distributed his benefits to everyone indiscriminately.*

As so often in Aristides, each simile conveys an interpretation of historical events, but the implication of the comparison with Triptolemus is especially meaningful in the *Panathenaicus*, which exults in Athens' cultural mission to the world. Triptolemus symbolized Athenian philanthropy through his connection with the myth of Demeter and the Eleusinian religion; he carried forth from Attica Demeter's dual gift of agriculture and the mysteries and distributed them throughout the world.[1]

In the passage alluded to in the lines cited above, Aristides tells the story of Triptolemus' mission in greater detail (I. 167):

> B. *The Athenians sent a religious procession all over the world to distribute the necessities of life from a sort of theoric fund.[2] They say that one of Demeter's nurslings was put in charge of this mission; and it was frequently reported that he had a winged chariot, since he moved everywhere faster than the wind. In fact, his progress was so completely unhindered that he does seem to have been conveyed through the clear air. This mission proved the truth of what had been a mere saying before*

> *by showing that 'generosity is naturally swift'; these Athenians, you see, actually spread their gift faster than those in need of their service could express a desire for help. I adduce the custom of the first fruits as a memorial and symbol of this divine mission, this generosity to all mankind. Every year in ancient times, the Greeks would send the first fruits of their seeds to Athens. There is, of course, a further proof that agriculture originated in Attica and spread to other places from there, namely, the oracles of the god that call Athens the mother-city of crops.*

Aristides was by no means unfamiliar with the story of Triptolemus, which appears three other times in the Aristidean corpus:

> C. *Ad Romam*, I. 336: *Thus, I have come to think of the so-called 'life before Triptolemus' as in fact life before you Romans; it was harsh, uncultivated, not very far away from primitive hill-culture. The city of the Athenians initiated our contemporary form of civilized life, but you Romans, though not the originators, are said to be better men and to have secured the good life.*[3]

D. *Eleusinus*, I. 416f., where Aristides tells what he can of the mysteries' ἄρρητα: 1. After the story of Demeter's search for Core:

> *Finally Demeter came to Eleusis and thus gave a name to the place, and, when she found her daughter, she instituted the mysteries. Furthermore, the two goddesses gave grain to the city of the Athenians, and from her in turn it was distributed to all Greeks and barbarians. To these Athenians we ascribe Celeus, Metaneira, and Triptolemus with his winged chariot of snakes borne over land and sea.*

2. After a brief interval,[4] one again finds the argument from Hellenic custom:

> *On each occasion, the Greeks repay Athens by sending the first fruits to her as though she were the mother-city of their very persons as well as their agriculture.*

E. *Athena*, I. 18: *Triptolemus, of course, was younger than Erichthonius; yet, even in his case, the seeds would have come from Demeter but the chariot from Athena.*

The interest in the mythical gifts of grain (σῖτος, σπέρματα, καρπός, ἥμερος τροφή) and the mysteries (μυστήρια, ἄρρητα, τελετή) which is exhibited in the foregoing passages places Aristides squarely in the panegyric tradition of fourth-century Attic oratory. Passages B and D and their contexts clearly reflect the very myth of Athens' intimate connection with the early cultural achievements of Eleusis that is found in Isocrates' *Panegyricus* and the extant *Epitaphioi,* especially the one in the *Menexenus.*[5] Aristides and the earlier orators believed the Athenians to have been not only autochthonous but also the first men born anywhere.[6] Attica put forth the first food to feed these first men and thus became known as their nurse or mother.[7] Athens can be called θεοφιλής because of the gifts that the gods gave her and φιλάνθρωπος, since she did not begrudge other men these gifts but spread them all over the world.[8] This concentration on Athens' philanthropic mission represents the heart of the matter, and in it Aristides was closest to Isocrates. Only these two orators employ Eleusinian myth without rationalization, Isocrates dwelling on Demeter and Core, Aristides on Triptolemus as well as the goddesses. Moreover, both authors adduce the Hellenic custom of sending the first fruits to Athens as evidence for Athenian primacy in agriculture, and both refer to a famous oracle. According to Isocrates, Delphi ordered the Hellenes to send the first fruits to Athens; in Aristides, the oracle designated Athens the mother-city of crops. Furthermore, Isocrates gives as important a place to the institution of the mysteries as to the gift of grain; Aristides does also in the *Eleusinus,* though not elsewhere.[9]

Although Isocrates and Aristides employ the Eleusinian myth extensively, they are both ill at ease in the world of myth. Isocrates, in particular, apologizes profusely for dragging out so hoary a tale as that of Demeter:

1. *Paneg. (4), 28: Even if the story has become 'mythical,' still, it is fitting that it be retold at this point.*
2. *Paneg. (4), 30: In the first place, the very reason that one might adduce for condemning the stories about these deeds, namely, that they are so old, ought more reasonably to prove that they are genuine. The fact that many people have retold and everyone has heard versions of these events should prove that the stories are trustworthy, albeit ancient.*

Aristides is similarly uncomfortable with the mythical elements in the panegyric context of passage B. He apologizes with the expressions ὡς λέγεται and φήμη κατέσχεν, and he partly rationalizes the myth of Triptolemus' winged progress. Nevertheless, as we noted in the preceding chapter, such apologies amount to conventional claims of historical accuracy amongst the orators.[10] Isocrates, at least, knew that for Athenian audiences a story's age and popularity in the city guaranteed that it was an integral part of the Athenian popular tradition and therefore reliable, and Aristides' close imitation of Isocrates in the present instance indicates that he was operating under the same assumptions.

The Eleusinian gifts of grain and the mysteries quite clearly formed a very old part of the Athenian popular tradition, and Aristides, together with the earlier orators, certainly reflects that tradition; yet two problems arise from the passages we have seen. The first is, of course, the presence of Triptolemus, whom none of the orators besides Aristides mentions in his account of the story.[11] The second problem is more relevant to our investigation of the Pentecontaetia; it concerns Aristides' reasons for bringing the myth of Triptolemus into the purely historical context of passage A. Other references to the gift of grain occur in the various orators' mythological sections, well before the historical period is treated. It is therefore possible that in Aristides' view the myth of Triptolemus carried specific political overtones for fifth-century Athenians which were lost or unimportant to the fourth-century orators. Thus, for the purposes of our investigation, two questions must be posed: were Triptolemus' connection with the primeval Attic gifts to humanity and his political significance in the Pentecontaetia true elements of the fifth-century popular tradition, and, if they were, does Aristides reflect that tradition accurately? Since these questions raise the possibility that Aristides presents a more accurate version of the fifth-century tradition than the earlier orators do, the identification of his sources for the story of Triptolemus becomes an important corollary question. In order to answer these questions, I propose to trace the evolution of the Athenian tradition of Triptolemus from the period of our earliest evidence until Aristides' day, with special emphasis on the political significance of the myth in fifth-century Athens.[12]

Black-figure pottery provides the earliest evidence for the myth of Triptolemus at Athens.[13] Fifteen vases from the last half of the sixth century portray Triptolemus as a bearded adult sitting on a chair that is equipped with a pair of wheels.[14] The painters always depicted the hero holding some ears of grain, which clearly symbolize his mission to distribute the gift of agriculture. In most scenes, Triptolemus is shown at a stop on his mission, where he is educating a group of people in the cultivation of grain.[15] This early Attic Triptolemus has little in common with the hero of that name in the *Homeric Hymn to Demeter*.[16] Demeter ordains the Triptolemus of the poem to be the minister of her mysteries; he has nothing to do with the discovery or distribution of grain. We cannot determine exactly how or when the earlier version of the myth evolved into the Attic form, and no artistic prototype of the vase paintings is known; yet it is probably fair to say that the popularity of the Attic conception reflects the same nationalistic tendencies of the period of the tyrants which turned Dionysus and Theseus into Attic cultural symbols.[17] As Dionysus became the Athenian symbol of viticulture, Triptolemus came to represent agriculture. In fact, black-figure representations of Dionysus being conveyed through the world in his wheeled chair and holding a bouquet of vines clearly influenced the artistic conception of Triptolemus.[18]

A new and quite different canon for the representation of Triptolemus on pottery began in the second decade of the fifth century and continued down to about 420, a period during which the theme of our hero was extremely popular. We are again ignorant of any artistic prototype, and some of the features that were popular amongst black-figure painters remain; yet the fifth-century painters focused their attention upon four aspects of the myth of Triptolemus that had been absent or unpopular in the previous century.[19] In the first place, red-figure painters portrayed Triptolemus as a beardless youth or even a boy.[20] Second, a pair of wings attached to the wheels of his chair conveys a notion of speed to the scene in red-figure ware.[21] In some cases, painters also added a pair of snakes to enhance the image of Triptolemus' vehicle even more.[22] Third, Triptolemus is often shown holding a phiale as well as the ears of grain that were common in black-figure. The phiale was relatively uncommon in the first part of our period, but it appears frequently and sometimes totally supersedes the grain later in the century.[23] Finally, the painters concentrated on a new aspect of the myth: instead of showing Triptolemus' arrivals, they stress his departure from Eleusis.[24] The hero, seated in his magic car, listens to Demeter and Persephone, who instruct him in the details of his upcoming mission. Demeter normally fills Triptolemus' phiale from an oinochoe, and Persephone often holds a torch. Other people holding these same objects join the three main actors on many vases.[25]

Fifth-century vase painters shared their conception of the well-worked myth of Triptolemus with other popular media of the period.[26] Two striking similarities to painting can be found in the fragments of Sophocles' *Triptolemus*.[27] First, Sophocles reproduced the popular image of Triptolemus' magic chair (fr. 596): δράκοντε θαιρὸν ἀμφιπλὶξ εἰληφότε. Second, the poet illustrated the favorite anecdote of the vase painters in a long episode during which Demeter attends to Triptolemus' departure and tells him which nations to visit. The scene itself has not survived, but we have a summary in Dionysius[28] and perhaps the beginning of Demeter's commands in the fragment, σὲ δ' ἐν φρενὸς δέλτοισι τοὺς ἐμοὺς λόγους (fr. 597). Sophocles clearly stressed Triptolemus' function as distributor of agriculture; numerous fragments refer to the various lands he is to visit, and elements of the cereal diet of various tribes receive brief attention.[29] There is one fragment, however, which exhibits an interest in the mysteries.[30]

In sculpture, the Grand Relief of Eleusis and fragments of three plaques from the Eleusinium in Athens illustrate the characteristics of the fifth-century tradition of Triptolemus. Although the hero's chair does not appear on the great relief, the other artistic elements are present: Triptolemus is a youth; Demeter stands before him and offers him an ear of grain; Core holds a torch and crowns Triptolemus with myrtle, a symbol of the mysteries.[31] Two of the plaques from the Eleusinium depict the normal scene of Triptolemus' departure.[32] Only the top of the hero's staff and Demeter holding a torch survive on one plaque. On the other, the lower halves of Demeter and Core and Triptolemus' chair with snakes around its axle survive. The third relief apparently shows Demeter and Athena together.

When we attempt to interpret the new and predominant characteristics of fifth-century representations of Triptolemus, his youth lends itself most easily to explanation. In archaic painting, the mature Triptolemus represents a more conservative version of the myth, one that is closer to the *Hymn*.[33] The youth of the classical period simply reflects the popular Athenian version of Triptolemus' parentage.[34] Pausanias, the *Marmor Parium*, Apollodorus, and a Scholion upon Aristides all confirm that in the Athenian tradition Triptolemus' parents were Celeus and Metaneira.[35] Thus, it seems that at Athens Triptolemus superseded the *Hymn's* Demophoon as Demeter's nursling.[36] As to the artistic attributes of Triptolemus' chair, the addition of wings should probably be interpreted as no more than the painters' attempt to convey the idea of movement on a long and speedy journey. The snakes, however, may be more significant. Since they are an agrarian symbol but perhaps also had a place in the mysteries, they may indicate that Triptolemus' mission had two purposes, the spreading of both agriculture and mysteries.[37] The double nature of the hero's mission became an important aspect of the myth in the fifth century. Indeed, the most significant new element in the fifth-century artistic conception of Triptolemus, namely, the elaborate scene of his departure, can certainly be described as an attempt to stress his dual connection with grain and mysteries. The agricultural side of Triptolemus was, of course, too firmly entrenched to be forgotten, even when the ears of grain are not depicted.[38] On the other hand, Triptolemus' phiale, Demeter's oinochoe, Core's torch, and the frequent appearance of these paraphernalia in the hands of other characters point to the ceremonial of the Eleusinian mysteries.[39] In spite of Mylonas' insistence that Triptolemus' mission had no part in the secret portion of the rites of initiation, these artistic attributes show that the hero was connected at least with the public ceremonies.[40] The phiale and oinochoe certainly represent the sacred potion which Demeter concocted in the *Hymn* and which was served to initiates on the sixth day of the Greater Mysteries.[41] Persephone's torch likewise recalls the initiation rites, and the other figures on the vases probably represent religious attendants and initiates.[42] Once we have identified the new elements in the scene of Triptolemus' departure as references to the mysteries, however, we are still left with the task of interpreting the reasons for the upsurge in popularity which the theme of Triptolemus experienced after around 480.

Dugas correctly applies a political interpretation to the fifth-century innovations in the popular view of Triptolemus: whereas a concentration on the hero's arrivals in archaic painting said little about his origin, the new scheme showed clearly that Demeter sent him out from Eleusis.[43] By stressing Triptolemus' connection with Attica and the world-renowned mysteries, the Athenians could emphasize the pious, civilizing mission of their city. It was precisely this political and nationalistic significance of the story that made it so attractive to official and popular media at Athens in the period of the expanding Athenian Empire. To be sure, the political importance of the Eleusinian gifts and Triptolemus had not been lost on Athenians of older generations; one can detect Athenian chauvinism in myths that go back at least to Eleusis' incorporation into the Athenian state. According to one myth, Triptolemus' association with the Lesser Mysteries at Athens goes back to their origin in the ceremony of initiation for Heracles at which Triptolemus acted as Hierophant.[44] The Athenians also believed that Triptolemus founded the festival of the *Proerosia*, which commemorated Demeter's salvation of all Greece from a famine.[45] Triptolemus was also considered the founder of the *Haloa* festival, during which the Athenians traditionally proclaimed that agriculture (ἥμερος τροφή) had originated in their land.[46] Furthermore, the demand that all Hellenes send the first fruits to Eleusis, where a portion was given to Triptolemus, became a regular, politically inspired feature of the *Eleusinia* at some time between 600 and 468.[47] In spite of this early evidence, however, the fifth-century conception of Triptolemus was unique, and Dugas' political explanation of this uniqueness is correct. In fact, I will suggest that in the fifth century the myth of Triptolemus not only symbolized Athens' civilizing mission in general but the Athenian Empire in particular.

No doubt a fifth-century Athenian felt a patriotic stir when he saw his city's goddess taking part in the traditional scene of Triptolemus' departure on a vase or other artistic work.[48] That Athenian would have been ecstatic at the production of Sophocles' *Triptolemus*. The play seems to have brought Sophocles his first victory in rather unusual circumstances: the board of generals led by Cimon awarded the prize directly to the playwright.[49] Not only is this a comment on the play's popularity, it may well tell us something about Cimon's image as a statesman and general. Perhaps it is not too far amiss to suggest that the poet created in Triptolemus a symbol of Athens' civilizing, anti-barbarian mission under the generalship of Cimon. In this respect, it is interesting to note that Cimon is said by Mylonas to have undertaken the restoration of the Eleusinian shrines destroyed by the Persians.[50] The implication may be that Cimon himself believed there was a parallelism between the missions of the characters in the Eleusinian pantheon and of Athens at the head of the Delian League.

The Cimonian Telesterion may never have been completed, but its plan was far exceeded by the structure that Pericles erected in its place as part of his building program.[51] Like so many of Pericles' buildings, his Telesterion should be interpreted as a symbol of Athens' wealth and power; it ought to be seen in its proper context as part of Pericles' plan to implement the Congress Decree.[52] Several of Pericles' important buildings and his exploitation of the religious practices that had long been associated with their sites symbolized the transformation of the wartime alliance, established in such documents as the Oath and Covenant of Plataea, into a religiously oriented union, an Athenian Amphictyony as it were.[53] When the League's treasury was transferred from Delos to Athens, the payments neither retained the character of contributions to the war effort nor became simply imperial tribute paid to Athens; they took on the aspect of religious duties owed to Athena. The special nature of the φόρος was also symbolized by its connection with specific religious institutions in various official documents relating to the collection of tribute. For example, the Cleinias Decree and the tribute reassessment of 425/4 required the allies to send a cow and panoply to the *Panathenaea*.[54] This festival was, of course, depicted on the Parthenon frieze, and the other decoration on the building commemorated Athens' pious, civilizing, anti-barbarian mission. This set of symbolic connections amongst tribute, festival, and Periclean building also existed in the Eleusinian context. In a decree whose wording reflects regulations for the collection of tribute, the allies were required to contribute the first fruits to the *Eleusinia* (*IG* I² 76 = *ML* 73):[55]

1. l.14: ἀπάρχεσθαι δὲ καὶ τὸς χσυμμάχος κατὰ ταὐτά.
The allies as well shall offer first fruits according to the same procedure.[56]

2. ll.24-26: κελευέτο δὲ καὶ ὁ ἱεροφάντες καὶ [ὁ] δαιδόχος μυστερίοις ἀπάρχεσθαι τὸς Ἕλλενας τὸ καρπὸ κατὰ τὰ πάτρια καὶ τὲν μαντείαν τὲν ἐγ Δελφῶν.
Let an exhortation be pronounced both by the Hierophant and the Daidouchos for the Hellenes to make offerings of the first fruits at the Mysteries in accordance with ancestral custom and the oracular response from Delphi.[57]

This document is surely evidence that the same sort of relationship obtained amongst first fruits, *Eleusinia* and mysteries, and Telesterion as did amongst cow and panoply, *Panathenaea*, and Parthenon. And, as if the political implications of the inscription were not already obvious, the benefits to be derived from the sacrifices of the first fruits are politically circumscribed (ll.44-46):

[τοῖ]ς δὲ ταῦτα ποιõσι πολλὰ ἀγαθὰ ἔναι καὶ εὐκαρπίαν καὶ πολυκαρπία[ν, οἵ]τινες ἂν [μ]ὲ ἀδικõσι Ἀθεναίος μεδὲ τὲν πόλιν τὲν Ἀθεναίον μεδὲ τὸ θεό.
For those who do this there shall be many benefits

in abundance of good harvests if they are men who do not injure the Athenians or the city of the Athenians or the two goddesses.

Isocrates maintains a genuine memory of the fifth-century practice in the passage noted earlier, where he mentions a Delphic oracle that commanded the Greeks to send the first fruits to Athens in compliance with ancestral custom.[58] In passage B cited above, Aristides similarly mentions oracles that called Athens the mother-city of crops. The Scholion on this passage connects Aristides' mention of the oracle with that of Isocrates and with other sources for the Athenian tradition by stating that, during a natural disaster, the god ordered the Hellenes to celebrate a festival with Athens, the mother-city of crops.[59] This, then, brings us back to Triptolemus, who, as we have seen, had a traditional connection with the *Eleusinia*. Moreover, our imperial inscription does not ignore that hero in its instructions for the use of the first fruits in the sacrifices of the *Eleusinia* (ll. 37-40):

τρίττοιαν δὲ βόαρχον χρυσόκερον τοῖν θεοῖν ἑκα[τέρ]-
[αι ἀ]πὸ τὸν κριθῶν καὶ τὸν πυρῶν καὶ τõι Τριπτολέμοι
καὶ τõι [θε]õι καὶ τε͂ι θεᾶι καὶ τõι Εὐβόλοι ἱερεῖον ἑκάστοι τέλεον
καὶ τε͂ι Ἀθεναίαι βõν χρυσόκερον.

(They shall sacrifice) the triple sacrifice, first a bull with gilt horns to each of the two goddesses separately, out of (proceeds from) the barley and the wheat; and to Triptolemus and to the god and the goddess and Euboulos a full-grown victim each; and to Athena a bull with gilt horns.

It cannot be accidental that this Triptolemus is the mythical character whose departure from Eleusis and connection with agriculture and the mysteries became such favored subjects in both official and private media during the very years when the Athenian Empire was at its height. Although one must exercise care in interpreting references to mythical figures as political symbolism, I believe that enough evidence exists to warrant the conclusion that during the fifth century Triptolemus was employed as a symbol of Athens' civilizing mission at the head of her imperial Amphictyony.[60] He was by no means the most significant symbol of the empire; that function was reserved for Athena. Even in the context of the Eleusinian pantheon, Demeter was more important than Triptolemus. Still, Triptolemus could symbolize specific aspects of the Athenian Empire very nicely, namely, its far-flung nature, its mission to visit places all over the world, and its ability to move to those places swiftly.

The evidence from the fourth century shows that a certain memory of the fifth-century political significance of the myth of Triptolemus continued to exist in official circles. Most importantly, Xenophon reports a political speech by a certain Callias, torchbearer of the Eleusinian mysteries (*Hell.* VI. 3. 6):[61]

> *They say that, when our ancestor Triptolemus showed the sacred and unutterable rites of Demeter and Core to foreigners for the first time, it was to your founding father Heracles and your fellow citizens the Dioscuri. Moreover, Triptolemus distributed the seed of grain to the Peloponnese ahead of every other place.*

Triptolemus' initiation of Heracles was an ancient tradition; the story even ranked as a minor theme on fifth-century pottery and may have received a literary treatment in Panyassis' *Heraclea*.[62] What is significant about Callias' speech is that it juxtaposes the story of Athens' early philanthropy, which we have seen in the *Panegyricus* and *Menexenus*, with the story of Triptolemus, whom the other fourth-century authors ignored. Furthermore, this juxtaposition occurs in a political context resembling that of our fifth-century sources. Unlike his fifth-century predecessors, however, the pompous and nostalgic Callias was relatively more concerned with the past than the present; like Isocrates and Aristides, he felt that his story belonged to the realm of historical tradition rather than contemporary mythological propaganda. Apart from Callias' own character, the main evidence for this assertion derives from his use of the word λέγεται, which presumably points to the popular tradition just as Isocrates' μυθώδης ὁ λόγος and Aristides' ὡς λέγεται do.[63] Besides Xenophon, we should also take note of two other fourth-century sources that seem to bear the stamp of official propaganda. First, two Panathenaic prize-amphoras which portray Triptolemus in the old manner exemplify the survival of the tradition in that conservative medium.[64] Second, Triptolemus is mentioned in a mid-fourth-century amendment to a now lost decree concerning the first fruits. This decree seems to have superseded the fifth-century order to the allies from which we quoted above.[65] It is perhaps not far amiss to attribute Triptolemus' presence in these sources to the same kind of nostalgia and reliance on an established historical tradition that influenced Callias. A wider examination of evidence from the fourth and later centuries will reveal that in fact

Triptolemus' popularity as a contemporary political symbol declined sharply after the fall of the Athenian Empire.

From around 420, vase painters began to portray Triptolemus much less frequently than before and in a different manner.[66] Most scenes from the last years of the fifth century and the first half of the fourth tend to exhibit the painters' virtuosity rather than any serious interest in Triptolemus' cultural mission. For the most part, paintings no longer depict the anecdote of the hero's departure; in fact, Triptolemus is often shown in the corner of an elaborate panorama of Eleusinian notables.[67] Scholars normally interpret this to mean that Triptolemus came to be considered a minor Eleusinian deity, and this hypothesis is confirmed by a fourth-century Eleusinian bas-relief, which shows Triptolemus receiving his worshippers as Demeter and Core look on.[68] To be sure, Athens continued to demand recognition for her philanthropic gifts of grain and the mysteries; it is simply that in most cases Triptolemus has dropped out of the popular story, and frequently all mythological elements have been rationalized. We already noted Triptolemus' absence from the orators, who assigned the traditional task of distributing the dual gift to the Athenian Demos.[69] The same tendency to ignore Triptolemus exists in an Amphictyonic decree dated to around 125 B.C.[70] The decree expresses gratitude to the Athenian Demos for the gifts of grain and the mysteries but does not mention Triptolemus or any other mythical figure. Similar passages appear in numerous Greek and Latin authors.[71]

After the fourth century, the legend of Triptolemus seems to have survived primarily in connection with the mystery religion at Eleusis, in the local historians of Attica, and in an Egyptianized version that made its way to Rome. The continuing presence of Triptolemus in Eleusinian art guarantees his importance for the mysteries, and we should not ignore Claudian's evidence for Triptolemus' presence in the ceremony that he witnessed.[72] As to the *Atthis*, the *Marmor Parium* and more especially Philochorus show that Triptolemus had a role in the local histories. In fact, a fragment of Philochorus may tell us quite a lot about his version of the Triptolemus myth (*FGrH* 328 F 104):[73]

> Celeus was king of Eleusis at the time when Triptolemus lived. Philochorus says that Triptolemus went out in a warship to the cities to distribute grain; his ship was supposedly a winged snake, but in fact it had some such figurehead.

Philochorus was obviously interested in Triptolemus' mission and his mode of conveyance, both of which were important elements in the fifth-century tradition. Although the name of Celeus is not actually part of the fragment, it may indicate that Philochorus accepted the Athenian genealogy of Triptolemus. Furthermore, Philochorus may well have recorded the oracle that ordered the Greeks to send the first fruits to the mother-city of crops.[74] We should not forget, however, that Philochorus was himself a μάντις and was consistently interested in the origins of Attic cults and festivals such as the *Proerosia* and *Haloa*.[75] Undoubtedly, then, he was more interested in religious than political history when he told the story of Triptolemus, and we should not expect to find in Philochorus a deliberate imitation of the fifth-century political symbolism.

An Apulian amphora, which is from the second half of the fourth century but predates Alexander, gives us our earliest evidence for Triptolemus in an Egyptian context.[76] The execution is rather exotic, but the traditional anecdote of Triptolemus' departure is clearly visible. He stands in a chariot drawn by two monstrous serpents; Demeter fills his phiale; two ears of grain adorn his hair; and two Horae holding stalks of grain observe the scene, which takes place beside the Nile. In the Greek literature of Egypt, Callimachus refers to Triptolemus' agricultural function (*Ad Dem.* 21): Τριπτόλεμος ἀγαθὰν ἐδιδάσκετο τέχναν.[77] Eratosthenes may have recalled from Sophocles the unpleasant incident between Triptolemus and Charnabon, the king of the Getae.[78] Finally, Diodorus gives a fairly complete description of the Egyptianized version of the myth. The historian makes Osiris, who was not originally an agricultural hero, the distributor of agriculture and Triptolemus his mere assistant.[79] It may have been this Triptolemus who was the object of a prayer in a papyrus from Antinoopolis and of Alexandrian date.[80]

There is some evidence to suggest that the Ptolemies and, in their turn, the Roman emperors adopted Triptolemus as a political symbol.[81] The *tazza Farnese*, from the end of the third century, depicts Triptolemus in the guise of a Ptolemy carrying seeds, a yoke, and a plow.[82] Beside him are Isis, who is the Egyptian Demeter, and the Nile. The attribute of the plow, although not widely represented before the Ptolemaic period, certainly recalls Triptolemus' agricultural function and does appear in Triptolemus' traditional scene of departure on an Attic crater from the middle of the fifth century and a skyphos from the end of that century.[83] On the Roman side, an Aquilean silver cup from the Julio-Claudian era portrays a member of the imperial family as Triptolemus.[84] He wears the costume of a sower and stands beside a chariot drawn by winged snakes. Demeter observes the scene, and the whole undoubtedly reflects the conception of the *tazza Farnese*.[85] Furthermore, Alexandrian coins from the age of the Antonines depict Triptolemus as a sower in his snake-chariot.[86] Finally, it should be noted that Latin writers borrowed the myth of Triptolemus from the Alexandrians. The hero appears as a sower in the *Rhetorica ad Herennium* and Ovid, as in Cornutus.[87] In Virgil, he is the *puer monstrator aratri* (*Georg.* I. 19), and in the *Fasti* Ovid makes him the hero of plowing, sowing, and reaping.[88] Only in Ovid's *Metamorphoses* does something like the traditional Triptolemus appear (V.652): patria est clarae mihi Athenae. Even this, however, lacks the specific political connotations of the Athenian tradition and cannot be viewed as a link in the chain by which that tradition was transmitted to Aristides.

We are now in a position to return to Aristides and view his remarks in the context of the whole tradition of Triptolemus. As is probably already evident, the orator captured the spirit of the Athenian popular tradition of the fifth century in a quite remarkable way. The image of the winged chair (passages A, B, D, and E) and the traditional Athenian genealogy (passage D) could, of course, reflect fifth-century media; yet both of these elements of the myth were far too common in the fourth and later centuries to prove an intimate connection between Aristides and the fifth-century tradition of Triptolemus. It is Aristides' conception of Triptolemus' mission that bears the true seal of the fifth-century political symbolism. Either Demeter and Athena (passages D and E) or the Athenians themselves (passage B) sent the hero to distribute the benefits of agriculture and the mysteries throughout the world. This philanthropic act was commemorated by the oracle about first fruits and the mother-city of crops (passage B). The gifts and the oracle, of course, were not lost on the propagandists of the fourth century; we have seen how similar Aristides' version is to that of Isocrates' *Panegyricus* and other representations of the epitaphic tradition. With the exception of a few conservative memories in later media, however, the fourth and subsequent centuries ignored Triptolemus' role as a symbol of imperial Athens' cultural and political mission. We can therefore say that Aristides has gone beyond his obvious sources and displays an understanding of this fifth-century example of political symbolism. His understanding appears to be most accurate in passage A, where he integrates the political aspects of the Cimonian Triptolemus with those of the Periclean. The Cimonian influence is obvious: Triptolemus as a symbol of Athens' anti-barbarian mission in the early part of the Pentecontaetia. The Periclean symbolism comes out when we consider the religious tone of the context of passage A. The orator opens his account of the Pentecontaetia with a comment on the outpouring and renewal of Hellenic religion that occurred after the war for freedom against Xerxes in Greece.[89] Naturally, Athens is the center of attention, and Aristides mentions in particular the religious buildings that were erected on the Acropolis after the war. Only a few lines later he brings in his comparison between the humanitarian missions of Triptolemus and Athens. This is a very apt comparison to apply to the pious leaders of the Periclean Amphictyony, the builders of the Telesterion as well as the Parthenon.

I hope that I have provided a viable solution to the chief problems that faced us at the beginning of this chapter by suggesting that Aristides accurately preserved the way in which the myth of Triptolemus was exploited as a political symbol in the fifth century. There remains the difficult question of Aristides' source. Literary *Quellenforschung* of the traditional kind would presumably look for the influence of Philochorus, Sophocles, or even Xenophon upon Aristides. On the side of the first, one can point to the scholiast's use of Philochorus to explain the text of Aristides, the rationalization of the fairy-tale elements in passage B, and Athena's gift of the chariot to Triptolemus in E.[90] The placing of passage A, however, suggests Sopholces: it occurs between Aristides' allusion to the early battles of the Pentecontaetia and his account of the Battle of Eurymedon, the very years to which Sophocles' production of the *Triptolemus* belongs. Finally, Callias' speech in Xenophon offers what appear to be verbal as well as thematic parallels to passage D.[91] Not only is the dual gift of grain and mysteries placed beside the initiation of Heracles and the Dioscuri in both passages, but the two have four words in common(ἀρρήτοις : : ἄρρητα ; ξένων : : ξένοις ; καρποῦ, καρπῶν : : καρποῦ, καρπόν; τροφῆς : : τροφῆς).[92]

The preceding evidence would seem to suggest that Aristides imitated different literary sources for his various references to Triptolemus; yet the apolitical nature of Philochorus' account and the tenuous conjecture in the case of Sophocles show the dangers of this kind of literary *Quellenforschung*. Moreover, the fullness of Aristides' account in passage D could not have derived from Callias' brief reference alone, and in fact there are serious differences between the passages. Triptolemus' functions as agricultural hero and Hierophant constitute Callias' whole point; for Aristides, Triptolemus is only one character in the larger Eleusinian story. In the light of these problems with the three possible literary sources mentioned and the absence of other extant ones, I should like to suggest that the thematic and even verbal parallels between Aristides and the earlier authors result, not from the direct influence of the latter, but from a common reliance on one major source, namely, the oral popular tradition of Athenian history. We noted earlier that the disclaimer ὡς λέγεται in Aristides and similar expressions in Xenophon and Isocrates point to the influence of a popular tradition.[93] Furthermore, Aristides mentions something about his sources for passage D (I.146): ... ποιηταὶ καὶ λογοποιοὶ καὶ συγγραφεῖς πάντες ὑμνοῦσιν.... We concluded in Chapter I that this kind of statement usually amounts to a conventional allusion to a living tradition of the sort that the Greeks were quite capable of transmitting orally over a long period of time and with a great deal of thematic and even verbal consistency.

The difficulty with the suggestion of the preceding paragraph is, of course, the lack of evidence for the tradition's transmission from the time of Xenophon to that of Aristides. There was indeed a renewal of interest in the tradition of Eleusis, the Eleusinian religion, and its political importance for Athens in the second century after Christ. The ancient Athenian demand for the first fruits was revived in Hadrian's day.[94] After the barbarian destruction of 170, which, by the way, elicited the *Eleusinus* from Aristides, Eleusis was restored to a greater magnificence and prestige than it had previously enjoyed.[95] Aristides himself provides the evidence for Triptolemus' continuing importance in this context. Unfortunately, we cannot easily discover how the ancient tradition of Eleusis survived to be reawakened in the second century. It is just possible, however, that one other aspect of the renewal in Hadrian's time may contain a clue to the transmission of the tradition. That emperor established an ephebic festival, the *Antinoeia,* at Eleusis.[96] It will be suggested in the final chapter that the patriotic speeches given by the ephebes on the occasion of such festivals were based on topics from the popular tradition. In fact, I will contend that the many ephebic speeches that were given throughout the long lives of these festivals constituted an oral form of the transmission of the popular tradition. It seems reasonable that Hadrian would have concerned himself, not only with Antinous and the Eleusinian religion, but also with the continuation of the ephebic political, military, oratorical, and athletic traditions which had been at least partially responsible for the transmission of the Athenian historical tradition so much admired by his classicizing age. It is this tradition that might well have carried on the fifth century's political view of Triptolemus.

1. For the story of Triptolemus, cf. Apollod. I. 5. 2, with helpful notes in the translation of Sir J.G. Frazer, *Apollodorus: The Library*, The Loeb Classical Library (New York: Putnam, 1921), p. 38, n. 2. Cf. F. Schwenn, *RE* Vol. VIIA, *s.v.* Triptolemos, cols. 213-30; G.E. Mylonas, *Eleusis and the Eleusinian Mysteries* (Princeton, 1969), pp. 20-22; N.J. Richardson, *The Homeric Hymn to Demeter* (Oxford, 1974), pp. 194-96 *et passim;* C. Kerényi, *Eleusis: Archetypal Image of Mother and Daughter*, trans. by R. Manheim (New York: Schocken Books, 1977), pp. 120-30.

2. For the particularly Athenian character of Aristides' reference to a theoric fund, cf. Oliver, *Civilizing Power*, p. 102. It is also interesting to note that the official delegations sent by the Greek cities to the Eleusinian mysteries were called 'theories': cf. Mylonas, *supra*, n. 1, p. 244.

3. For the chronological relationship between this oration and the *Panath.*, cf. *infra*, Chapter VI, n. 75.

4. 'Heracles and the Dioscuri were the first foreigners to be initiated. The athletic contest was first established at Eleusis of Attica, and there was the contest of the appearing fruit (καρποῦ), with men testing how much they might increase in strength from the benefits of agriculture (ἡμέρου τροφῆς).'

5. The relevant passages are: Isoc. *Paneg.* (4), 28-31; Pl. *Menex.* 237b-238a; Hyp. *Ep.* (6), 4f.; Demosth. *Ep.* (60), 4f.

6. Aristid. *Panath.* I. 163. Cf. Isoc. *Paneg.* (4), 24; Pl. *Menex.* 237b; Lys. *Ep.* (2), 2.

7. Aristid. *Panath.* I. 165. Cf. Isoc. *Paneg.* (4), 24, 28, 33; *Menex.* 237b and d. At *Paneg.* 25, Isocrates calls Attica, τροφός: Aristides' explicit rejection of this title at I. 165 may be an intentional correction of the older orator.

8. Aristid. *Panath.* 1. 166f. Cf. Isoc. *Paneg.* (4), 28f.; *Menex.* 237c, 238a; Hyp. *Ep.* (6), 5; Demosth. *Ep.* (60), 4f.

9. For Aristides' reliance on Isocrates for this matter in the *Eleusinus:*

   a. Isoc. *Paneg.* (4), 28: περί τε τῆς τοῦ βίου τελευτῆς ... ἡδίους τὰς ἐλπίδας ἔχουσιν ....

   b. *Eleus.* I.421: περὶ τῆς τελευτῆς ἡδίους ἔχειν τὰς ἐλπίδας....

10. Isocrates' very apology in the present case formed part of my argument: cf. *supra*, Chapter I, p. 7f.

11. This is true, despite the opinions of Oliver, *Ruling Power*, p. 880, and Schwenn, cf. *supra*, n. 1, col. 222, who maintain that, although Triptolemus is not actually mentioned in *Paneg.* 29, his presence is implied or assumed to exist in the minds of the audience. Cf. Mylonas, *supra*, n. 1, p. 21.

12. There were other traditions, all of which have yet to be studied carefully either in themselves or in relation to the dominant Athenian tradition. Pausanias (I. 14) mentions several, most importantly the Argive version. Also from Pausanias and from the *Marmor Parium* (ep. 14f.) we know the Orphics had a version of their own. Plato's *Apology* (41a) makes Triptolemus a judge in the underworld, a function confirmed by two vases. There was also an Egyptianized version: cf. *infra*, n. 79.

13. A catalogue of Triptolemus in vase paintings from the 6th, 5th, and 4th centuries at Athens appears in C. Dugas, "La mission de Triptolème," *Mélanges d'Archéologie et d'Histoire* (École Française de Rome), 62 (1950) 23-31. Other important collections include E. Buschor in A. Furtwängler and K. Reichhold, *Griechische Vasenmalerei*, Ser. III (Munich: Bruckmann, 1932), p. 260; J. Overbeck, *Griechische*

Kunstmythologie (Repr. Osnabrück: Biblio, 1968), pp. 530-89; B. Grossman, *The Eleusinian Gods and Heroes in Greek Art* (Diss. Washington Univ., 1959).

14. In only one case (Dugas, *ibid.*, no. 28), Triptolemus is not bearded. A.B. Cook, *Zeus*, Vol. I (Cambridge Univ., 1914), pp. 225ff., calls attention to the fact that the wheels are usually shown in profile, so that only one wheel appears. Cook connects this single wheel with the solar wheel, a symbol of the sun, but overlooks the passage in the *Epitaphios* of Hyperides where Athens distributing the gift of grain is said to resemble the sun: cf. *supra*, n. 5.

15. This is the older scheme, which does not make its way into red-figure ware. It vaguely recalls the Triptolemus of the *Homeric Hymn*, a mature king dispensing gifts to the people (cf. Dugas, *supra*, n. 13, p. 9).

16. *Ad Dem.* 153 (where Triptolemus is named as an Eleusinian chief) and 474ff. (where Demeter teaches her mysteries to T. and the other Eleusinian lords). Cf. Richardson, *supra*, n. 1, *ad loc.*

17. Cf. Schwenn, *supra*, n. 1, col. 219.

18. Attic painters certainly borrowed Triptolemus' wheeled chair from Dionysus. Two vases (Dugas, nos. 5 and 12) show both T. and Dionysus dispensing their gifts and borne on nearly identical chairs. Cook, cf. *supra*, n. 14, p. 214f., reproduces both paintings. The figure of Theseus as a cultural hero also influenced the myth of T.: cf. M. Nilsson, "Die eleusinischen Gottheiten," *Arch. f. Rel.* 32 (1935) 86 and 128.

19. For hints of the new style in black-figure pottery, cf. Dugas, *supra*, n. 13, p. 10.

20. There are only two exceptions. Dugas no. 28 and the obviously archaizing pelike (Dugas, no. 45), which is discussed by D. Feytmans, "Une représentation inusitée du départ de Triptolème," *L'Antiquité Classique* 14 (1945) 286-318.

21. The wing, probably taken from representations of Dionysus, became current in the first quarter of the fifth century (cf. Dugas, *supra*, n. 13, p. 10f.). Numerous examples from the Berlin Painter survive.

22. The snakes, which are unimportant in the first quarter of the fifth century, are first seen on a pair of vases from around 490/80. As the century advances, almost all representations portray the snakes. The source of the snakes is unknown. O. Kern, *Eleus. Beitr.* (Halle, 1909), p. 11, states that Sophocles (*Tript.* fr. 596) borrowed them from the Eleusinian mystery play. Triptolemus' hissing snakes certainly played a prominent part in the ceremony which Claudian witnessed (*De Rapt. Pers.* I, 12-14):

angues Triptolemi stridunt et squamea curvis
colla levant adtrita iugis lapsuque sereno
erecti roseas tendunt ad carmina cristas.

23. I would stress the distinction between grain and phiale less than Dugas, cf. *supra*, n. 13, pp. 9-19. Dugas overemphasizes the difference between the agrarian Triptolemus of the first part of the fifth century and the ministerial hero who holds the phiale (cf. *supra*, p. 20f.). There is, in fact, no contradiction between grain and mysteries. Even though T.'s agrarian mission may not have been part of the secret rites of Eleusis (cf. Mylonas, *supra*, n. 1, p. 269f.; Kerényi, *supra*, n. 1, pp. 120-30), grain certainly occupied an important position in the Eleusinian myth in general (Mylonas, pp. 238, 260f., 271, and 275), and T. had a place within the Athenian Eleusinium (cf. *supra*, p. 20).

24. Besides Dugas, cf. T.B.L. Webster, *Potter and Patron in Classical Athens* (London: Methuen, 1972), p. 257.

25. Cf. Dugas, no. 31.

26. I exclude from my text Panyassis of Halicarnassus, who was, properly speaking, outside the Athenian tradition; yet, since his city was a member of Athens' league, mention should be made of a comment about him by Apollodorus (I. 5. 2 = fr. 24 Kinkel): Πανύασις δὲ Τριπτόλεμον Ἐλευσῖνος λέγει·φησὶ γὰρ Δήμητρα πρὸς αὐτὸν ἐλϑεῖν. Panyassis apparently identified Eleusis with the Celeus of the *Homeric Hymn* and his Triptolemus with the *Hymn's* Demophoon. In this case T. was a youth for Panyassis, as he was for the red-figure painters.

27. I cannot accept the suggestion of F. Brommer ("War der *Triptolemus* des Sophokles ein Satyrspiel?", *Philologus* 94 [1939-40] 336-38), that the *Triptolemus* was a satyr play. His only cogent reason for taking it as such is the presence of a dancing Silenus on a vase with Triptolemus. The Silenus is probably borrowed from representations of Dionysus, as are so many of Triptolemus' characteristics. For the fragments, cf. A.C. Pearson, *Fragmenta* (Cambridge Univ., 1917), Vol. II.

28. Dion. Hal. *Ant. Rom.* I. 12. 2: μαρτυρεῖ δέ μοι τῷ λόγῳ Σοφοκλῆς μὲν ὁ τραγῳδοποιὸς ἐν Τριπτολέμῳ δράματι. πεποίηται γὰρ αὐτῷ Δημήτηρ διδάσκουσα τὸν Τριπτόλεμον, ὅσην χώραν ἀναγκασϑήσεται σπείρων τοῖς δοϑεῖσιν ὑπ' αὐτῆς καρποῖς διεξελϑεῖν (ed. C. Jacoby).

29. For the lands, cf. frs. 598, 600, 601, 602, 603 (?), 604, 617. For the diets of the local tribes, cf. frs. 600, 601, 603 (?), 605, 606, 607, 608, 609, 610.

30. Cf. fr. 611, ἀπυνδάκωτος οὐ τραπεζοῦται κύλιξ. A synonym for ἀπυνδάκωτος is ἀπύϑμενος (Pollux 10. 79), a term which Athenaeus (*Deipnos.* 501a) applies to phialai, whose importance for the mysteries we shall note *supra*, p. 21.

31. Cf. Mylonas, *supra*, n. 1, p. 192f. For the myrtle, cf. Dugas, *supra*, n. 13, p. 19.

32. Cf. T.L. Shear, *Hesp.* 8 (1939) 208f., fig. 9.

33. Cf. *supra*, n. 15.

34. Mylonas, cf. *supra*, n. 1, p. 193. Cf., however, Dugas,*supra*, n.13, p. 11.

35. Paus. I.14.2; *Marmor Parium*, ep. 12; Apollod. I.5.1; Schol. Aristid. III. 53. For Panyassis, cf. *supra*, n. 26. Sophocles, too, may have accepted this genealogy: cf. Schwenn, *supra*, n. 1, col. 221; Pearson, *supra*, n. 27, p. 242.

36. Cf. Richardson, *supra*, n. 1, p. 195f.

37. Cf. Dugas, *supra*, n. 13, p. 11f. For the snakes in the mysteries, cf. *supra*, n. 22 for Claudian. Feytmans, cf. *supra*, n. 20, p. 297, suggests the influence of Sophocles on vase painters.

38. As Sophocles shows, one of Demeter's functions in the scene of departure is to instruct the hero about his agricultural mission. Cf. Feytmans, *ibid.*, p. 300.

39. Cf. Dugas, *supra*, n. 13, pp. 13-16.

40. For Mylonas, cf. *supra*, n. 23.

41. For the *Hymn*, cf. ll. 49, 200f., 208ff. Cf. Dugas, *supra*, n. 13, pp. 12-14; Mylonas, *supra*, n. 1, p. 259f.; A. Delatte, *Le cycéon: Breuvage rituel des mystères d'Éleusis* (Paris: Société d'Édition "les Belles Lettres," 1955).

42. Cf. Dugas, *ibid.*, p. 15.

43. *Ibid.*, p. 10f.

44. Cf. Mylonas, *supra*, n. 1, p. 204f.; Feytmans, *supra*, n. 20. For the possibility that Panyassis described Triptolemus' initiation of Heracles in his *Heraclea*, cf. R. Rapetti, "Paniassi ed Eracle iniziato ai misteri eleusini," *La Parola del Passato* 21

(1966) 131-35. However, V.J. Matthews, *Panyassis of Halikarnassos: Text and Commentary, Mnemosyne* suppl. vol. 33 (Leiden: Brill, 1974), p. 116f., sees a weakness in Rapetti's arguments and assigns the fragment in question (24) to the *Ionica* rather than the *Heraclea*.

45. For Triptolemus' part, cf. the *Marmor Parium*, ep. 12: ἀφ' οὗ Δημήτηρ ἀφικομένη εἰς Ἀθήνας καρπὸν ἐφ[εῦρ]εν καὶ προ[ηροσία ἐ]πρά[χθη πρ]ώτη ὁ[εἴξαντος] / [Τ]ριπτολέμου τοῦ Κελεοῦ καὶ Νεαίρας... βασιλεύοντος Ἀθήνησιν Ἐριχθέως. Cf. F. Jacoby, *Das Marmor Parium* (Berlin: Weidmann, 1904), pp. 6f., and 63. For the *Proerosia*, cf. Mylonas, *supra*, n. 1, p. 7, n. 3.

46. Again the *Marmor Parium* is our source (ep. 13): ἀφ' οὗ Τριπτό[λεμος ἐθέρισε τὸν καρπόν, ὃν]ἔσπειρεν ἐν τῆι Ραρίαι καλουμένηι Ἐλευσῖνι, ἔτη Χ[Η]ΔΔΔΔΓ, βασιλεύοντος Ἀθηνῶν [Ἐριχθέως. For the *Haloa*, cf. Jacoby, *ibid.*, pp. 65-68. Pausanias confirms all this by speaking of the sacred threshing floor (ἅλως) of Triptolemus (I. 38. 6) and by repeatedly referring to T. as the distributor of agriculture (I. 14. 2; VII. 18. 2; VIII. 4. 1). Himerius (*Or.* 23. 6, ed. Colonna) also connects Triptolemus with the ἥμερος καρπός. Isocrates (*Paneg.* 28) mentions the traditional ἥμερος καρπός without Triptolemus. Cf. Schol. Luc. *Dial. Mort.* 7. 4. (= *Rhein. Mus.* 25 (1870) 559: ... τὰς ἡμέρους τροφὰς παρὰ αὐτῶν εὑρεθῆναι καὶ πᾶσι κοινωνηθῆναι τοῖς ἀνθρώποις παρ' αὐτῶν [the Athenians]).

47. Cf. Mylonas, *supra*, n. 1, pp. 238 and 244. It should also be mentioned that Triptolemus had temples in the vicinity of the Eleusinia in Athens (Paus. I. 14. 1-4) and at Eleusis (I. 38. 6). Unfortunately, the age and political significance of these buildings are problematic. For sacrifices received by T. at the Eleusinian games: cf. *IG* I² 5 = F. Sokolowski, *Lois sacrées des cités grecques* (Paris: École Française d'Athènes, 1969), no. 4. For the political significance of *IG* I² 5, cf. R.M. Simms, "The *Eleusinia* in the Sixth to Fourth Centuries B.C.," *GRBS* 16 (1975) 269-79, who suggests that the reorganization of the *Eleusinia* into an Athenian propagandistic festival dates either to 560-27 or interestingly, 480-68.

48. For such a vase, cf. the reproduction in M. Verrall and J. Harrison, *Mythology and the Monuments of Ancient Athens* (London: Macmillan, 1890), p. 99. For other artistic works, cf. Mylonas, *supra*, n. 1, p. 193.

49. Our three testimonia for the play's production are:
   a. The *Triptolemus* was produced within one year of 468 (Pliny, *H.N.* XVIII, 65).
   b. Sophocles won a victory in 469/8 (*IG* II² 2325 and *Marmor Parium*, ep. 56). Cf. the *Fasti, IG* I², p. 277.
   c. Cimon and his fellow generals awarded Sophocles his first victory for his first production, apparently in 469/8 (Plut. *Cim.* 8. 8).

Cf. W. Schmid and O. Stählin, *Geschichte der griechischen Literatur*, Part I, Vol. II (Munich: Beck, 1934), p. 313f.

50. Cf. Mylonas, *supra*, n. 1, pp. 106-13.

51. *Ibid.*, pp. 113-28.

52. I accept the view of A.E. Raubitschek, "The Peace Policy of Pericles," *AJA* 70 (1966) 37-41. Cf. *infra*, Chapter VI, pp. 158-60; Mylonas, *ibid.*, p. 127.

53. On the surface, of course, the very rebuilding of the shrines destroyed by the Persians was in violation of the oath at Diod. XI.29.3 and part of the program of the Congress Decree (cf. Plut. *Per.* 17. 1).

54. *IG* I² 66 = *ML* 46, and *IG* I² 63 = *ML* 69, respectively. Cf. the decree concerning the colony at Brea: *IG* I² 45 = *ML* 49.

55. For the date of the decree, possibly towards the end of the Archidamian War, cf. Meiggs, *Athenian Empire*, p. 304. If my theories are correct, there should have been a similar decree passed near the middle of the century. L. Preller, *Griechische Mythologie*, Vol. I (Berlin: Weidmann, 1894), p. 773 and n. 3, believes that the oracle mentioned in the decree was historical and should be dated to the middle of the fifth century. For the parallelism between this decree and those governing the tribute, cf. *ML.* p. 220. Cf. Sokolowski, *supra*, n. 47, no. 5.

56. For the translations, cf. C.W. Fornara, *Archaic Times to the End of the Peloponnesian War*, Vol. I of E. Badian and R.K. Sherk (eds.), *Translated Documents of Greece and Rome* (Baltimore: Johns Hopkins, 1977), p. 157f.

57. The allies must comply, whereas there is merely a strong suggestion made to the other Greeks: cf. Meiggs, *Athenian Empire*, pp. 303-05.

58. *Paneg.* (4), 30f.

59. Schol. Arist. *Panath.* III.55.24ff.: ...λοιμοῦ ἐνσκήψαντος τοῖς Ἕλλησιν, ἔχρησεν ὁ θεὸς μὴ προτέρου ἂν πεπαῦσθαι τὴν νόσον, εἰ μὴ σὺν τῇ μητροπόλει τῶν καρπῶν προηροσίας θύουσι τῇ Δήμητρι,δεικνὺς ἐντεῦθεν πρώτους Ἀθηναίους δεδέχθαι τὸν σῖτον. The Scholion may reflect Philochorus: cf. Lenz, *Aristeidesscholien*, p. 65f. and n. 1. Diodorus confirms this as the Athenian version (I. 29. 3f.): ὁμολογεῖν δὲ καὶ τοὺς Ἀθηναίους ὅτι βασιλεύοντος Ἐρεχθέως καὶ τῶν καρπῶν διὰ τὴν ἀνομβρίαν προηφανισμένων ἡ τῆς Δήμητρος ἐγένετο παρουσία πρὸς αὐτοὺς καὶ ἡ δωρεὰ τοῦ σίτου. He goes on to mention, in the same vein as the *Marmor Parium*, the invention of the mysteries and the institution of the agricultural festivals. In a later passage (V. 68f.), Diodorus mentions that festivals (which ones?) were established in gratitude to Demeter for returning the gift of grain and assigning its distribution to Triptolemus after she had withheld it because of her daughter's rape: cf. also, V. 4. 4.

60. This may be true even in so mundane a matter as the imperial grain trade. Around 450, Triptolemus appeared in his magic chair on the coinage of Cyzicus, an important emporium for grain in the empire: cf. B.V. Head, *Historia Numorum*² (Oxford, 1911), p. 525.

61. For the only other fourth-century literary reference to Triptolemus' mission, cf. Pl. *Leg.* 782b: ... καὶ τὰ Δήμητρός τε καὶ Κόρης δῶρα ... Τριπτόλεμόν τέ τινα τῶν τοιούτων γενέσθαι διάκονον.

62. For the pottery, cf. Feytmans, *supra*, n. 20, p. 311. For Panyassis, cf. *supra*, n. 44.

63. Cf. *supra*, p. 17f.

64. Cf. Dugas, *supra*, n. 13, p. 21; J.D. Beazley, "Panathenaica," *AJA* 47 (1943) 464 and n. 4.

65. *IG* II² 140, ll. 20-22: τῶ[ι δὲ Διὶ καὶ τῆι Δήμη]- / τρι καὶ τῆ[ι Κόρηι καὶ τῶι Τριπτο]- / λέμωι καὶ [τῶι θεῶι ... κτλ. The tradition of calling for and receiving the first fruits continued well into the fourth century (*IG* II² 1672) and either survived, or was revived, in the time of Hadrian (*IG* II² 2956-57): cf. *supra* p. 30. Moreover, the call for international recognition of the sacred gifts continued to be made as a preliminary to the Greater Mysteries (*IG* II² 1235-36).

66. Cf. Dugas, *supra*, n. 13, p. 20f.

67. *Ibid.*

68. *Ibid.*: cf. Mylonas, *supra*, n. 1, p. 195f.

69. For the orators, cf. *supra*, n. 5. So also Diodorus, who mentions the gifts in many places (I. 29. 1; V. 69. 1f.; XIII. 26. 3) and in different ways (cf. *supra*, n. 59), can assign the function of distributing grain and establishing festivals to the city of Athens rather than Triptolemus (V. 4. 4).

70. Cf. Oliver, *Civilizing Power*, p. 18, for text, translation, and references to published editions.

71. The passages are noted by Oliver, *ibid.*, p. 18f.

72. For art, cf. Mylonas, *supra*, n. 1, p. 197f. For Claudian, cf. *supra*, n. 22.

73. A Scholion upon Aristides probably refers to this very passage of Philochorus (III. 54): καὶ ὅμως Ἀριστείδης οὕτως ἔδοξεν, εἶναι πτερωτὸν τὸ ἅρμα, ὅτι ταχέως ἄνω τε καὶ κάτω κατήρχετο. Φιλόχορος δὲ ἱστορεῖ ὅτι ἡ ναῦς, ἔνϑα ἦν ὁ Τριπτόλεμος, διὰ τοῦτο ἐνομίσϑη ὑπόπτερος, ἐπειδὴ ἐξ οὐρίας ἐφέρετο.

74. Cf. *supra*, n. 59.

75. L. Pearson, *The Local Historians of Attica* (Philadelphia: APA, 1942), pp. 112-14.

76. Cf. Cook, *supra*, n. 14, p. 222f.; Overbeck, *supra*, n. 13, p. 551, no. 51, Atlas, Plate XVI, no. 13.

77. The 'good art' refers either to the art of the plow or agriculture in general.

78. Hygin. *Astr.* 2. 14, narrates the story of Charnabon's plot against Triptolemus. Sophocles' *Triptolemus* likewise told the story of Charnabon (fr. 604 P). It is generally believed that Eratosthenes influenced the *Astronomica* to a considerable extent, and though Hyginus quotes Eratosthenes in 2.14 for a variant version, Eratosthenes himself could have given variant versions.

79. Diod. I. 18. 2; Demeter is twice identified with Isis (I. 14. 1 and V. 69. 1) in defense of Egypt's claim to the invention of agriculture. That Osiris' agricultural function was a Greek import from the myth of Triptolemus was proved by O. Rubensohn, "Triptolemus als Pflüger," *Athen. Mittheil.* 24 (1899) 61. Cf. also, J.G. Griffiths, *Plutarch's De Iside et Osiride* (Cambridge Univ.: University of Wales, 1970), p. 309.

80. C.H. Roberts, *The Antinoopolis Papyri*, Vol. I (London: Egypt Exploration Society, 1951), pp. 39ff., no. 18, contends that the papyrus reflects a branch of the Eleusinian mysteries in Alexandria. This is denied by A. Delatte, "La papyrus d'Antinoopolis relatif aux mystères," *Académie Royale de Belgique—Classe des Lettres*, Ser. 5, 38 (1952) 202f. (Cf. the same title in *Comptes Rendus de l'Académie des Inscriptions et Belles Lettres*, 1952, pp. 251-58). Cf. M. Nilsson, "The Royal Mysteries," *Harvard Theol. Rev.* 50 (1957) 66; Griffiths, *supra*, n. 79, p. 91f. If we accept one of Delatte's conjectures, that the papyrus represents a literary exercise involving the initiation of Heracles, Panyassis could be a literary source. At any rate, a prayer to Triptolemus seems to reflect the fourth-century phenomenon of his deification.

81. Besides the article by Ch. Picard, "La patère d'Aquileia et l'Éleusinisme à Rome au début de l'époque impériale," *Antiquité Classique* 20 (1951) 362f., I am indebted to the work of G. Cart, "Triptolème d'après deux lampes antiques de Musée du Louvre," *Mélanges Picard* (=*Revue Archéologique*, 1948), pp. 142-53.

82. Cf. Picard, *ibid.*, p. 362f.; Delatte, *supra*, n. 80, *Académie Royale*, p. 203.

83. Delatte, *ibid.*, p. 201, and Cook, cf. *supra*, n. 14, p. 223. Both scholars oppose O. Kern, "De Triptolemo Aratore" in *Genethliacon Gottingense* (Halle: Niemeyer,

1888), pp. 102-05, who makes the plow an Alexandrian invention. Moreover, there may have been some identification at Athens between Triptolemus and Epimenides the Bouzyges: cf. Schwenn, *supra,* n. 1, col. 214; Delatte, *ibid.,* p. 201.

84. Cf., however, G. Hafner, "Der Silberteller von Aquilei," *Arch. Anz.* 82 (1967) 213-19, who maintains that the main figure is Ploutos, not Triptolemus.

85. Picard, cf. *supra,* n. 81, p. 363f.

86. R.S. Poole, *Catalogue of the Coins of Alexandria* (Repr. Bologna: A. Forni, 1964), pp. xlii, 49, 71, 82, 120, 148, 163, and 264.

87. The passages are, respectively: *Rhet. ad Her.* IV.6.9; *Trist.* III. 8. 1f.; *Epid.* 28 (p. 53, 22, Lang).

88. Cf. *Fast.* IV. 393-620.

89. I. 239-42.

90. Athena's original gift of the chariot to an Athenian was a part of the tradition of the *Atthis.* Cf. Oliver, *Civilizing Power,* p. 104f.

91. Cf. *supra,* p. 16, and n. 4.

92. Another interesting parallel may be that between Callias' δεῖξαι and ὁ[είξαντος] of the *Marmor Parium:* cf. *supra,* n. 45.

93. Cf. *supra,* p. 25.

94. Cf. *supra,* n. 65.

95. Cf. Mylonas, *supra,* n. 1, pp. 156-86.

96. *Ibid.,* p. 155; P. Graindor, "Études sur l'éphébie attique sous l'empire," *Musée Belge* 26 (1922) 185-88.

CHAPTER III
THE DEPARTURE OF THE SPARTANS

Chapter II began with a citation of the passage from Aristides' *Panathenaicus* about the opening of the offensive war which the Hellenes launched against the Persian Empire once they had expelled Xerxes from Greece. Aristides portrayed the beginning of the crusade against Persia as a whirlwind campaign which recalled to his mind the winged progress of the Athenian cultural hero Triptolemus. My study of the rest of the war will continue in accordance with the methodology laid down previously: the framework of Aristides' narrative will provide the framework for my discussion, and quotations from his text will supply the starting points for the sections of my analysis. Our next task, therefore, will be to examine the refusal of the Spartans to participate further in the war. Expanding upon the theme of 'speed' that characterized his reference to Triptolemus, Aristides reports that the Spartans and other contingents from mainland Greece found it so difficult to maintain the momentum of the struggle against Persia, that they left the war to Athens and her new allies from Asiatic Greece (I. 246):

> *With the intention (of thus improving upon Triptolemus), the Athenians swiftly skirted the coast of Asia and immediately sailed up the navigable rivers; no sooner were they reported to be somewhere than they were actually seen. They really seemed to be participating in a spectacle like a war dance in full armor. They leaped into their movements so frequently and intensely that even the Spartans, who had stayed with them throughout the first phases, fell back like men who could not keep up with winged compatriots. In just the same way, the other Greeks, the ones who had sailed out with the Athenians earlier, fell reeling out of the contest. But the Athenians kept on going and made do with new partners, the Ionians, who had been under the King's sway and were led by him against those other Greeks and Greece herself earlier in the war. The fact is*

that out of his own resources the King supplied the Athenians with materiel for the war against himself: his naval bases, fortresses, armed camps, everything went over to them; his arms and ships became theirs.

Beecke assumes that the preceding passage refers to the transfer of the hegemony from Sparta to Athens, the renunciation of the command by the Spartans, and the foundation of the Delian League, all of which Thucydides narrates in a straightforward manner.[1] The tenor of the passage does not seem to reflect events prior to the transfer of the hegemony, and the last line refers to the tribute and other resources which the eastern Greeks made available to the masters of the Delian League. Thus, Beecke's conclusions are accurate insofar as the passage marks the point in history where the Spartans terminated their active participation in the war against Xerxes and left everything to the Athenians; yet the assumption of agreement with Thucydides could be deceiving. To be sure, Aristides appears to define significant chronological divisions in the same manner as Thucydides. For both authors, the Battle of Plataea represents a major chronological break, before which there had been 'the war' and after which a new period began.[2] Just as Thucydides opens his digression on the distinct period of the Pentecontaetia with the sieges of Sestos and Byzantium, Aristides inserts a long rhetorical interlude between Plataea and the first events of the next period, namely, the Battle of Mycale and the attacks on Sestos and Byzantium.[3] The two authors agree that the next important historical development was the departure of the Spartans.[4] In spite of these similarities, however, I hope to demonstrate in this chapter that the dissimilarities outweigh them enough to warrant the conclusion that Aristides was relying on a tradition of fifth-century chronology and events that was independent of Thucydides.

Modern accounts of the departure of the Spartans rely on Thucydides and supplement him with other historical sources.[5] These sources, however, assign little intrinsic value to the Spartan departure, which assumes importance only in the context of more significant events: Pausanias' misconduct, the transfer of the hegemony, the foundation of the Delian League, and the institution of the Athenian Empire. Beecke, for example, drew on the historical tradition for such terms as the transfer, the Delian League, and *phoroi*. These terms do not appear in our passage of Aristides, who seems to be uninterested in giving the Spartan departure any of the significance that historians have recognized in it. Moreover, Aristides' reticence about the implications of the Spartan withdrawal becomes quite serious when we note that the lacuna was intentional. Aristides was a careful writer: he would not have been so inadvertent as to omit events about which he knew, unless he had wanted to omit them. Casual references throughout his discourses prove that he was fully aware of the effects of Pausanias' misconduct,[6] the story of the allies offering the hegemony to the Athenians,[7] and the assessment of Aristides the Just.[8] Furthermore, Aristides the Rhetor not only purposely ignored the significance of the formal transfer of the hegemony, he added an apparently unhistorical and confusing detail to his version of the event: the siege of Eion, the first action of the Delian League according to Thucydides, precedes the departure of the Spartans in Aristides.[9] Moreover, the context of the passage cited above will not allow the reader to attach any practical importance to the Spartan departure. Throughout Aristides' narrative of the period following Plataea, the Athenians originate and implement a plan to humble the Persian king.[10] The Spartans simply attended the designs of the Athenians.[11] There was, in effect, no transfer of the hegemony, since the Athenians held the hegemony even before the Spartans left.

What could have motivated Aristides to construct a narrative so openly contradicted by the historians? He might have been engaging in a bit of tendentious boasting on behalf of the city he was praising. However, in so allusive an author as Aristides, one must search for sources; and if the preceding chapters are not too far from the mark, we ought to examine fifth-century tradition as a possible source. Such an examination will constitute the main theme of this chapter; yet, since a genuine fifth-century tradition standing behind Aristides' attitude to the transfer of the hegemony could be important for our understanding of the chronology of the first half of that century, the subject of chronology will constitute a secondary theme. Aristides' silence about the transfer of the hegemony, after all, represents only one part of his chronological analysis of the fifth century, which differs substantially from that of Thucydides. Rhetorical and historical elements combine in Aristides' narrative to minimize the break at Plataea and to demonstrate that the many battles fought against Persia from Marathon to the Peace of Callias constituted a single war, throughout which Athens maintained a *de facto* hegemony. Since Sparta's earlier hegemony was purely formal and totally unreal, Aristides could gloss over the apparent transfer of the hegemony in a few ambiguous words and divide the century into two nearly equal periods, the Persian War and the Greek War. Thucydides developed a different set of chronological divisions, in which the transfer of the hegemony was the pivotal point that introduced a fifty-year period of Athenian growth between the war against Persia and the twenty-seven-year war against Sparta.

Aristides twice states explicitly his belief in the unity of the entire conflict with Persia. For him the first half of the fifth century was taken up with the Persian War, which had three parts: the campaign of Marathon, the struggle in Greece against Xerxes, and the counterattack that led to the Peace of Callias:

1. I. 250: *Such was the war that Athens prosecuted against the barbarians both in Greece and in their own country; but such also was the Peace that she made. In both she showed that she did not march out in pursuit of wealth nor even for the pleasure of gain, but with this one goal in mind: to secure the freedom of the Greeks from the barbarians. And yet who could name a nobler crowning act of war or peace with Greeks or with barbarians than that by which Athens concluded her business in those days?*

2. I. 276: *Apart from this, Athens' excellence was proved in all three phases of the war. In the first part, she alone accomplished the task. In the second, she stood in the forefront of danger against the King and received the prize of valor. The final phase once again belonged to her alone; this included the naval and land battles off Cyprus and Pamphylia and the great drive between them. So it is that Athens, standing alone, was first to conquer the barbarians; then, when she stood beside others, she outdid her allies no less than her enemies; and she alone remained to the end.*

These direct statements merely repeat and summarize a concept of unity which underlies Aristides' narrative from Marathon to Callias. Aristides achieves this unity by weaving into his account four partly historical and partly rhetorical themes: σωτηρία and ἐλευθερία; the fear that the war inspired; the punishment of the King's hybris; and the true hegemony of the Athenians. I shall trace these themes in the *Panathenaicus* and then attempt to demonstrate how they and the chronological system they imply derive from a true popular tradition of the fifth century, which was independent of, and certainly older than, the highly personal analysis of Thucydides.

1. Σωτηρία and ἐλευθερία. Aristides quite naturally presents the campaigns of 490 and 480/79 as Athenian struggles on behalf of Greek salvation and freedom. In a preface to his account of the Persian War, Aristides calls that conflict, ὁ ἀγὼν ὑπὲρ τῆς σωτηρίας.[12] At Marathon, Athens single-handedly preserved Hellenic freedom and safety,[13] and her wisdom and superiority at Salamis meant that in that battle, too, she alone was responsible for the salvation and freedom of Greece.[14] Aristides, however, thematically connects his account of the two earlier phases of the war with the final phase by insisting that the desire for freedom, peace, and safety motivated the Athenians to lead an offensive campaign against Persian domains (I. 244):[15]

Thus, to avoid suggesting anything untoward, I will just say that, in her conduct of the next phase no less clearly than in the first, Athens conducted the war as a proof of her true justice and courage. Moreover, she undertook the task of protecting the security and safety of the Greeks; yet she also reasoned that an honorable and real peace could be had by all only if the Greeks pushed the barbarians as far as possible from Greece. This was impossible if she reined in the allies and guarded them in the home territory or if she accomplished nothing on their behalf and they did nothing for themselves. The Athenians arrived at this accurate conclusion by correctly analyzing the nature of the situation, since normally the only people who are truly at peace are those who show that they do not always insist on living in peace.

Moreover, in a passage cited earlier,[16] Aristides summed up Athens' conduct of the whole war from Marathon to Callias by stressing his belief that the Athenian goal had always been the freedom of Greece rather than profit. This directly contradicts Thucydides' judgment about the purpose of the Delian League: πρόσχημα γὰρ ἦν ἀμύνεσθαι ὧν ἔπαθον δῃοῦντας τὴν βασιλέως χώραν.[17] Whether or not Aristides intended to correct Thucydides, he certainly conceived of a single conflict from Marathon to Callias motivated by an admirable singleness of purpose in the Athenians.

2. The theme of fear (φόβος or δέος). As we shall see in greater detail in Chapter VI, Aristides carefully frames his account of the last phase of the war with two rhetorically significant expansions on a theme of fear. In the earlier passage, which serves as an introduction for the last part of the war, Aristides shows that Athens intended to transfer fear from the Greeks to the King: τοὺς φόβους

καὶ τοὺς κινδύνους εἰς τὴν ἐκείνων μεταστῆσαι (I.243). From 490 to 479 Greece feared Persia; from 479, Athens acted in such a way that Persia increasingly feared Greece. At the end of this last phase of the war, the Athenian policy had succeeded: the King conceived such a fear for his own person that he accepted the terms of the Peace of Callias.[18] What is significant for my present argument is that Aristides does not confine the theme of fear to the last part of the war. He employs it in a similar manner to frame his account of the second phase. Before Thermopylae, Aristides predicts that Xerxes will find Athens at Artemisium and Salamis and that the King, ἐκπλαγεὶς ἔδεισεν οὐ μόνον περὶ τῶν λοιπῶν, ἀλλὰ καὶ περὶ τοῦ σώματος (I. 212). Later, at the sight of his disaster at Salamis, the King, ἐκπλαγείς, sings a recantation and flees (I. 230). The theme of fear, therefore, constitutes a thematic bond between the last two phases of the war and is intimately related to an even more unifying motif, namely, the punishment of the King's hybris.

3. *The punishment of the King's hybris.* Aristides introduces the campaign of 480/79 with a damning criticism of Xerxes as a man of hybris. A similar judgement was passed upon Darius,[19] but Xerxes τοσοῦτον ὕβρισε τῇ περιβολῇ ὥστ' ἔγνω τὸν πρότερον στόλον ὡσπερεὶ παιδιὰν ἀποφῆναι (I. 206). Aristides expatiates primarily upon Xerxes' attempt to serve his mad ambitions by turning nature topsy-turvy and vying with Zeus (I. 209): ἐδέχετο δ' αὐτὸν οὔτε γῆ οὔτε θάλαττα ἱκανῶς, καὶ ταῦτα εἶχε πρὸς τὴν ἐκείνου χρείαν καὶ μετέβαλλεν εἰς ἄλληλα. The greatest atrocities were the bridging of the Hellespont and the channelling of Athos.[20] The story of the *peripeteia* of the hybristic King occupies an important position in Aristides' narration of the whole war. Athenian involvement with Persia began as a desire to punish (δίκην λαβεῖν) the King for daring to enslave the Ionians,[21] and Aristides repeats the Athenian intention in his introduction to the war's final stage (I. 245):

> They went about punishing those who deserved it. Thus, they clearly understood that mankind would receive great benefits from their inflicting punishments on the violent barbarians, who had overstepped their proper bounds.

During the course of the war, the Athenians engulf the King in a downfall that draws together all the themes we have seen: Athens saves and frees Greece by forcing the King to fear for himself. The Peace of Callias, of course, represents the climax of the *peripeteia*.[22]

4. *The true hegemony of the Athenians.* Aristides' most

convincing argument for the unity of the war lies in his insistence that Athens held the true hegemony throughout the war (I. 223):

> To be sure, the Athenians did not give the hegemony over to others in the actual accomplishment of deeds as they did in the matters of the title and the wing of the battle-line. How could they? The truth is that the Spartans had a nominal hegemony, but the Athenians had the real one. The nobility of the Athenians' position is evident in the fact that they held the hegemony over the hegemones; in fact, no command was valid unless it was approved by a certain Athenian. So it was that the Spartan admiral commanded the commanders of the other contingents, but the Athenian ruled over the commander of the commanders.

The Spartan hegemony was a phantom title, whereas the ἀληθινὴ ἡγεμονία always rested with Athens.[23] Aristides supports this explicit statement by constructing his whole narrative to illustrate his thesis that Athenian excellence in every aspect of the war proved that the true hegemony belonged to Athens. In fact, Aristides pictures the Persian War as a contest of excellence, in which the Athenians defeated both their allies and the enemy (I. 195):

> When the case was being decided between Greeks and barbarians and a small part of the world was engaged in a contest with a large part, the issue was not only safety but also excellence. Athens conquered each race in a more noble way than could have been hoped for: the Greeks were shown to provide her with very little assistance and the larger race appeared to be as inferior as it was large.

The Athenians exhibited their excellence in several ways. Athens stood alone against the Persians at Marathon and won the ἀριστεῖα for Artemisium and Salamis.[24] The Athenian presence was so vital to the allied cause, that Aristides repeatedly voiced the sentiment that, if the Persians could have subdued Athens, the rest of Greece would have fallen. Since both Darius and Xerxes knew this, they sent embassies to demand Athens' submission before their respective wars.[25] Xerxes tried twice more after his initial attempt failed: once between Thermopylae and Salamis and again shortly before Plataea.[26] The Athenians demonstrated further excellence by teaching the other Greeks how to oppose the barbarians. Marathon served as the initial paradigm for the valor of the later contests,[27] in which the Athenians restrained and encouraged the Spartans as though they were children.[28]

The conclusion which Aristides draws from this litany of Athenian virtues appears in a hypothetical debate concerning the hegemony which the Athenians might have, but did not, put forward on the eve of the Battle of Salamis. The rhetorical purpose of the debate is to demonstrate how the Athenians conquered their allies in fairness, gentleness, and high-mindedness by not demanding the titular hegemony even though it belonged to them on account of their excellence at Marathon and the superiority of their preparations for the upcoming battle at Salamis.[29] To be sure, they had already provided the three prerequisites for the Greek victory at Salamis: the best general,[30] the majority of the triremes,[31] and the boldest courage.[32] Nevertheless, the Athenians accepted the titular leadership of the Spartans. Aristides recognizes the virtue in the Athenians' refusal to contest the hegemony and in the rest of their behavior, and so he concludes his hypothetical debate with the explicit statement of Athens' true hegemony that we noted above.[33] For Aristides, therefore, excellence and superiority alone show where the true hegemony lies; and the Athenians exercised such an hegemony throughout the Persian War, during which no transfer of a purely formal hegemony could have had any serious impact.[34]

Although no continuous version of the Persian War as extensive as Aristides' has survived in a popular medium, careful study of the poetic, artistic, and particularly the oratorical traditions of the fifth and fourth centuries will elucidate consistent references to the four themes that we have seen in Aristides' account. Moreover, it will become apparent in the following discussion that the popular tradition agreed with Aristides in not totally denying the existence of a transfer of hegemony, but in glossing over it at its proper place in the narrative and implying strongly that Athens held the true hegemony from Marathon to Callias.[35] The similarity between the accounts of Aristides and those in the various popular media should confirm that the former presents an accurate version of the popular tradition of the fifth century, although it will not necessarily indicate his specific source. I shall begin by discussing the history of the four themes that we have seen in Aristides' narrative.

1. Σωτηρία and ἐλευθερία. It is not difficult to show that these two words, especially the latter, served as catchwords for describing the aims and achievements of the Greeks during the first two phases of the war. Freedom or slavery was the issue at Marathon, and the stated purpose of the Hellenic League was the liberation of Greece.[36]

The Oath of Plataea bound its adherents to fight for the freedom of Greece, and the Covenant of Plataea called on its signatories to commemorate their victories in Greece by conducting the games of the *Eleutheria* and to continue the war against Persia.[37] The catchwords were applied especially to the Athenians, who, according to Pindar, established φαενναν κρηπιδ' ἐλευθερίας at Artemisium (fr. 77 Snell). Moreover, Herodotus' judgment is well known (VII. 139. 5):

> However, if one were to say that the Athenians became the saviors of Greece, he would not miss the mark of truth. In fact, whichever side the Athenians supported was likely to predominate. Thus, by deciding that Greece should remain free, they, after the gods of course, were the ones responsible for stirring up Greece (that portion of it which had not medized) and repelling the King.

Since Herodotus admitted that his opinion was likely to be ἐπίφθονον μὲν πρὸς τῶν πλεόνων ἀνθρώπων, we can probably assume that he took it from popular Athenian tradition. For our purposes, however, it is essential to demonstrate that the catchwords σωτηρία and ἐλευθερία were popularly extended to the final phase of the war and realized completely only with the Peace of Callias. The orators of the fourth century unanimously reflect the popularity of such an extension in their own century. Lysias, in his *Epitaphios*, says that the Athenians freed Greece at Salamis and Plataea and then continued to keep her free by enforcing on the Persians the terms of the Peace of Callias.[38] For Isocrates the act of salvation came first and was followed by the liberation (*Paneg.* (4), 83): οὐ μόνον δὲ τὰς αὐτῶν πατρίδας διέσωσαν, ἀλλὰ καὶ τὴν σύμπασαν Ἑλλάδα ἠλευθέρωσαν. Isocrates normally uses σωτηρία to describe the Athenian aim in the war up to Plataea[39] and ἐλευθερία for the Athenian achievement after the expulsion of Xerxes from Greece.[40] In the *Menexenus*, on the contrary, Plato speaks of ἐλευθερία as the Athenian goal throughout the war and σωτηρία for the battles which lead directly to Callias.[41] Lycurgus follows Lysias in maintaining that the Athenians liberated the Greeks at Salamis and then set the boundaries for Greek freedom with the Peace of Callias.[42] Furthermore, one should note the motivation that Ephorus assigns to Themistocles for carrying on the war: τοὺς ἄλλους τοὺς κατὰ τὴν Ἀσίαν Ἕλληνας ... ἐλευθερώσειν (Diod. XI. 41. 4).

Most scholars balk at accepting the fourth-century orators as evidence for fifth-century traditions, since the Attic orators frequently are thought to have constructed tendentious accounts of fifth-century history to satisfy the requirements of their highly programmatic literature. The catchwords 'salvation' and 'freedom' might be examples of rhetorical distortion when they are applied to the last phase of the war. Orators like Isocrates spoke in favor of a new Athenian hegemony to replace the Spartan domination, which had failed to secure the freedom of the Greeks. To make the concept of another Athenian Empire palatable, the orators had to portray the fifth-century empire as a champion of freedom and autonomy by applying to it the panhellenic catchwords of the Persian War.[43] The possibility of such unreliability in the orators makes it incumbent upon us to examine fifth-century sources, if we wish to assure ourselves that the popular tradition of the fourth century derived from the popular tradition of the fifth. This procedure, however, creates a serious stumbling block to any who would argue that fifth-century Athenians applied the catchword ἐλευθερία to the offensive campaigns against Persia. Thucydides, in his analysis of the originally published purpose of the Delian League, ignored liberation and concentrated on the motive that Aelius Aristides explicitly rejected, namely, vengeance and reparation (I. 96. 1): πρόσχημα γὰρ ἦν ἀμύνεσθαι ὧν ἔπαθον δηοῦντας τὴν βασιλέως χώραν.

Mr. Sealey has accepted Thucydides' statement at face value and rejected as later propaganda all claims that the league was also formed to liberate the eastern Greeks from Persia.[44] A number of scholars, however, have refuted Sealey's thesis by returning to a variation on the theory of J.A.O. Larson: the organization of the Delian League within the older Hellenic League shows that the former's purpose was to serve merely as an instrument of the latter for the conduct of the naval war against Persia.[45] Larson may have stated the case too strongly, but clearly most Greeks believed that the Delian League was intended to carry on the ideals of the Hellenic League. Just as in the earlier alliance, the members simply bore the title, the Hellenes, and their financial officers were called Hellenotamiai.[46] The Athenians felt that they did not invalidate their relationship with the Hellenic League until they withdrew from that organization after the incident at Ithome during the revolt of the Helots.[47] Most scholars, therefore, oppose Sealey and insist that Thucydides' statement on the published purpose of the Delian League is incomplete. The liberation of Greece was as important an element of the allies' program in the early days of the Delian League as it had been in the elder league, which was created as Xerxes' invasion was threatening Greece. This explains how Spartan propaganda of later years could meaningfully taunt Athens, the tyrant city, with the league's early catchword, liberation.[48] Brasidas' audiences, for example, would remember the failure of Athens' promise of freedom.

Those who oppose Sealey, of course, must explain why Thucydides omitted liberation from his own description of the purpose of the Delian League. Sealey himself comes close to the truth in his discussion of two other Thucydidean passages which do make mention of liberation as a purpose of the league.[49] Both statements appear in polemical speeches in which the speakers are able to strengthen their anti-Athenian sentiments by pointing to the hypocrisy of the earlier promise of liberation. Sealey believes that Thucydides placed these references to liberation in oratory because they represent the kind of popular opinion that is too suspicious to be accepted as authentic; Thucydides' own conception leaves no room for the claim of liberation. Sealey is essentially correct in his analysis of Thucydides' historical method; yet I would carry his judgment one step farther in the light of our discussion of Thucydides' disdain for the popular tradition in Chapter I. Our findings there would seem to indicate that, although Thucydides could comfortably place elements of the popular tradition in the mouths of the speakers whom he quoted, he refused to admit into his own narrative any element tainted with the stain of popularity. I now suggest that, as a result of this unvarying practice of his, the historian was led into an unfortunate hypercorrection in the case of the goals of the Delian League: by rejecting the popular claim of liberation, he rejected an authentic element of the historical tradition. Moreover, it should be noted that the claim of liberation at this point would ill suit Thucydides' narrative, which is about to launch into its central theme: the inexorable process whereby Athens transformed the league into a tyranny.

The implication of the preceding argument is, of course, that the popular tradition transmitted a genuine element of history that Thucydides ignored. We have still to discuss, however, one important fifth-century testimonium for the fact that, both popularly and officially, Athenians believed that the offensive campaigns against Persia formed the final phase of a crusade for freedom which had begun long before the transfer of the hegemony. The argument derives from the literary and archaeological evidence for the area of the Stoa of Zeus Eleutherios in the northwest sector of the Athenian agora.[50]

The most impressive remains on the site are those of the stoa itself, which was begun around 430, completed perhaps about 420, and decorated with acroteria at the turn of the century. An archaic altar and the base of a statue, which stand very near the stoa, have been identified as belonging to a precinct of Zeus Soter. The altar survived Xerxes' destruction and continued in use, but the statue was lost and presumably replaced in the 470's.[51] The later stoa was meant to enhance the precinct of Zeus, and the official cult title remained Zeus Soter.[52] Some time after the foundation of the precinct, however, Zeus Soter received a new title, Eleutherios, which rapidly replaced the older title in popular parlance. If we accept the testimony of Didymus as reported by Harpocration, the new name came about as a result of the defeat of the Persians: ἐκλήθη γὰρ ἐλευθέριος διὰ τὸ τῶν Μηδικῶν ἀπαλλαγῆναι τοὺς Ἀθηναίους.[53] Pausanias implies that the stoa took its name from the pre-existing statue of Zeus, which the evidence of archaeology proves was the focal point of the whole monument.[54]

Difficulties about interpreting the invention of the title Eleutherios arise because of the impossibility of fixing the event securely before or after the transfer of the hegemony. Didymus seems to imply a time soon after the repulse of Xerxes, and the excavators suggest that the new title began with the new statue. If the Athenians turned their attention to such practical matters as walls, dockyards, and houses immediately after Plataea, it seems reasonable to assume that statues would appear somewhat later. Apparently, we can only state that the popular name Eleutherios probably originated around the time of the transfer of the hegemony. However, we can learn more from the new title by examining the popular meaning which it was meant to carry. The name Eleutherios almost certainly evidences an Athenian attempt to emulate the foundation of Zeus Eleutherios which the Spartans established after the Battle of Plataea.[55] The Plataean *Eleutheria*, however, were not simply a festival of thanksgiving for the freeing of European Greece. The Covenant of Plataea demanded two things of its signatories: the conducting of the *Eleutheria* and the furnishing of forces to carry on the war against Persia. The 'freedom' celebrated in these games looks forward to the liberation of eastern Greeks, the continuation of the crusade against Persia, as well as backward to the expulsion of Xerxes from mainland Greece. The Athenians must have borrowed both connotations when they added the title Eleutherios to their traditional Zeus Soter. The new name, although it could evoke memories of Marathon in a popular source,[56] obviously remained in vogue long after the transfer of the hegemony and symbolized the policy of the Delian League, which amounted to a continuation of the Hellenic League's policy of liberating all Greeks.[57] Even if we cannot precisely date the addition of the new title to the old cult of Zeus, therefore, the source and popularity of the new title demonstrate the continuity of the popular concept of liberation as a catchword in the war against Persia.

In the light of what has been said about the catchword ἐλευθερία in the fifth century, we can accept the evidence of the fourth century with greater confidence. Of course, Isocrates and the others might have supported fourth-century programs with a vague reminiscence about a fifth-century catchword which could be molded to fit the rhetorical exigencies without regard to accuracy. We have seen, however, that the orators were relying on an old and familiar tradition in their claims that the Delian League served the cause of Greek freedom, and, what is more interesting, the later evidence from the Stoa of Zeus shows either that they were partaking in a general effort to revive the old tradition or that the older stories had remained in vogue for over a century. Freedom from Persia certainly became a catchword in the fourth-century panhellenic movement, but fourth-century additions to the stoa indicate that the word was meant to recall in detail its fifth-century popular meaning as exemplified in the title Zeus Eleutherios. Isocrates himself mentions that statues of the panhellenic heroes Conon and Evagoras stood in front of the stoa; Pausanias confirms Isocrates' remark and adds that Conon's son and successor, Timotheus, was also present.[58] Moreover, the decree establishing the second naval confederacy of Athens was placed before the stoa.[59] If fifth-century traditions were very much alive for those responsible for the publication of decrees and the erection of statues in the fourth century, we should not assume that the orators operated in a vacuum. In the case of the catchword ἐλευθερία, they have accurately preserved a significant theme of the fifth-century tradition, all of which shows that Athenians had a stronger conception of the unity of the Persian War than Thucydides did.

2. The theme of fear. Since this matter, which forms a major part

of Chapter VI, cannot detain us here, I shall only anticipate briefly my conclusions in that chapter. The basic point, the one which forces the audience to view the Delian League as an instrument for the continuation of the Persian War and the war itself as a unity from Marathon to Callias, is that in all popular sources Darius' invasion of Greece issued in a period of fear for the Greeks, which did not terminate until the fear had been transferred to Persia by Athenian campaigns leading up to the Peace. The orators all elaborate on the theme of fear, which can be traced in extant popular media to the speech of the Athenians at Sparta as reported by Thucydides.[60]

3. The hybris of the King. It is a commonplace of Greek literature that the Persian monarchs, especially Xerxes, exhibited hybris. Athenian writers never tired of pointing out how the royal hybris manifested itself in impious and unnatural activities such as Xerxes' bridging of the Hellespont and channelling of Athos, and the Athenians believed that they were the agents of a nemesis which involved the monarchy in a downfall that began with Marathon and culminated with Callias. The theme was popular enough in Aristides' era for Lucian to satirize its overuse, and Plutarch could blithely say that Cimon brought on the Battle of Eurymedon simply to deflate the King's pride.[61] The topic had established itself by the fourth century in popular Attic sources, as Isocrates, the *Epitaphioi*, and the *Marmor Parium* indicate.[62] Even Herodotus constructed his accounts of the Persian kings, especially Cyrus and Xerxes, in Aeschylean terms of hybris and self-destruction; and Aeschylus himself made Xerxes the tragic hero of the *Persae*.[63] In fact, our earliest direct reference to the theme of hybris occurs in the *Persae*, for which Pericles served as choregus in 472.[64] For the purposes of the present discussion, it might be sufficient to have demonstrated that from around 472 the Athenians popularly accepted the story of the King's hybris, which would contribute to the concept of one war from at least 480 to the Peace of Callias. I believe, however, that this theme of hybris had been ingrained in the popular mentality as long as the theme of freedom and that consequently, as long as there was fighting against Persia, Athenians continued to view the struggle in terms of these themes and to think of the whole war as a unity.

Although Greeks naturally understood events in tragic modes, Themistocles seems to have played an important role in popularizing the tragic view of the Persian king. If we can accept Herodotus' authority, the Athenian statesman made a speech soon after Salamis in which he spoke of the King's hybris and called for the liberation of Ionia. He said that the gods had punished the King for attempting too much (to rule Europe as well as Asia) and for impiety (in destroying temples and religious statues). This speech of Themistocles may have influenced Aeschylus in his *Persae*, a play which is full of praise for the victor of Salamis. In a particular passage, Aeschylus seems to have transferred Themistocles' sentiments as cited by Herodotus to the ghost of Darius.[65] The poet's vocabulary is different from the historian's, but the essence is the same: condemnation of the Persian hybris and impiety in having burned temples and overthrown religious statues. This seemingly conscious recollection of Themistocles' moralizing and Aeschylus' general good will to that Athenian statesman open the possibility of a similar connection between Themistocles and another dramatist. Glaucus of Rhegium maintained that the *Persae* was adapted from Phrynichus' *Phoenissae*, which had been produced in 476 with Themistocles himself as choregus.[66] Both plays, therefore, may well have made an issue of the King's hybris, and both poets, while composing in political terms familiar to their audiences, could have reproduced Themistocles' judgment of the Persian king. The opinions of these three men certainly look forward to Herodotus and the epitaphic tradition; yet they might also look backward to popular attitudes from the period of the Ionian Revolt. In 493/2, Themistocles was archon and Phrynichus brought out his *Capture of Miletus*, which apparently chided the Athenians for failing to secure the liberation of Ionia.[67] Both men could have been speaking of the King's hybris even then, and what evidence we have suggests that the two themes, hybris and the liberation of Ionia, were too closely bound together to be separated.

In the first place, Themistocles and Phrynichus were certainly among those Athenians who had pressed for involvement in the Ionian Revolt and continued to be interested in freeing Ionia even after Lade. It should also be noted that Themistocles persuaded the Athenians to build a fleet to counter Persian as well as Aeginetan encroachment in the Aegean.[68] After Mycale, Themistocles at first argued on behalf of the Ionians against the Spartan proposal of mass migration and then accepted them into the alliance which was to develop into the Delian League with its openly stated purpose of freeing Ionia.[69] Finally, from at least 476, there seem to have been annual productions of a new tragedy about the Battle of Salamis, and the only extant example, the *Persae*, combines the themes of hybris and liberation.[70] Hybris is obvious in the *Persae;* liberation may not be. In one passage, however, the chorus recognizes that Salamis spells the beginning of the end of the Persian domination of Ionia, and the poet is even political enough to ignore normal Greek usage and call the Ionians 'Hellenes,' in accordance with the official terminology of the Delian League.[71] The basic theme of the play is, of course, the effect of the Battle of Salamis on King Xerxes; but the battle itself, its victors, and its political consequences are constantly before the audience.[72]

I believe that, in the light of the preceding discussion, it is reasonable to conjecture that a pair of ideas, the freedom of Ionia and the hybris of the King, together formed an integral part of Athenian popular tradition since at least the Ionian Revolt. Just as Xerxes committed the ultimate act of hybris by invading Greece, the conquest of Ionia and the reduction of the Ionian Revolt had also been shocking examples of hybris.[73] For Phrynichus and his choregus, for Aeschylus and his,[74] and presumably for the Athenian playgoer in general, Athenian policy towards Ionia and Persia was a continuum from the Ionian Revolt to the Peace of Callias. That policy was the instrument of $ἄτη$ in the hands of the gods: it punished the King's hybris by freeing Ionia from his domination. This conclusion derives some additional support from the lack of distinction found in the Athenian tradition between Xerxes and Artaxerxes.[75] The latter was certainly not guilty of aggression against Greeks; yet the Peace of Callias, which was concluded during his reign, was universally looked upon as the just punishment of a hybristic king. Moreover, no popular source mentions Artaxerxes by name or distinguishes him in any way from Xerxes. It therefore appears that the unity of the war against Persia and the punishment of the King's hybris constituted such pervasive themes in the Athenian popular tradition, that the transfer of the sovereignty at the Persian court was not considered any more relevant than the transfer of the hegemony from Sparta to Athens.

4. *The true hegemony of the Athenians.* We now come to the fourth and final theme which served to unify the Persian War in the Athenian popular tradition. The Athenians portrayed themselves as having possessed a *de facto* hegemony in the war from Marathon to Callias on account of their consistent superiority over their allies as

well as the Persians. As a result, the formal transfer of the hegemony, even when it is noticed, does not bear the kind of significance that Thucydides assigns to it. The theme includes six common motifs.

a. No one could have questioned Athens' superiority at Marathon. The Athenians themselves, however, regularly augmented their deed with the tendentious boast that they had fought the battle alone, without the aid of the Plataeans, whose presence is confirmed by reliable sources.[76] Our earliest evidence for this claim seems to come from the Athenian speech before the Battle of Plataea as reported by Herodotus, and the next occurs in Thucydides' version of the speech of the Athenians at Sparta in 432.[77] The boast became such a commonplace in fourth-century oratory that Theopompus felt constrained to chide the Athenians for their chauvinism (ἀλαζονία) in the matter.[78] Whatever the origin of the boast might have been, it clearly became a part of the epitaphic tradition. Several extant *Epitaphioi* repeat the boast, and other orations containing it consistently employ the chauvinistic topics which have long been recognized as belonging to the epitaphic tradition.[79] *Epitaphioi*, however, were not the only popular media to voice the Athenian claims about Marathon. A famous epigram commonly attributed to Simonides contains in its brief scope numerous topics which appear throughout the epitaphic tradition:[80]

Ἑλλήνων προμαχοῦντες Ἀθηναῖοι Μαραθῶνι
ἔκτειναν Μήδων εἴκοσι[? ἐννέα] μυριάδας.

The epigram cannot be dated firmly, but if its thematic similarity to the so-called Marathon epigrams is any indication, it was probably inscribed in the first third of the fifth century and may have been composed soon after the battle itself.[81] The claim that Athens defended Greece, the use of a verb with the prefix προ-, and the stress on the number of Persians all appear in most of the speeches in the epitaphic tradition.[82] More specifically, however, the absence of any mention of Plataean aid and the boast contained in προμαχοῦντες probably amount to the claim of having fought alone.[83]

b. The popular tradition maintained that the other Greek cities recognized Athens' superiority in the Persian War by granting her the ἀριστεῖα. Thus, in summarizing the whole Persian War, Isocrates can say that the Athenians εὐθὺς μὲν τῶν ἀριστείων ἠξιώθησαν (*Paneg.* (4), 72).[84] Athenian sources were especially fond of claiming the first prize for Salamis, which became popular in Athens as the decisive victory in opposition to Sparta's claim for Plataea.[85] Although Herodotus states that the Aeginetans made off with the first prize for Salamis, while the Athenians came in second,[86] Lysias, certainly relying on fifth-century sources, awarded the prize to Athens.[87] Plato, who preferred land to naval power and therefore Marathon and Plataea to Artemisium and Salamis,[88] phrases his reference to the ἀριστεῖα more cleverly (*Menex.* 240e):

> *To* (*the men of Marathon*) *we ought to dedicate the first prize of valor in our speech; but the second prize goes to those who fought and won the naval battles at Salamis and Artemisium.*

In this way Plato compromises between the claim for the prize which every *Epitaphios* must contain and Herodotus' conception of the truth. Finally, Aelius Aristides specifies what relevance the claim for the first prize has for a discussion of the hegemony and in so doing he seems to be making explicit the implication that had always resided in the tradition (I. 223f.):

> *The Greeks were fully aware of Athens' superiority and therefore awarded her the prize for valor for the naval battles. In this way those who were actually present and saw the fighting gave testimony as to who had led them to safety. Moreover, Athens passed the other cities and an Athenian surpassed all other individuals. So it is that the Athenians gained a reputation for politic behavior by yielding and at the same time were awarded the true hegemony by all.*

c. Another aspect of Athenian superiority appears in the often voiced sentiment that the rest of Greece would have succumbed to Xerxes' power if the Persians could have persuaded the Athenians to capitulate. Herodotus betrays his Athenian bias by repeating this judgment twice: once in his own words and once through Mardonius, who came to understand Athens' pivotal position and consequently sent Alexander I of Macedonia to persuade the Athenians to join the Persians.[89] Although Herodotus' version reflects the common Athenian tradition, the Athenians tended to bring the motif into a much closer relationship with the Battle of Salamis.[90] An early instance occurs in the *Persae*, in which Salamis shatters the King's hope of conquering all of Greece through conquering Athens alone (233f.):

Ἀτόσσα: ἀλλὰ μὴν ἵμειρ' ἐμὸς παῖς τήνδε θηρᾶσαι πόλιν·
χόρος· πᾶσα γὰρ γένοιτ' ἂν Ἑλλὰς βασιλέως ὑπήκοος.

The play, of course, goes on to glorify Athens' exploit at Salamis. Such a joining of this motif to the primacy of Salamis in the fifth-century tradition probably led the fourth-century orators to misplace the story of Alexander's embassy to Athens.[91] The orators all accepted a version which amplifies the Athenian achievement at Salamis by placing the embassy before that battle rather than Plataea.[92] Finally, we should note that it is again Aristides who gives voice to the implication behind the stories of Athens' indispensability to the Greek cause and the consequent Persian embassies. He says that after Athens had rejected Xerxes' offer, she τοῖς εὖ φρονοῦσι τῶν Ἑλλήνων ἡγεμὼν τῆς ἀποκρίσεως ἐγένετο (I.211).[93]

d. Athens' superiority and virtual command over the other Greeks receives more support from another motif in the popular tradition: the Athenians taught the other states how to behave towards the Persian invaders. Isocrates says that at Artemisium the Athenians showed the Hellenes that naval warfare was no less conducive to ἀρετή than hoplite fighting.[94] Similarly Salamis no less than Marathon proved to everyone that numbers cannot stand against ἀρετή.[95] The Peloponnesians, however, had to be shamed by the Athenians into contributing their ships at Salamis.[96] The fourth century clearly took this topic from the epitaphic tradition, where its inherent idealism caused it to receive special emphasis in the two most carefully constructed *Epitaphioi*, namely, Thucydides' version of Pericles' oration and the one in Plato's *Menexenus*.[97] Pericles, of course, almost totally ignores earlier history, but who can forget the famous pronouncement (II. 41. 1): ξυνελών τε λέγω τήν τε πᾶσαν πόλιν τῆς Ἑλλάδος παίδευσιν εἶναι? The *Epitaphios* in the *Menexenus* presents the Athenians of the 490's and 480's as the Platonic paradigm of ἀρετή which ought to be imitated by everyone.[98] Idealistic as the notion is, Plato carefully relates it to truly popular motifs by saying, for example, that at Artemisium and Salamis the Athenians taught the Greeks how to fight at sea.[99] Such statements as these influenced the Athenians to have the *Menexenus* read annually.[100] This practice could have had a profound effect on the later epitaphic tradition, which in turn influenced Aristides, in whom the motif of teaching retains its Platonic vigor.[101]

e. I have referred twice to the important part Salamis played in Attic versions of the Persian War.[102] It remains only to point out the triple motif with which popular sources described the Athenian contributions to the battle: the Athenians supplied the bulk of the fleet, the best commander, and the most outstanding courage. The actual numbers of ships vary from author to author, but usually about two-thirds are recognized as Athenian.[103] Themistocles played the decisive role in bringing about the victory; he is described as the commander of the commanders.[104] The Athenians exhibited a remarkable courage, especially in abandoning their homes to the Persians and taking to their ships.[105] These three topics nearly always appear together. They clearly constitute the canonical epitaphic statement about Salamis, which every Athenian orator would roll forth in one breath when his story came around to Salamis. The Athenian ambassador to Sparta knew the canon so well, that he could reproduce its elements with an amazing succinctness (Thuc. I. 74. 1): τρία τὰ ὠφελιμώτατα ἐς αὐτὸ παρεσχόμεθα, ἀριθμόν τε νεῶν πλεῖστον καὶ ἄνδρα στρατηγὸν ξυνετώτατον καὶ προθυμίαν ἀοκνοτάτην.

f. By virtue of the five achievements mentioned above, the Athenians popularly claimed to have defeated their allies in excellence and the Persians in battle. Isocrates and Lycurgus both insist that the Athenians beat their allies and enemies, ὡς ἑκατέρων προσῆκε (*Paneg.* (4), 72; *Leoc.* 70). Isocrates repeatedly states that during the Persian War Athens and Sparta competed to see which city could benefit Greece more; Athens, of course, left her competitor far behind.[106] Aristides reproduces this traditional theme of a double ἀγών against both friends and enemies (*Panath.* I. 217): ἀμφοτέρας γὰρ τὰς νίκας ἀνείλοντο σαφέστατα ἀνθρώπων ... τοὺς μὲν γὰρ ἐχθροὺς τοῖς ὅπλοις, τῇ δ' ἐπιεικείᾳ τοὺς φίλους ἐνίκησαν.[107] However, two similar and extraordinary claims for originality accompany Aristides' version of this old topic: he says that other writers have passed it over or at most failed to do it justice.[108] If these claims have any meaning, they must refer to the debate concerning the hegemony which Aristides places between them, and which appears to be quite original.[109] As we noted earlier, it is set dramatically before the Battle of Salamis and consists of the argument that the Athenians might have made if they had wanted to demand the formal hegemony from Sparta. Aristides includes some words by a hypothetical Athenian speaker as well as his own analysis, both of which justify the cause of the Athenians by showing how they conquered their allies in fairness, gentleness, and highmindedness, since they gave up their just claim to the hegemony and did not make an issue over it when they could quite profitably have done so.

The conclusion of Aristides' hypothetical debate on the hegemony has important ramifications both for the immediate discussion about the double ἀγών and the thesis of this whole chapter. All the points made in the debate show how Athens won the double ἀγών, but those points amount to the very four themes which we have been examining for some time. For Aristides, these four themes inexorably led the debate to its conclusion, which we have in fact already seen (I. 223):[110] ἀλλ' οἱ μὲν (Spartans) ὄνομα ἡγεμόνων, οἱ δ' (Athenians) ἔργα παρείχοντο, καὶ τοσούτῳ κάλλιον αὐτοῖς τὸ σχῆμα καθίστατο ὅσῳ τῶν ἡγεμόνων αὐτῶν εἶχον τὴν ἡγεμονίαν. ... We return to the idea that cumulatively the four themes are meant to force the audience to believe that Athens always had the ἀληθινὴν ἡγεμονίαν (I. 224). Aristides, however, closes the chapter with the ambiguous remark: καὶ μὴν καὶ πρὸς τὰ λοιπὰ τοῦ πολέμου τὴν πόλιν ἤδη καθαρῶς προεστήσαντο οἱ Ἕλληνες. Apparently this refers to the actual transfer of the hegemony; yet in the narrative it comes before Salamis, whereas Aristides almost ignores the transfer at its proper point in the narrative, as we saw at the beginning of the chapter.

The evidence which we have seen so far leads to the conclusion that Aristides recreated in his *Panathenaicus* a detailed, accurate, and continuous version of the popular tradition concerning the transfer of the hegemony. A tradition which seemed to be hidden away in casual references in drama and oratory, possibly spurious *Epitaphioi*, lost buildings and works of art, and fragments of lost historians, in fact exists in the pages of the *Panathenaicus*. Aristides has constructed his narrative of the Persian War with four potent themes, which played an equally important role in the early popular versions of that war. In both Aristides and the earlier popular media, these themes lead effectively, if somewhat emotionally, to the conclusion that the transfer of the hegemony was not terribly significant. The *Menexenus* could ignore the event completely.[111] Other popular sources misplace it in their narratives or simply treat it as a trivial point.[112] Between the four themes and the playing down of the transfer of the hegemony, of course, logic demands two intermediate conclusions: the unity of the war and the idea that Athens held the true hegemony throughout that war. As we have seen, Aristides draws both conclusions from the four themes. We must now try to determine in greater detail whether those are merely his own conclusions or, as has been intimated above, he derived them from the ancient popular tradition. Let us turn first to the question of the true hegemony and then to the unity of the war.

Did Aristides invent the conclusion of his hypothetical debate about the hegemony from a number of disparate themes copied carefully from various media, or did he reproduce the conclusion which the ancient tradition itself had drawn from its understanding of Athenian history? I believe that the second alternative is closer to the truth, because Aristides' idea of a debate for the hegemony and presumably the debate's conclusion are not as original as he would have us suppose and in all probability derive from the epitaphic tradition. In fact, Aristides possessed at least one authority for a debate about the hegemony. Isocrates constructed his *Panegyricus* as a major statement in the fourth-century debate over who should receive the hegemony in the proposed new crusade against Persia, and his major argument was that Athens deserved the new hegemony, since she had held the position of ἡγεμών in ancient times and throughout the Persian War (*Paneg.* (4), 99):[113]

> So then, with a campaign about to begin against the barbarians, who should have the hegemony? Should it not belong to those who achieved the greatest renown in the former war; to those who were considered worthy to receive the prize of valor in the common struggles?

Isocrates' version of the debate, of course, must raise the same question as Aristides'. Did the older orator invent the debate by drawing untraditional conclusions from the four traditional themes, or did he employ a traditional set of motifs, which fit his argument perfectly even in their pre-existing form? As in the case of Aristides, I believe the latter possibility is closer to the truth and that evidence is forthcoming from speeches reported by Herodotus and Thucydides.

Something very similar to a debate for the hegemony occurs in Herodotus, where the Athenians argue with the Tegeans over the place of honor in the battle line at Plataea.[114] The speaker treats Athens' legendary achievements and Marathon in the traditional manner of the *Epitaphios*, but nothing beyond Marathon is mentioned.[115] The speech of the Athenians at Sparta as reported by Thucydides is a more detailed and, for our purposes, a more important gauge of the popular tradition.[116] The first part of the speech includes the traditional Athenian version of the Persian War, as we have seen in detail above. The Athenian speakers conclude that their behavior in the Persian War entitled them to their Empire (I. 75. 1): Ἀρ᾽ἄξιοί ἐσμεν, ὦ Λακεδαιμόνιοι, καὶ προθυμίας ἕνεκα τῆς τότε καὶ γνώμης ξυνέσεως ἀρχῆς γε ἧς ἔχομεν τοῖς Ἕλλησι μὴ οὕτως ἄγαν ἐπιφθόνως διακεῖσθαι; There follows a detailed defense of the Athenian Empire and Athens' treatment of her imperial subjects, and this defense was no anomaly. Most extant *Epitaphioi* and speeches derived from the epitaphic tradition contain justifications of the Empire which, although they are less bold and more sophistic than those of Thucydides, show that the motif of defending the ἀρχή formed a part of the tradition.[117] Numerous common themes appear in the fourth-century justifications: the Spartans abused their hegemony worse than the Athenians had;[118] the affairs of Melos and Scione were trivial or deserved. Even the most noble funeral oration contains a defense, admittedly an idealistic one, of the ἀρχή. Pericles concludes his defense as follows (Thuc. II.41.3):

Athens, alone of all contemporary states, comes to the test stronger than she is reputed to be. Only her enemies do not complain about the quality of the city that defeats them when they attack her; only her subjects do not find fault with the virtues of their rulers.

We therefore have evidence that in the fifth century Athenians generally believed, as the speakers at Sparta did, that Athens acquired her empire on account of her superiority in the Persian War and, as Pericles said, that Athens maintained her empire on account of her superiority. These beliefs closely parallel Isocrates' and Aristides' idea that on account of her superiority Athens acquired first a *de facto* and then a *de iure* hegemony in the Persian War. Indeed, I would suggest that, for purposes of discussing the popular tradition, the terms hegemony and empire can be equated. I maintain that 'acquiring the ἀρχή' should be considered, in a popular source, simply a bolder, fifth-century expression for which a later, more careful and panhellenic author would substitute 'acquiring the ἡγεμονία.'[119] These conclusions, in the light of corroborating evidence from our discussion of the four themes, lead me to postulate that neither Aristides nor Isocrates invented the idea of a debate about the hegemony with its conclusion that Athens acquired a virtual hegemony early in the Persian War because of her superiority. The idea that Athens' political position came from her superiority was inherent in the earliest debates about the legitimacy of that position. The natural result of such an attitude was the belief that no formal transfer of hegemony could be nearly as important as the story of Athens' continuous virtue.

In closing this chapter, I should like to discuss what most historians would probably consider the most serious implication of the popular failure to emphasize the transfer of the hegemony, namely, its disagreement with Thucydides' carefully designed chronological divisions. Emotionally, of course, the themes of freedom, fear, hybris, and Athenian superiority induce a belief that the Persian War was a unity from Marathon, or even the Ionian Revolt, to the Peace of Callias; but let us turn directly to the chronological problem. In attempting to divide the fifth century into intelligible periods, the popular tradition adopted a set of chronological divisions which Thucydides consciously rejected. We moderns have wholeheartedly accepted Thucydides' chronology and consequently have lost sight of the standard Athenian view.

Thucydides based his chronological divisions on his own interpretation of the causes of the Peloponnesian War; and, since he believed the war was mainly caused by Athenian power, he wrote the Pentecontaetia to explain the growth of Athens' power. That period of fifty years was separated from the earlier period, the Persian Wars, by the transfer of the hegemony and related events. Hostilities had erupted between Sparta and Athens during the Pentecontaetia, but Thucydides distinguished these from his twenty-seven-year war which began in 431. The fifth century, therefore, contained three distinct periods: the Persian Wars, the Pentecontaetia, and the Peloponnesian War. The popular tradition adopted a simpler chronology, which, if less analytical than Thucydides', explains a great deal about Athenian attitudes. In the popular mind, the fifth century admitted only one important division into two periods, the Persian War and the Greek War. Unfortunately, the tradition failed to pinpoint the date of the crucial division between the two periods and in fact could not do so. The last event of the Persian War, the Peace of Callias, must follow the first event of the next period, the Battle of Tanagra, whatever actual dates we assign to these events. Exactness in chronology, however, was not the hallmark of popular conceptions of history, and so the popular tradition continued to commit the kind of illogicality in chronology which so exasperated Thucydides in Hellanicus' account of the Pentecontaetia.[120]

Plato most clearly exemplifies the nature, and the problems, of the popular chronology (*Menex.* 242a):

> *So this was the war that a unified Athens waged on behalf of herself and all her fellow Greeks against the barbarians. However, after there was a Peace and the city was properly honored, first rivalry and then its result, envy, was directed against Athens. It is, after all, practically human nature for this to happen to great benefactors. The result was that the city was quite unwillingly placed in a state of war against the Greeks. A little later, during this war, the Athenians fought a battle at Tanagra against the Spartans and on behalf of the freedom of Boeotia.*

Such a chronology forces Plato to place Tanagra after Callias. The same division, the same conglomerating of campaigns against Persia as opposed to actions against other Greeks, occurs in Lycurgus and the *Epitaphios* of Demosthenes.[121] A similar impression even survives in Thucydides' brief survey of Greek history in Book I and especially in Pericles' *Epitaphios,* where the two categories, foreign and Greek wars, clearly appear (Thuc. II. 36. 4):[122]

> *I shall avoid boring a well-informed audience with a digression on the wartime deeds by which we Athenians came into the possession of our empire. (You all know about) the battles that we ourselves or our fathers fought so nobly to ward off any barbarians or Hellenes who attacked us.*

As E. Schwartz pointed out long ago, Isocrates and Lysias accepted the same chronology as Plato and the others, but their rhetorical skill and the exigencies of their situations caused them to arrange the traditional material in a rather unusual pattern.[123] In the *Panegyricus,* for example, the Persian War precedes an extended justification of the Athenian Empire, after which the Peace of Callias is compared with the Peace of Antalcidas. Nevertheless, the traditional chronology remains in essence and the transfer of the hegemony loses its significance.

As a final example of the popular tradition, let us turn to a fragment of Philochorus, which is indispensable to a discussion of the transfer of the hegemony and the chronology of the popular tradition (fr. 117): ὁ δὲ Φιλόχορός φησι καὶ τὴν ἡγεμονίαν τοὺς Ἀθηναίους λαβεῖν διὰ τὰς κατασχούσας τὴν Λακεδαίμονα συμφοράς.[124] The fragment alludes to a famous series of events from near the middle of the fifth century: the Laconian earthquake, the Messenian revolt, Cimon's expedition to aid Sparta, Sparta's rejection of that aid, and the consequent breach between Athens and Sparta.[125] The fragment should be all the more significant because it appears to pinpoint these events as the opening of a new period in the historian's analysis. In fact, Jacoby believes that the fragment belongs to the beginning of Book IV of Philochorus' *Atthis*, a book which includes the period from the affair at Ithome to the end of the Peloponnesian War.[126]

To be sure, the mere fact that Philochorus stressed the chronological significance of the incident at Ithome can be reconciled with Thucydides' account, in which the affair marked the first major breach between Sparta and Athens.[127] However, no mention of a transfer of the hegemony near the middle of the century can reflect Thucydidean influence. Moreover, Thucydides did not assign the value of a major historical division to Ithome. The first break between Sparta and Athens certainly receives due attention, but for Thucydides the major themes of the Pentecontaetia predominate for another thirty years. As we have seen, the great historian recognized only two vital chronological divisions in the fifth century: the original transfer of the hegemony and the affairs of Corcyra and Potidaea. Fragment 117 of Philochorus must therefore represent a chronological interpretation which is independent of Thucydides and combines the so-called First Peloponnesian War with Thucydides' twenty-seven-year war into a single period. The new period commenced with the affair at Ithome, which led to a second transfer of hegemony to Athens. The new hegemony, however, was unqualified, as the previous one had been, by such expressions as τῆς θαλάττης or τῶν συμμάχων.[128] The old hegemony, the original Delian League, had been a dependent unit of the Hellenic League,[129] which was now defunct as far as Athens was concerned.

According to Jacoby, Philochorus' treatment of the second transfer of the hegemony represents the final stage in a continuous development of Attic chronological theory between the time of Thucydides and that of Philochorus. The *Atthis* became ever more subject to a classicizing interpretation of Athens' golden age, a period which could be described as 'The Rise and Fall of the Athenian Empire.' Such an era would comprise the years from the affair at Ithome to the end of the Peloponnesian War—exactly the same as the scope of the fourth book of Philochorus' *Atthis*.[130] Jacoby's perception of the chronological divisions in the *Atthis* are undoubtedly correct, but I believe he incorrectly labels them novel and post-Thucydidean. In the light of the evidence presented in this chapter, I would suggest that in his chronological analysis Philochorus was simply attempting to rationalize the illogical chronology of the *Epitaphios*. As we have seen, the popular tradition failed to pinpoint a chronological division between its two qualitative rather than chronological categories of events: war against Persia and war among the Greeks. Philochorus hit upon an excellent solution to the impasse in the popular chronology by choosing the affair at Ithome as the dividing line. Although Tanagra was closer than Ithome to the Peace of Callias, Ithome contained the vital matter of the change of hegemony. Before Ithome, the Athenians and their allies acted as the agents of the Hellenic League with a mandate to use the hegemonial system to carry on naval warfare against Persia and to free the Asiatic Greeks. After Ithome, Athens exercised an absolute hegemony over her imperial subjects and led them into war against Sparta and her allies. Philochorus, therefore, either blatantly accepted the main tenet of the epitaphic and popular chronology, the completion of the Persian War before the start of the Greek War, or he satisfied himself with a qualitative rather than a strictly chronological analysis. In either case, the Atthidographer clearly succumbed to the pressure of the popular tradition and divided the fifth century into periods of Persian War and Greek War.

1. Beecke, *Historischen Angaben*, p. 46f.; cf. Thuc. I. 95-97.
2. It seems that for Thucydides the period known as τὰ Μηδικά began with Marathon and ended with Plataea: cf. N.G.L. Hammond, "τὸ Μηδικόν and τὰ Μηδικά," *CR* N.S. 7 (1957) 101. Aristides seems to accept the same division by referring to the period up to Plataea as ὁ πρότερος πόλεμος (I. 243). At I. 251, however, πράξεις Μηδικαί refers to the period from Marathon to the Peace of Callias.
3. Aristid. I. 245 (cf. *supra*, Chapter II, p. 15), and Thuc. I. 89, 94. The separation of Plataea from Mycale, which occurred on the same day, shows that Aristides was more concerned with interpretation than chronology.
4. It should be noted that Herodotus implicitly accepts the same chronological division as Aristides and Thucydides by terminating his work with the siege of Sestos.
5. Aristot. *Ath.Pol.* 23. 4-5; Diod.XI. 44-47, 50; Plut. *Ar.* 23-25. 1, *Cim.* 6. 2-7; Nepos, *Ar.* 2.2-3.
6. Aristid. I. 339; II. 318.
7. I.258; 339. Cf. Thuc. I. 96. 1; Isoc. *Areop.* (7), 17; *De pace* (8), 30; *De bigis* (16), 27; Demosth. *Olyn.* III (3), 24.
8. Aristid. I. 279f., 317. Cf. II. 115f., 200, 232.
9. I. 245.
10. Cf. I. 244: ὁ μὲν λογισμὸς οὗτος ὁ τῆς πόλεως· 246: γνόντες δὲ οὕτως. . . .
11. Cf. I. 246: Λακεδαιμόνιοι τοῖς μὲν πρώτοις τῶν ἔργων παρεγένοντο, ἔπειτ' ἀπῆραν, ὥσπερ πτηνοῖς ἀκολουθεῖν οὐ δυνάμενοι.
12. I. 195; cf. I. 205.
13. I. 203.
14. I. 213, 223; cf. the discussion about Athens' true hegemony based on her consistent superiority and excellence, *supra*, pp. 54ff.
15. Cf. I. 248, where the Athenians act as the protectors of Greece, and their aim is ἀσφαλία.
16. Cf. the first passage cited on p. 42. A similar idea seems to be present in Aristides' rather convoluted discussion of the quality of the final portion of the Persian War (I. 243). Athens initiates the action but not for selfish purposes.
17. For a more detailed analysis of the purpose of the Delian League, cf. *supra*, pp. 48ff.
18. I. 248-50. Note the reversal of the theme of σωτηρία: it is now the King's safety that is in danger.
19. I. 197.
20. I. 209f.
21. I. 196.
22. Just as the other writers in the popular tradition, Aristides makes no distinction between Xerxes and Artaxerxes: cf. *supra*. p. 54.
23. I. 224.
24. Marathon, I.200; Artemisium and Salamis, I. 223, 231, 276. Note especially I. 231, where the ἀριστεῖα are connected with the hegemony: οἱ (the Greeks) μὲν γὰρ τὰ ἀριστεῖα ἔδοσαν τῇ πόλει καὶ ταῦτα ἡγεῖσθαι ἐφ' ὧν ἦν.
25. I. 197.
26. I. 227, 233f. Cf. *supra*, p. 56f.

27. I. 204.
28. I. 223, 227.
29. I. 217f. For Marathon, cf. I. 220.
30. I. 219, 223.
31. I. 219.
32. I. 218, 222f.
33. I. 223f.
34. It cannot be denied that the conclusion of the debate contains a reference to the transfer of the hegemony (I. 224): καὶ μὴν καὶ πρὸς τὰ λοιπὰ τοῦ πολέμου τὴν πόλιν ἤδη καθαρῶς προεστήσαντο οἱ Ἕλληνες· πάντες γὰρ οἱ σύλλογοι καὶ αἱ σύνοδοι πρὸς Ἀθηναίους καὶ παρ' Ἀθηναίων ἐκ τούτων ἐγίγνοντο, καὶ κατέστη κοινὸν βουλευτήριον ἡ πόλις τοῦ πρὸς τὸν βάρβαρον πολέμου. One must note, however, that this transfer of the hegemony appears in Aristides' narrative *before* the Battle of Salamis, not after Plataea as in Thucydides. Aristides has contrived a highly rhetorical narrative which glosses over the transfer of the titular hegemony in its proper chronological position and stresses the unity of the war under Athens' true hegemony. Cf. *supra*, p. 59.
35. Elements of the oratorical tradition appear in And. *De myst.* (1), 107f.; Lys. *Ep.* (2), 42-57; Isoc. *Paneg.* (4), 57-123, the most extensive version outside of Aristides; *Panath.* (12), 47-67; Demosth. *Ep.* (60), 9-11; Plato, *Menex.* 239b-242a; Lycurg. *Leoc.* 70-72. Moreover, careful historians such as Thucydides and Herodotus borrowed from the true oratorical tradition for speeches like those at Thuc. I. 73ff., VI. 82f.; Hdt. IX. 27.
36. For Marathon, cf. Hdt. VI. 109. 3, 6. For the Hellenic League, cf. J.A.O. Larson, "Federation for Peace in Ancient Greece," *CP* 39 (1944) 153f.; A.E. Raubitschek, "The Peace Policy of Pericles," *AJA* 70 (1966) 39f. Also cf. the discussion of the purpose of the Delian League, *supra*, pp. 48f.
37. For the oath of the Acharnae stele, cf. M.N. Tod, *Greek Historical Inscriptions*, Vol. II (Oxford, 1948), No. 204, pp. 303-07; G. Daux, *Studies Presented to D.M. Robinson*, Vol. II (St. Louis, 1953), pp. 775-82; *ATL* III. 104f.; Gomme, *HCT* II. 205; P. Siewart, "The Ephebic Oath in Fifth-Century Athens," *JHS* 97 (1977) 102-11, and his references. For the literary evidence for the oath, cf. Lycurg. *Leoc.* 81; Diod. XI. 29.3, both of whom may have employed Ephorus (so H.T. Wade-Gery, "The Peace of Kallias," *Athenian Studies Presented to W.S. Ferguson: Harvard Studies in Classical Philology*, Suppl. vol. I (1940), p. 125, n. 1). F.W. Schlatter, S.J., *Salamis and Plataea in the Tradition of the Attic Orators* (Diss. Princeton, 1960), p. 187f., believes that the portion of the orators' version of the oath which concerns ἐλευθερία is most likely to be historical. Cf. also, Meiggs, *Athenian Empire*, pp. 504-07. For the Covenant of Plataea, cf. Plut. *Ar.* 21. 1; for its historicity and place in the popular tradition, cf. A.E. Raubitschek, "The Covenant of Plataea," *TAPA* 91 (1960) 178-83. The historicity is accepted by J.A.O. Larson, "The Constitution and Original Purpose of the Delian League," *HSCP* 51 (1940) 175ff., but rejected by P.A. Brunt, "The Hellenic League against Persia," *Hist.* 2 (1953-54) 153-56 and *ATL* III. 101-04. For the cult of Zeus Eleutherios at Plataea, cf. Diod. XI. 29. 1; Plut. *Ar.* 21. 1; Paus. IX. 2. 5.
38. Lys. *Ep.* (2), 42; 47; 55-57.
39. For the sentiment that Athens surpassed Sparta in their rivalry over who should contribute the most to the salvation of Greece, cf. *Paneg.* (4), 85; 87; 91. At *Paneg.* 85,

91, 93, 99, and *Panath.* (12), 52, σωτηρία is used for the first two phases of the war. Σωτηρία would seem to be the Athenian aim in the earlier and more desperate stages of the war: cf., for such uses of the word, Thuc. V. 111. 2; VIII. 53. 3; Lys. *In Erat.* (12), 69; H.T. Wade-Gery, "Classical Epigrams and Epitaphs," *JHS* 53 (1933) 91, who believes that the Zeus Soter of the Athenian agora received his cult title in honor of his aiding in the recovery of Athens from the Persians. The title Soter, on the contrary, antedates the Persian War: cf. *infra,* n. 50. Plato, *Leg.* 707b-c, speaks of σωτηρία as beginning with Marathon and ending with Plataea. The first Marathon epigram, however, stresses freedom: cf. *infra,* n. 81.

40. Ἐλευθερία is applied to the later period at *Paneg.* (4), 106; 117; and, by implication, *Panath.* (12), 59f. The exception is *Paneg.* (4), 95, where the term is applied to Salamis.

41. Ἐλευθερία at 239b; σωτηρία at 240c; both at 240e. For freedom in the first two phases of the war, cf. Hyp. *Ep.* (6), 37.

42. *Leoc.* 70, 73.

43. Isoc. *Paneg.* (4), 117f.; *Panath.* (12), 68.

44. R. Sealey, "The Origins of the Delian League," *Ancient Society and Institutions: Studies Presented to Victor Ehrenberg on his 75th Birthday* (Oxford: Blackwell, 1969), pp. 233-55.

45. Larson, cf. *supra,* n. 37, p. 175. Similarly, N.G.L. Hammond, "The Origins and Nature of the Athenian Alliance of 478/7 B.C.," *JHS* 87 (1967) 41-61. Cf. H.D. Meyer, "Vorgeschichte und Gründung des delisch-attischen Seebundes," *Hist.* 12 (1963) 404-46; Brunt, *supra,* n. 37, p. 149f., shows that the terms of the Hellenic League's treaty are analogous with those of the Delian League. Raubitschek, cf. *supra,* n. 37, p. 183, points out that the Covenant of Plataea was the direct predecessor of the league of 478. Cf. D. Kagan, *The Outbreak of the Peloponnesian War* (Ithaca, N.Y.: Cornell, 1969), p. 41: "the purposes of the Delian League were almost identical with those of the Hellenic League." Cf. also, V. Martin, *La vie internationale dans la Grèce des cités* (*Publication de l'Institut universitaire des hautes études internationales,* Geneva, no. 21 [Paris, 1940]), p. 151: the Delian League was "l'émanation ou, si l'on vent, dédoublement de la coalition formée contre Xerxès." De Ste. Croix, *Origins,* p. 302, strengthens the case by analyzing the internal policies of Sparta. For rebuttals of Sealey which do not stress the continuity of the leagues, cf. A.H. Jackson, "The Original Purpose of the Delian League," *Hist.* 18 (1969) 12-16, and Meiggs, *Athenian Empire,* pp. 462-64.

46. Cf. Thuc. III. 13.1; And. *De pace* (3), 38.

47. Thuc. I. 102.

48. Larson, cf. *supra,* n. 37, p. 208.

49. Cf. Sealey, *supra*.n. 44, p. 239f. The speeches are those of the Mytilenians (III. 10. 3: ξύμμαχοι μέντοι ἐγενόμεθα οὐκ ἐπὶ καταδουλώσει τῶν Ἑλλήνων Ἀθηναίοις, ἐπ' ἐλευθερώσει ἀπὸ τοῦ Μήδου τοῖς Ἕλλησιν) and of Hermocrates (VI. 76. 3-4).

50. For a summary of scholarship, cf. J. Travlos, *Pictorial Dictionary of Ancient Athens* (New York: Praeger, 1971), p. 527. For the physical evidence, cf. H.A. Thompson and R.E. Wycherley, *The Agora of Athens,* Vol. XIV of *The Athenian Agora* (Princeton: ASCS, 1972), pp. 96ff. For literary evidence, cf. R.E. Wycherley, *Literary and Epigraphical Testimonia,* Vol. III of *The Athenian Agora* (Princeton: ASCS, 1957), pp. 25-30.

51. H.A. Thompson, *Hesp.* 6 (1937) 74.
52. *IG* II² 689 and 690.
53. Harpocration appears to preserve the most reliable text. Similar versions appear in the Souda, *s.v.* ἐλεύθερος ; Hesychios, *s.v.* ἐλευθέριος Ζεύς ; Schol. Plato, *Eryxias,* 392a; Schol. Paus. I. 3. 2. For the text and translation, cf. Wycherley, *Testimonia, supra,* n. 50, p. 26. Harpocration cites Hyperides for an opposing version, that the stoa was built by freedmen and so received its title.
54. Paus. I. 3. 1-3.
55. Cf. Wade-Gery, *supra,* n. 39, p. 92. For the *Eleutheria,* cf. Posidipp. 29; Diod. XI. 29; Paus. IX. 2. 6; and, of course, the text of the covenant, *supra,* n. 37.
56. Aristides himself at *Panath.* I. 204: ὥστ' εἰκότως εἰπεῖν εἶναι τὴν μὲν πόλιν τὸν ἐλευθέριον Δία τιμᾶν ἐπὶ τοῖς πραχθεῖσι προσήκειν, τοῖς δὲ ἄλλοις Ἕλλησι τὴν πόλιν, καὶ νομίζειν τὸν Ἀθηναίων δῆμον ὥσπερ ἐλευθέριον τοῖς Ἕλλησιν εἶναι. J.H. Oliver, *Demokratia, the Gods, and the Free World* (Johns Hopkins, 1960), p. 165f., sees a marked similarity between this statement and the paintings in the Stoa of Zeus.
57. Since Zeus Eleutherios gave his name to the new stoa, which Pericles included in his building program, I would tentatively suggest that the structure reflects Pericles' panhellenic policy as reflected in the Congress Decree.
58. Isoc. *Evag.* (9), 57; Paus. I. 3. Four statue-bases remain, presumably one for both Conon and Timotheus, one for Evagoras, one for the Zeus, and a later one for Hadrian.
59. *IG* II² 43; cf. line 65, where the title Eleutherios is used.
60. I. 75. 3: ἐξ αὐτοῦ δὲ τοῦ ἔργου κατηναγκάσθημεν τὸ πρῶτον προαγαγεῖν αὐτὴν ἐς τόδε, μάλιστα μὲν ὑπὸ δέους. ... Notice just above, at 75. 2, where the speaker calls the Persian campaigns of the Pentecontaetia, τὰ ὑπόλοιπα τοῦ βαρβάρου.
61. Plut. *Cim.* 12. 1. Lucian, *Rh. pr.* 18, *DMort.* 414, playfully advises aspiring young orators who want to make a splash in Athens to go through all the stock themes.
62. References to Xerxes' hybris are numerous. A rather remarkable instance is the recurrence of a single pair of words to describe the bridging of the Hellespont and the channelling of Athos. Isocrates has (*Paneg.* (4), 89): τὸν μὲν Ἑλλήσποντον ζεύξας, τὸν δ' Ἄθω διορύξας. Lysias (*Ep.* (2), 29) uses the same forms of the verbs and the *Marmor Parium* (ep. 51) has ἔζευξεν and διώρυξε. References to the punishment meted out by Athens are equally common, but the very word of Aristides (I. 245), κολάζω, appears twice in *Epitaphioi.* Gorgias, who called Xerxes ὁ τῶν Περσῶν Ζεύς in his *Epitaphios* (H. Diels, *Die Fragmente der Vorsokratiker,* Vol. II (Berlin: Weidmann, 1952), p. 284), later refers to the Athenians as κολασταὶ δὲ τῶν ἀδίκως εὐτυχούντων (Diels, p. 286). Hyp. *Ep.* (6), 5, has: ...οὕτως (as the sun) καὶ ἡ πόλις ἡμῶν διατελε[ῖ το]ὺς μὲν κακοὺς κολάζο[υσα. ...Cf. Is. (4), 89; Aristid. I. 563; Dio Chrys. 14 (I. 254); 17 (I. 276).
63. For Cyrus and Cambyses in Hdt., cf. H.-P. Stahl, "Learning Through Suffering? Croesus' Conversations in the History of Herodotus," in *Yale Classical Studies,* Vol. XXIV, *Studies in the Greek Historians* (Cambridge University, 1975). Xerxes' case is obvious, although one should note that Herodotus presents a more amplified version of the theme of hybris than Aeschylus. The dramatist does not mention the channelling of Athos, and his references to the chains on the Hellespont (lines 71f.; 745ff.) are, according to A. Sidgwick (ed.), *Aeschylus: Persae* (Oxford, 1957), p. 43f., "only

picturesque and figurative expressions for the bridge of boats itself." Herodotus, however, takes the chains literally and has the angry king beat and fetter the Hellespont (VII. 35). Moreover, the historian narrates the incident at Athos as an example of the king's μεγαλοφροσύνη(VII. 24).

64. Aeschylus won with the *Persae* in the year of Menon (cf. Hypoth.), which was 473/2. The *Fasti Theatri Atheniensis* (*IG* II² 2318) lists Pericles as Aeschylus' choregus for that year.

65. Hdt. VIII.109; *Pers*. 801-14. For the basic similarities, cf. H.D. Broadhead, *The Persae of Aeschylus* (Cambridge University, 1960), p. 201. For the implications of the similarities, cf. A.J. Podlecki, *The Political Background of Aeschylean Tragedy* (Ann Arbor: Michigan, 1966), pp. 23ff. The following argument owes much to this book and, by the same author, *Themistocles* (Montreal: McGill—Queens University, 1975), where, at p. 125, attention is called to a late, rhetorical progymnasma on the King's hybris. For a view opposed to drawing inferences from apparent connections between Themistocles and the *Persae*, cf. R.J. Lenardon, *The Saga of Themistocles* (London: Thames and Hudson, 1978), pp. 121-25.

66. Cf. Hypoth. of the *Persae;* Plut. *Them.* 5; and Podlecki, *Aeschylean Tragedy*, p. 157, n. 16. E. O'Neill, Jr., *CP* 37 (1942) 425ff., suggests that the production of the *Phoenissae* helped celebrate Themistocles' restoration of the Theater of Dionysus.

67. Cf. Podlecki, *Aeschylean Tragedy*, p. 14 and n. 18, and *Themistocles*, p. 6. H.T. Wade-Gery, *Essays in Greek History* (Oxford, 1958), p. 177f., places the play in the year before Themistocles' archonship. G. Freymuth, "Zur Μιλήτου Ἅλωσις des Phrynichos," *Philologus* 99 (1955) 51ff., denies the political tendency of the play. Cf., however, Lenardon, *supra*, n. 65, pp. 38 and 105f.

68. Thuc. I. 14. 3: Ἀθηναίους Θεμιστοκλῆς ἔπεισεν Αἰγινήτας πολεμοῦντας, καὶ ἄμα τοῦ βαρβάρου προσδοκίμου ὄντος, τὰς ναῦς ποιήσασθαι. Certainly a Persian invasion was expected when the ships were built (Hdt. VII. 20, 138).

69. Hdt. IX. 106. 3.

70. G. Murray, *Aeschylus: The Creator of Tragedy* (Oxford, 1940), p. 114f., suggests that these plays formed a series of national celebrations of victory, whereas Podlecki, *Aeschylean Tragedy*, pp. 13ff., would see in them Themistoclean propaganda against Cimon. For the latter suggestion, cf. Aristot. *Pol.* 1304a22; *Ath. Pol.* 25. For a good general interpretation of the poetry of the *Persae*, cf. D.J. Conacher, "Aeschylus' *Persae:* A Literary Commentary," in J. Heller (ed.), *Serta Turyniana* (University of Illinois, 1974), pp. 143-68. One wishes that more of the *Persae* of Timotheus of Miletus survived: cf. Podlecki, *Themistocles*, p. 62f.

71. *Pers.* 897-907; cf. Broadhead, *supra*, n. 65, p. 221.

72. Cf. Podlecki, *Aeschylean Tragedy*, p. 12ff.

73. It is interesting to note that Herodotus connects the disease of royal hybris with those oriental monarchs who, one by one, came to harm Ionia and then mainland Greece: Croesus, Cyrus, Cambyses, etc. Cf. Stahl, *supra*, n. 63, p. 19.

74. For Pericles' early support of Themistocles' policy, cf. Podlecki, *Aeschylean Tragedy*, pp. 99ff.

75. The tradition, of course, distinguishes between the two persons, Darius and Xerxes, but not between their hybristic motives: cf. Lys. *Ep.* (2), 21; Pl. *Menex.*

239c-240a; Hdt.VII.8.a.1; Diod.X.19.5; Aristid. *Panath.* I.197.

76. Hdt. VI. 108.The Plataeans appeared on the painting of the battle in the Stoa Poikile; cf. Paus. I. 15. 3. The Plataean presence received regular notice in the celebration of the greater *Panathenaea;* cf. Hdt. VI. 111. There was also, of course, the Plataean grave at Marathon; cf. Paus. I. 32. 3. Even an orator could mention the Plataean aid, if it suited his purpose: cf. Demosth. *In Neae.* (59), 94.

77. Hdt. IX. 27; Thuc. I. 74; cf. Hdt. VII. 10. β. 1.

78. And. *De myst.* (1), 107; Lys. *Ep.* (2), 20; Isoc. *Paneg.* (4), 86f.; *Areop.* (7), 75; Pl. *Leg.* 698b-699d; *Menex.* 240d; Demosth. *De cor.* (18), 208; Lycurg. *Leoc.* 104, 108. For this as the boast which upset Theopompus in *FGrH,* 115 F 153, cf. K. Walters, "We Fought Alone at Marathon," (see, *supra,* Chapter I, n. 1) p. 20, n. 21, and W. Connor, *Theopompus and Fifth Century Athens* (Washington: Center for Hellenic Studies and Harvard, 1968), p. 88; 172, n. 32. In support of this idea, I should like to mention Aristides' belief that some people might see ἀλαζονία in the Marathon epigram, which, as we shall see in a moment, contains by implication at least, the boast of Athenian singlehandedness at Marathon (Περὶ τοῦ Παραφθέγματος, II. 511).

79. E. Meyer, *Forschungen,* pp. 219ff., noticed the similarity between the contexts of *Epitaphioi* and such speeches as those at Hdt. VII. 161; IX. 27; and Thuc. I. 73-78. The common topics of the funeral orations have been listed by H. Strasburger, "Thukydides und die politische Selbstdarstellung der Athener," *Hermes* 86 (1958) 22-26. Cf. O. Schroeder, *De laudibus Athenarum a poetis tragicis et ab oratoribus epidicticis excultis* (Diss. Göttingen, 1914), pp. 68-76. Cf. *infra,* Chapter VII, n. 21.

80. The version here is from Aristides, cf. *supra,* n. 78, and the Souda, s.v. Ποικίλη. Lycurg. *Leoc.* 109, gives the second line as χρυσοφόρων Μήδων ἐστόρεσαν δύναμιν. Cf. *Anth. Pal.* 167, p. 812 (Iacobs). N.G.L. Hammond, "Marathon and the Marathon Campaign," *JHS* 88 (1968) 52ff., suggests the Atthidographer Demon as the Souda's source.

81. For the extensive bibliography on the epigrams, cf. *SEG* X (1949) 139-40; XII (1955) 23; XIII (1956) 29. B.D. Meritt, "Epigrams from the Battle of Marathon," in *The Aegean and the Near East,* ed. by S. Weinberg (Locust Valley, New York: Augustin, 1956), p. 270f., restores the epigrams as follows:

A. Ἀνδρῶν τῶνδ᾽ ἀρετὲ[όόχοσει κλέος ἄφθιτον]αἰεὶ[:]
[hοῖς ἂν hυ]πὲρ χ[συνὸν σκλερὰ νέμοσι θεοί·]
ἔσχον γὰρ πεζοί τε[καὶ ὀκυπόρον ἐπὶ νεῶ]ν :
hελλά[δα μ]ὲ πᾶσαν δούλιο[ν ἔμαρ ἰδέν].

B. Ἔν ἄρα τοῖοτ᾽ ἀδάμ[ας ἐν στέθεσι θυμός,]hότ᾽ αἰχμὲν
στέσαμ πρὸσθε πυλῶν ἄν[τία μυριάσιν,]
ἀνχίαλομ πρέσαι β[ολευσαμένον ἐρικυδὲς]
ἄστυ βίαι Περσῶν κλινάμενο[ι στρατιάν].

Meritt maintains that 'A' was inscribed first (ca. 485-470, according to P. Amandry, "Sur les épigrammes de Marathon," in Θεωρία, *Festschrift Schuchhardt* (1960), p. 4, based on lettering), but 'B' was composed earlier and later added to the present stone (ca. 475-460, according to Amandry).

82. Cf. *supra,* n. 77f. For the defense of the Greeks, cf. Hdt., And., Lys., and Isoc. References to the Persian myriads occur in Isoc. and Lys.; the same idea with the word πλῆθος appears in And., Lycurg., and Aristides. For the verb with the prefix προ-, cf. προτάττω in And., Isoc., and Aristides, I. 197 (Lycurgus has παρατάττω); for

προκινδυνεύω, cf. Thuc., Isoc., and Demosth. *De cor.* I have been unable to discover a significant difference between προμαχέω and the other words beginning with προ-. The former simply seems to have been a poetic and epigrammatic word, which writers of prose did not adopt. Certainly προμαχέω and ἐν προμάχοισι were standard terms for describing the perfect heroic act in military poetry (Tyrtaeus and Callinus), Pindar (*Isth.* 7. 35), and epitaphs: cf. D. Young, *Pindar, Isthmian 7, Myth and Exempla: Mnemosyne,* Suppl. 15, 1971, esp. p. 23 and the appendix facing p. 48.

83. I would like to see in all this a definite connection between prose *Epitaphioi* and poetic epigrams and elegies. Such a connection certainly exists between poetic encomia, which were first applied to living individuals in Simonides' day (cf. H. Smyth, *Greek Melic Poets* (Repr. New York: Biblo and Tannen, 1963), p. lxxvi *seq.*), and prose encomia such as the *Evagoras,* in which Isocrates openly states his intention of competing with the related poetic genre (section 11). C.M. Bowra, *Greek Lyric Poetry*^{2} (Oxford, 1961), p. 347, notices a similarity between the form of consolation in Simonides' poem on the dead of Thermopylae (Smyth, Sim. I), and Pericles' *Epitaphios* (Thuc. II. 43. 2). I am confident that many other similarities exist.

84. Isocrates repeats the sentiment in section 99.

85. For the relative places of Salamis and Plataea in the popular tradition of the fifth and fourth centuries, cf. Schlatter, *supra,* n. 37, pp. 67-86.

86. Hdt. VIII. 93, 122.

87. One such earlier source may appear in a fragment of an epigram which A.J. Podlecki, "Simonides: 480," *Hist.* 17 (1968) 270, assigns to Salamis and Simonides:

εἰ δ'ἄρα τιμῆσαι, Θύγατερ Διός, ὅστις ἄριστος,
δῆμος Ἀθηναίων ἐξετέλεσσα μόνος.

88. Cf. *Leg.* 707b-c.

89. For Hdt.'s personal judgment, cf. VII. 139. For Mardonius' embassy, cf. VIII. 136.

90. For the primacy of Salamis as the decisive battle in the popular tradition of the fifth century, cf. Schlatter, *supra,* n. 85.

91. *Ibid.,* pp. 131-52.

92. Isoc. *Paneg.* (4), 94; *Archid.* (6), 43; Lys. *Ep.* (2), 33; Demosth. *De cor.* (18), 202; *Phil.* II (6), 11; Lycurg. *Leoc.* 71.

93. Schlatter, cf. *supra,* n. 37, pp. 138-49, discusses this version of an earlier embassy in the later tradition.

94. *Paneg.* (4), 91 (which is very similar to Pl. *Menex.* 241b).

95. Lys. *Ep.* (2), 41; Lycurg. *Leoc.* 108; cf. *supra,* n. 82.

96. Isoc. *Paneg.* (4), 97.

97. Cf. Oliver, *Civilizing Power,* pp. 9-11.

98. *Menex.* 241c; cf. Ilse von Loewenclau, *Der platonische Menexenus* in *Tübinger Beiträge zur Altertumswissenschaft,* 41 (1961).

99. 241b.

100. Cic. *Orat.* 151.

101. Marathon was a paradigm for the later contests (*Panath.* I. 204); Athens restrained the other Greeks at Salamis as though they were children (I. 223).

102. Cf. *supra,* p. 56 and n. 85; p. 57 and n. 91.

103. Hdt. VIII. 44. 1, 48, 82. 2; Thuc. I. 74. 1; Lys. *Ep.* (2), 42; Isoc. *Paneg.* (4), 98; 107; *Panath.* (12), 50; Demosth. *De cor.* (18), 238 (although cf. Demosth. *Sym.* (14), 29). For the origin of the figure two-thirds, cf. Beecke, *Historischen Angaben,* p. 32, and Schlatter, *supra,* n. 37, p. 170f.

104. Thuc. I. 74. 1; Lys. *Ep.* (2), 42; Isoc. *Panath.* (12), 51; Demosth. *De cor.* (18), 204; Diod. XI. 58f. For Themistocles' role according to Aeschylus in the *Persae,* cf. Podlecki, *Aeschylean Tragedy,* pp. 12ff.

105. Thuc. I. 74. 2; Lys. *Ep.* (2), 33; Isoc. *Paneg.* (4), 96; 99; *Panath.* (12), 50; Demosth. *De cor.* (18), 204; Lycurg. *Leoc.* 70.

106. Cf. esp. *Paneg.* (4), 85.

107. Beecke, *Historischen Angaben,* p. 25, sees Plut. *Them.* 7. 3, as the source of this statement.

108. I. 217, 224f.

109. I. 217-25. Cf. *supra,* p. 46.

110. *Supra,* p. 45.

111. Pl. *Menex.* 241d. Lycurg. *Leoc.* 70-72, likewise seems unaware of the transfer, and his ninety year term of Athenian hegemony must have *ended* in 404. Demosth. *Ep.* (60), 10 also ignores the transfer, but his narrative is too brief to be significant.

112. Lysias mentions the transfer only in ambiguous terms as a sequel to the Battle of Plataea (*Ep.* [2], 47). Isocrates, like Aristides, was more careful. He knew of the transfer (*Paneg.* [4], 71f.), but placed it right after Salamis (*Panath.* [12], 52) and generally handled it just as Aristides, as we shall see below. The speech of the Athenians at Sparta (Thuc. I. 74ff.) seems to fail as a representative of the popular tradition in this case: obviously, the transfer could not be slighted in front of a hostile Spartan audience. In a similar manner, Euphemus disregards the niceties which the Athenian public would expect (Thuc. VI. 83. 2) and speaks openly about the transfer (82. 3).

113. Cf. also *Paneg.* (4), 57; 63; 65f.; and 71. The whole context of Aristides, I. 217ff., and Isoc. *Paneg.* (4), 93ff., are very similar. A trace of the debate appears in Lysias' summary of the Persian War (*Ep.* [2], 57): ὧν ἕνεκα δεῖ μόνους καὶ προστάτας τῶν Ἑλλήνων καὶ ἡγεμόνας τῶν πόλεων γίγνεσθαι.

114. IX. 27. A similar debate was purposely avoided by the Athenians before Artemisium (VIII. 3). According to Oliver, *Civilizing Power,* p. 121, Aristides had both passages in mind: he corrected Herodotus by placing the debate before Salamis. Such a correction, however, reflects *fifth-century* attitudes, which glorified Salamis over the other battles.

115. For the epitaphic elements of this speech and the speech of the Athenians at Sparta, cf. *supra,* n. 79. Herodotus, it should be noted, carefully avoids the anachronism of bringing popular references to Salamis into a speech that was delivered before the tradition had had time to assimilate the glorification of that battle in comparison with Marathon.

116. I. 73-78. For the best discussion of this speech in relation to my argument, cf. A.E. Raubitschek, "The Speech of the Athenians at Sparta," in *The Speeches in Thucydides,* ed. by P. Stadter (Chapel Hill: UNC, 1973), pp. 40-42.

117. Lys. *Ep.* (2), 54ff.; Isoc. *Paneg.* (4), 100ff.; *Panath.* (12), 56ff.; Pl. *Menex.* 241e; Demosth. *Ep.* (60), 11; cf. Lycurg. *Leoc.* 72; Demosth. *Phil.* III. (9), 23.

118. The germ of this idea appears in Thuc. I. 76. 1: the Spartans would have created an empire just as bad as the Athenian if they had had the opportunity.

119. Cf. *supra*, p. 63, for Philochorus, fr. 117, which clearly applies the word 'hegemony' to the period of undisguised empire.

120. I. 97. 2: Hellanicus wrote τοῖς χρόνοις οὐκ ἀκριβῶς.

121. Lycurg. *Leoc.* 72f.; Demosth. *Ep.* (60), 11; cf. Isoc. *Paneg.* (4), 117f. Without wishing to incur a charge of circular argument, I should confine the evidence from Aristides to a footnote. He does, however, split the narrative into two distinct periods: the Persian War (through I. 250) and the Greek War (from I. 251).

122. Cf. Thuc. I. 18. 2f., where the Persian Wars precede the division of Greece into two camps. Gomme, *HCT* I. 133, points to a parallel notion in Hdt. VI. 98. 2, where two great evils are portended for Greece in the fifth century: war against Persia and then war περὶ τῆς ἀρχῆς.

123. E. Schwartz, "Kallisthenes Hellenika," *Hermes* 35 (1900) 115-117.

124. Jacoby, *FGrH*.III B, 328 F 117, from Schol. Aristoph. *Lys.* 1138.

125. Cf. Thuc. I. 101-03.

126. *FGrH*, III B Supp. I, p. 459f.; cf., by the same author, *Atthis* (Oxford, 1948), pp. 96 and 103.

127. *FGrH*,III B Supp. 1, p. 457, Supp. II, p. 367.

128. *Ibid.* Supp. I, p. 460. Cf., e.g., Aristot. *Ath. Pol.* 23. 2.

129. Cf. *supra*, p. 48 f.

130. *FGrH*, III B Supp. 1, p. 459f. Jacoby believes that, in Philochorus at least, the previous period began in 479/8.

CHAPTER IV
THE BATTLE OF EURYMEDON

After Aristides duly recorded in the *Panathenaicus* the departure of the Spartans, he proceeds with his main narrative of the final phase of Athens' grand campaign to humble the Persian king. The next event to receive full treatment is the Battle of Eurymedon, known in the tradition and in fact to have been the greatest Athenian victory of the period. Aristides refers to the battle again later in the oration and deals with it in considerable detail in the *Pro Quattuorviris*. In this chapter, I will analyze Aristides' three accounts of the battle and employ the results of my analysis to interpret some of the problems that ancient and modern scholars have raised concerning the tradition of the Eurymedon. The main goal of my discussion will, of course, continue to be to search for Aristides' sources and to explicate his relation to the popular tradition.

Aristides' earlier reference to the battle in the *Panathenaicus* displays an understanding of the unique, double nature of the victory at the Eurymedon (I. 246f.):

> There was even a time when the Athenians put up two trophies on one day: the land battle was just as great as the naval fight. The only benefit that the King gained in all this was that his empire and especially certain places in it became better known thanks to the Athenians' victories. So it is that the Eurymedon is famous because of these Athenians.

Although, as we shall see later, the orator expanded on the theme of the Eurymedon in the *Pro Quattuorviris*, the actual description of the battle in that work is similar to the one in the preceding passage (II. 209): ἐπὶ δὲ Εὐρυμέδοντι ποταμῷ ναυμαχίας καὶ πεζομαχίας μνημεῖα ἔστησεν ἀμφότερα ἡμέρᾳ μιᾷ νικῶν. These two passages exhibit an economy and understanding of the battle's unique feature that recall Thucydides' account (I. 100. 1):[1]

> *After this the Athenians and their allies fought a land and a*

naval battle against the Medes at the Eurymedon River in Pamphylia. Under the command of Cimon, the son of Miltiades, the Athenians won both battles on the same day and captured or destroyed all the Phoenician triremes, two-hundred of them.

Another version of the Battle of Eurymedon similar to the accounts of Aristides appears in Plutarch's *Cimon*.[2] In the manner of Thucydides, Plutarch records a great amphibious victory by Cimon at the Eurymedon River and he measures the magnitude of the victory in terms of Persian ships (two hundred captured and destroyed in Thucydides; two hundred captured and more destroyed in Plutarch). Beyond this Thucydidean outline, the biographer presents a detailed narrative of the battle, its antecedents, and its consequences that is too lengthy to cite in full. To summarize: Cimon launched an attack from Cnidus and Triopium upon the Persians, who were known to be on the Pamphylian coast. He brought Phaselis into the League and then attacked the Persian fleet at the Eurymedon, before Phoenician reinforcements totalling eighty ships could be brought up from Cyprus. There follows a detailed account of the amphibious encounter at the Eurymedon and an otherwise unattested fight in which Cimon defeated the reinforcing squadron at Hydrus. The question of Plutarch's sources for all the details not found in Thucydides must, of course, intrude itself upon our analysis, especially since, as we shall see below, his account is remarkably similar to that of Aristides in the *Pro Quattuorviris*.

Plutarch mentions Ephorus and Phanodemus, but their contributions appear to be cited as variants rather than major sources for the narrative.[3] Theopompus may well have affected Plutarch's account, but Callisthenes' *Hellenica* seems to have had a truly pervasive influence.[4] In the matter of the Persian commanders' names, Ephorus merely supplies a variant, but Plutarch blends Callisthenes' statement into his own narrative (12.5):

> Now Ephorus says that Tithraustes was commander of the royal fleet, and Pherendates of the infantry; but Callisthenes says that it was Ariomandes, the son of Gobryas, who, as commander-in-chief of all the forces, lay at anchor with the fleet off the mouth of the Eurymedon, and that he was... waiting for eighty Phoenician ships to sail up from Cyprus. Wishing to anticipate their arrival, Cimon.... (Perrin's Loeb trans.)

Later, after his account of the battle itself, Plutarch records Callisthenes' theory that one result of the battle was a *de facto* peace with Persia (13.4):

*And yet Callisthenes denies that the Barbarian made any such
terms, but says he really acted as he did through the fear which
that victory inspired, and kept so far aloof from Hellas....*[5]
(Perrin's Loeb translation)

Although Plutarch himself believes in a *de iure* peace and thus disagrees with Callisthenes, it is interesting that he notes the latter's stress of fear (διὰ φόβον) as the motivating factor behind the Persian acceptance of a *de facto* peace. At 12.2, Plutarch recorded that, before the battle, Cimon was planning to force the Persians to remain, ὑπὸ φόβου, east of the Chelidonians.[6] This parallelism argues strongly that Callisthenes or his source supplied Plutarch with a rhetorical framework as well as numerous details for the Battle of Eurymedon. Unfortunately, Callisthenes' source remains problematic, although Ctesias and Hellanicus have been mentioned for factual details, and I shall suggest the influence of the oral tradition in subsequent pages.[7]

Aristides' third reference to the Eurymedon does not seem to reflect the same tradition of the battle's tactical details that we have noted in his other accounts, in Thucydides, and in Plutarch (I. 276):
τὰ δ' αὖ τελευταῖα αὐτῆς ἐστιν ἴδια, αἱ περὶ Κύπρον καὶ Παμφυλίαν ναυμαχίαι καὶ πεζομαχίαι καὶ ὁ πολὺς δρόμος. Although Aristides purports to be describing the whole final phase of the Persian War, comparison with sources for the Battle of Eurymedon makes it clear that he worded his description in terms that apply only to that battle. If this is true, the reference to Cyprus and the 'long run' between Cyprus and Pamphylia force us to turn away from Thucydides and Plutarch as possible sources for Aristides and look towards the only other extant, detailed account of the battle, that of Diodorus.[8]

Diodorus' version of the Eurymedon is also too extensive to cite, but again a summary seems appropriate.[9] In 470 B.C., Cimon liberated Eion, conquered Scyros, and, μειζόνων πράξεων ἄρξασθαι διανοούμενος (XI. 60. 3), set out to liberate the East. He freed many of the cities of Caria and Lycia by persuasion or by force and then found the Persians. Their fleet was lying off Cyprus and the army was encamped on the Eurymedon River. The ambitious Athenian general attacked the Persian fleet near Cyprus with the following result (60. 6): ἐνίκων οἱ Ἀθηναῖοι, καὶ πολλὰς μὲν τῶν ἐναντίων ναῦς διέφθειραν, πλείους δὲ τῶν ἑκατὸν σὺν αὐτοῖς τοῖς ἀνδράσιν εἷλον. Later on the same day, Cimon sailed his force to the Eurymedon and defeated the Persian army by using a stratagem under cover of darkness. Subsequently the Athenians employed the booty from this whole campaign to set up a dedication which bore the following version of a well-known epigram:[10]

ἐξ οὗ γ' Εὐρώπην Ἀσίας δίχα πόντος ἔνειμε
καὶ πόλιας θνητῶν θοῦρος Ἄρης ἐπέχει,
οὐδέν πω τοιοῦτον ἐπιχθονίων γένετ' ἀνδρῶν
ἔργον ἐν ἠπείρῳ καὶ κατὰ πόντον ἅμα.
οἵδε γὰρ ἐν Κύπρῳ Μήδους πολλοὺς ὀλέσαντες
Φοινίκων ἑκατὸν ναῦς ἕλον ἐν πελάγει
ἀνδρῶν πληθούσας, μέγα δ' ἔστενεν Ἀσὶς ὑπ' αὐτῶν
πληγεῖσ' ἀμφοτέραις χερσὶ κράτει πολέμου.

For the whole time that the sea held Europe apart from Asia and fierce Ares has been attacking the cities of men, no such deed has ever been accomplished by earthborn men on the mainland and over the sea at the same time. The reason is that these men destroyed many Medes on Cyprus and captured a hundred Phoenician ships complete with their crews in the open sea. When Asia was struck by these men on both hands and with the strength of war she wailed loudly.

As in the case of Plutarch, we are able to trace Diodorus' version of the Eurymedon back to a fourth-century source. Although we can no longer blithely accept the presence of Ephorus behind every statement of Diodorus, it does seem that Ephorus was his source for the Battle of 'Cyprus-Eurymedon'.[11] In the first place, certain general considerations suggest Ephorus. We know that he employed epigrammatic evidence and that he arranged his material by topic rather than chronologically.[12] The latter would explain Diodorus' compression of such widely separated events as the capture of Eion and the Battle of Eurymedon into the same archon year. More important, the details of the battle which Plutarch assigns specifically to Ephorus correspond to those in Diodorus. Ephorus named Tithraustes as the Persian admiral and Pherendates as the general.[13] Diodorus at first calls Tithraustes the overall commander but later he inattentively refers to Pherendates as ἕτερος στρατηγός (XI. 61. 3).[14] Ephorus said 350 Persian ships engaged in the battle.[15] Diodorus gives 340, but no other source gives a similar number.[16] Moreover, the number 340 as well as an almost certain restoration of the name of Pherendates and a fragment of the epigram appear in a papyrus fragment that describes the battle in almost the same words as Diodorus used.[17] Most scholars accept the papyrus as an epitome, or perhaps even the text, of Ephorus.[18]

If we were to halt our investigation of Aristides' sources for the Battle of Eurymedon at this point, we could safely conjecture that he followed Callisthenes, Plutarch, or Thucydides in the earlier passage of the *Panathenaicus* and in the *Pro Quattuorviris,* and Diodorus or Ephorus in the other passage.[19] Further investigation, however, will reveal that this picture is too simplistic. The chief complicating factor arises, not in consideration of the tactical details of the battle, but in the matter of its chronology. The context of the earlier passage in the *Panathenaicus* shows that Aristides was relying on a chronology that was at least superficially in agreement with both Thucydides and Ephorus. Their accounts of the period from the transfer of the hegemony until the end of the war (the Peace of Callias in Ephorus) indicate that the Battle of Eurymedon and the expedition to Egypt were the two greatest Athenian undertakings in that period, and that there were other events, notably the attack on Cyprus which cost Cimon his life. Aristides seems to agree, in that the Eurymedon and Egypt are the very campaigns he mentions specifically for the same period. The later passage in the *Panathenaicus* and the account in the *Pro Quattuorviris,* however, seem to reflect a different chronology. In the former, the reference to the Eurymedon serves as Aristides' only reference to action in the last phase of the war; thus, that battle and the Peace of Callias are thrown into close juxtaposition. After the account of the Eurymedon battle itself in the *Pro Quattuorviris,* Aristides praises Cimon and introduces a clear reference to the Peace as the result of the battle (II.210):

> Well, Plato, this is the kind of protection that Cimon carefully and assiduously provided for all of Greece, not just his own city. So it is that, as long as Cimon lived, the barbarians were literally frightened to death of the Greeks; the Persians were much too busy looking out for their own safety to attempt to subvert our allies and place them under the King's domination. The Athenians freed all of the cities from the Persians and led most of the coastal region of Asia into revolt; this was the very opposite of the way the Spartans capitulated later.... [20]

In these latter two passages, Aristides seems to have adopted a chronological scheme similar to that of Callisthenes and Plutarch, who, as we noted above, considered the Peace (either *de facto* or *de iure*) to be a result of the Eurymedon.

Our analysis of the chief sources for the Eurymedon and their relation to Aristides has brought out most of the serious historical and historiographical problems concerning the battle. Modern scholarly opinion has generally concentrated on explaining the factual variations in geography and tactics amongst the sources by postulating the existence of more than one independent tradition of the battle.[21] The most successful of these attempts was that of Peek, who distinguished in Ephorus a tradition that included the incident at Cyprus from one in Thucydides, Callisthenes, and Plutarch that did not. A second dichotomy in the sources, the battle's chronological relation to the Peace of Callias, seems to admit the same explanation.[22] Ephorus separated, and one can see how Thucydides would have separated, the two events by inserting the Athenian campaigns in Egypt and Cyprus, while Callisthenes associated the Eurymedon closely with his *de facto* peace. Unfortunately, if we accept the hypothesis of two independent traditions along the lines of Thucydides/Ephorus and Callisthenes/Plutarch, we will doubtless be forced to explain the texts of Aristides in terms of a rather clumsy contamination of literary sources. This explanation, however, would be less than satisfactory. On the one hand, if we admit the influence of Ephorian chronology in the *Panathenaicus*, there remain an actual account of the battle that is decidedly not Ephorian, a version of the epigram that is different from Ephorus', and, in the later passage, the very connection between the Eurymedon and the Peace that Ephorus avoided. On the other hand, the 'tradition' of Callisthenes and Plutarch seems close enough to the account of the *Pro Quattuorviris*, but that tradition alone cannot explain the presence of the 'Eurymedon' epigram which Aristides cites with significant variant readings.[23] This sort of literary contamination is not what the conclusions of the previous chapters have led us to expect of Aristides; yet, if we accept the thesis of two traditions, we shall have to abandon our theory of a single, continuous popular tradition that predated and superseded all literary accounts and continued to exert a compelling influence at least until Aristides' time.

The remainder of this chapter will consist of an attempt to reinterpret the literary tradition for the Eurymedon in a way that takes into account the evidence of Aristides and of the earlier popular tradition. It will be my conclusion that there never was more than one fifth-century tradition of the battle and its chronology. A closer examination of the historical sources will reveal that they can be reconciled to the concept of an archetypal tradition; and a study of the oratorical sources and the famous epigram will point to the existence of a single oral tradition that stands behind all of the literary sources and explains away the apparent dichotomies. Finally, I shall return to Aristides, whose narratives contain evidence of the continuing vitality of the old oral tradition in his day.

We should perhaps imitate Peek's method and begin by

considering the manner in which the sources diverge concerning the tactical details of the Battle of Eurymedon. Fortunately this task is simplified by the fact that Ephorus is very much the odd man out in this matter: the only sources that confirm his version are late and almost certainly depend on his own narrative. These include, besides Diodorus: Frontinus and Polyaenus, who are only interested in Cimon's stratagem of disguising his men as Persians;[24] the Scholia on Aristides marked A and C in Dindorf, which know of only a land battle at the Eurymedon River;[25] and, possibly, Aristides himself, who seems to associate the Eurymedon and Cyprus in the later passage of the *Panathenaicus*. All the other sources are either mute on this point or join Thucydides in placing both the land and sea fights at the Eurymedon.[26] Clearly, therefore, if Ephorus did employ an independent tradition, the only clues to its existence will be found in the text of Diodorus.

Apart from the tactical absurdity of Diodorus' account, our suspicions about its historical value are aroused most by its remarkable similarity to that historian's version of the major battle during Cimon's last campaign to Cyprus.[27] The two narratives have the following features in common:

1. The Persian fleet is found tarrying (διατρίβειν) off Cyprus.
2. The Greeks liberate several cities from Persian control before the battles in question.
3. The naval battles are described in the same terms used by the epigram cited above: πλείους τῶν ἑκατὸν σὺν αὐτοῖς τοῖς ἀνδράσιν εἷλον for the Eurymedon and, for the other, ἑκατὸν σὺν αὐτοῖς τοῖς ἀνδράσιν εἷλε.
4. After the battles, the Athenians pursue their enemy to the opposite coast and force a landing.
5. After these land battles, the Athenians sail back to Cyprus.

These two narratives clearly form a doublet; and, if our earlier discussion of Diodorus' source is accurate, Ephorus stands behind the doubling effect.[28] The only question is whether one event has been described twice or two events have been described similarly. The second alternative would seem to be the more likely, when one observes that Thucydides could have provided the germ of this doubling by describing the amphibious battles at the Eurymedon and off Cyprus in similar terms.[29] Ephorus, however, may have duplicated elements of the Cyprus expedition in his Eurymedon narration. In fact, Ephorus may have been the first to accept the existence of a truly pervasive parallelism between the battles, and he may have done so because he noticed that Cyprus was actually mentioned in two of his sources for the Eurymedon. The first was probably Ctesias or Hellanicus, who preserved certain details that Thucydides ignored.[30] This source may well have contained a version of the detail reported by Plutarch about a Phoenician squadron lying off Cyprus before the Battle of Eurymedon and being beaten after the battle by Cimon at 'Hydrus.'[31] Ctesias' or Hellanicus' comments may have been vague or confused, but they did not contradict Thucydides' insistence that both the land and sea fights took place at the mouth of the Eurymedon River; this is assured by the presence of the detail in Plutarch's account. Ephorus, however, must have felt that he had found in the epigram which he cited a major source for the Battle of Eurymedon that made a naval fight at Cyprus an integral part of the battle narrative. He accepted the epigram's testimony for the number of captured enemy ships, and he imitated the poem's language of praise;[32] clearly, then, nothing would have prevented him from finding an important role in his narrative for Cyprus in imitation of the epigram. Once Ephorus had decided to include Cyprus, both Thucydides and the details of the epigram would have led him to construct his account of the amphibious Battle of Eurymedon in imitation of the tactically similar Battle of Cyprian Salamis, during the course of which Ctesias and/or Hellanicus had the Athenians fight an infantry action on the nearby mainland.

On the assumption that our reconstruction of Ephorus' historiography is correct, the epigram is clearly the key to our argument. If it was an Athenian dedication for the Eurymedon, and if Κύπρῳ was the original reading in the fifth line instead of γαίη as Aristides read in the *Pro Quattuorviris,* the poem would seem to be an early representative of an independent tradition that confirms Ephorus' version. If, on the other hand, the first of the above conditions does not prevail, the poem would seem to be an irrelevant accretion added to the Eurymedon tradition probably for rhetorical purposes. If the second condition is untrue, then the poem would have to be taken as a further testimonium in support of Thucydides' and Callisthenes' version of the Eurymedon.

The style, structure, and text of the epigram raise several problems that have received considerable scholarly attention.[33] For example, the sententious boastfulness seems to some scholars impossible in an epigram of the middle of the fifth century.[34] To others, however, the poem appears Aeschylean in date and quality.[35]

In particular, the personification of Asia and the division of earth between Asia and Europe may recall Aeschylus' *Persae*.[36] The boastfulness of the epigram certainly corresponds to the quality of the other epigrams on the Eurymedon,[37] and the stylistic requirements for a funeral epigram of some sort are present, if somewhat exaggerated.[38] Moreover, the epigram was popular enough to inspire imitations early in the fourth century.[39]

While some scholars concerned themselves with the question of the epigram's authenticity as a mid-fifth-century document, students of its structure have also introduced the problem of its unity. Schwartz believed that the first half represented a spurious accretion influenced by the panegyric tradition of the fourth century.[40] Wade-Gery similarly divided the poem, although he concluded that both halves were genuine dedications in themselves: the first half for the Eurymedon and the second for Cimon's last campaign to Cyprus.[41] One of Wade-Gery's strongest points was that the excessive praise of the uniqueness of the achievement in the first quatrain seems to be appropriate *only* to the Eurymedon. Friedländer, however, destroyed this argument by pointing out that the poem need not refer to the Cyprian expedition merely as a successful event in itself, but rather as the glorious conclusion of a long series of successful campaigns that included the Eurymedon and Egypt.[42] Moreover, both Friedländer and Peek argue convincingly for the thematic unity of the epigram.[43] They point out that neither half of the poem can stand alone: the lack of specificity in the first half demands the explanation introduced by γάρ in the second. The third and fourth distichs, therefore, supplement the description of action in the second rather than introduce new material in the manner of a continuous narrative.[44] If, then, we accept the unity of the epigram, our most serious problem becomes its object: the Eurymedon or Cyprus. In this regard, of course, the reading of the fifth line is of paramount importance.

A minority of scholars accept the γαίη of Aristides as the original reading.[45] They believe that Κύπρῳ first appeared as a gloss intended to define γαίη according to Ephorus' narrative. Diodorus or some intermediary source brought the gloss into the text in the place of γαίη. If this is correct, the object of the poem's praise becomes problematic. Was it the Eurymedon, the expedition to Cyprus, or some other campaign? Assuming for the sake of argument that the epigrammatist had the Eurymedon in mind, we would seem to have discovered independent confirmation of Ephorus' account against that of Thucydides and Plutarch. This confirmation, however, derives from the variation in the number of captured Persian ships: one hundred in the epigram and 'more than one hundred' in Ephorus; two hundred in Thucydides and Plutarch. Unfortunately, this numerical difference provides only a minor variation between our two 'traditions,' which are primarily distinguished by the presence or absence of Cyprus in the account of the battle. If γαίῃ is read, then, the essential difference between the versions of Ephorus and Thucydides remains unexplained, and we cannot claim that the epigram represents an early version of Ephorus' 'tradition.'[46] This is, of course, to repeat in reverse what was just said above: if Ephorus had read γαίῃ, there would have been no reason for him to make a sea battle at Cyprus an integral part of his narrative of the Battle of Eurymedon. Since he must have read Κύπρῳ, however, we are probably justified in believing that Κύπρῳ represents the original reading; γαίῃ was very possibly a change introduced to bring the poem into agreement with Thucydides' account of the battle.

If we accept the opinion of the majority of scholars and read, correctly as I believe, Κύπρῳ instead of γαίῃ,[47] there can be little doubt that the epigram refers to Cimon's last expedition to Cyprus and that it stood as a whole on a monument erected in Athens after Cimon's death.[48] We have seen, however, that Wade-Gery would challenge this identification on the grounds that the excessive praise in the first quatrain could be applied only to the Battle of Eurymedon.[49] To be sure, the praise in the other epigrams on the Eurymedon seems to support Wade-Gery's argument, and we must not forget that even Isocrates knew that the Egyptian expedition and Cimon's last campaign to Cyprus were hardly complete Athenian successes.[50] I would argue, however, that it was precisely this sort of reasoning, rather than the original intention of the epigrammatist or his patron, which created a connection between the poem and the Eurymedon in the minds of many Athenians. In the years after the monument was erected, people must have assumed that an amphibious battle that received so much praise should be the Eurymedon. This popular tendency is probably what influenced Ephorus to associate the poem with the Eurymedon, and we shall see more of this later. In any case, the epigram was apparently a later accretion to the Eurymedon tradition; it offers no confirmation that Ephorus was relying on an independent tradition. The evidence for the naval portion of the battle, therefore, suggests that there was never more than one tradition of the Eurymedon.

The chronology of the Battle of Eurymedon presents a more complicated problem than the tactical details did. Although I am aware of the dangers of circular argumentation, I should like, first, to state my own hypothesis about the chronology and, subsequently, to discuss the support for it that can be derived from the sources. As in the case of the tactics, I maintain that there was originally only one tradition about the chronology. However, two versions of that archetypal chronology were invented to explain the apparently ambiguous relationship in the tradition between the battle and the greatest event of the period, namely, the Peace of Callias. Some preferred to date the Peace soon after the Eurymedon, virtually as a result of that battle; others delayed the Peace to the period after Cimon's death. A second dichotomy closely followed the lines of the first: some considered the Peace to have been Cimon's great achievement, while others gave the credit for it to Callias, who was supposed to have negotiated it in Pericles' name after Cimon's death. It is my belief that in both of these dichotomies the former version represents the original popular tradition, while the latter came about as a result of serious historical inquiries. At least as early as the fourth century, these inquiries had been made, and the accounts of Ephorus and Callisthenes can be viewed as more or less awkward attempts to preserve as much as possible of the popular tradition while taking into account the results of their historical analyses. Let us begin with these fourth-century compromises.

As we have seen, Ephorus did not juxtapose the Eurymedon and the Peace. He knew that the Peace had to mark the end of the war; yet he also knew that fighting had continued in Cyprus and Egypt long after the Eurymedon. What is more, he was aware of, and is in fact our only source for, the one stipulation in the Peace of Callias that could be called favorable to Persia (Diod. XII. 4. 5): μὴ στρατεύειν τοὺς Ἀθηναίους εἰς τὴν χώραν, ἧς βασιλεὺς ἄρχει. Popularizing authors could ignore this serious qualification upon Athens' victory, but the historian could not avoid the implications of the stipulation.[51] The Athenian attacks on Egypt or Cyprus would have been a blatant violation of this term, so Ephorus had to date the Peace after the end of the Egyptian affair.[52] Ephorus also knew that Callias, not Cimon, negotiated the Peace, and the historian may have known that the former was a member of Pericles', not Cimon's, party. Thus, Ephorus could not ignore the tradition that the Peace represented the triumph of Pericles *after* Cimon's death on Cyprus. In spite of all this evidence, Ephorus' well-known Athenian bias caused him to minimize the results of Egypt and pass over the discomfiture of the Athenians on Cyprus. Moreover, he very nearly capitulated to the other version of the chronology by appending a notice of Cimon's death as a mere footnote *after* the conclusion of the Peace.[53]

Callisthenes also seems to have avoided the popularizing chronology. Although Plutarch probably imitated him in juxtaposing the Eurymedon and the Peace, Callisthenes seems to have separated the two events by employing the simple expedient of denying the *de iure* existence of the latter.[54] Since no firm evidence supports the often repeated theory that Callisthenes was bowing to Theopompus in denying the Peace,[55] one wonders whether his motive were not rather a desire to correct the popular chronology. In this regard, Plutarch's reasons for rejecting Callisthenes' testimony could prove interesting (*Cim.* 13. 5):

> But in the decrees collected by Craterus there is a copy of the treaty in its due place, as though it had actually been made. And they say that the Athenians also built the altar of Peace to commemorate this event, and paid distinguished honors to Callias as their ambassador. (Perrin's Loeb translation)

Meiggs has suggested that Plutarch, quite unaware of any controversy about the authenticity of the Peace, concerned himself solely with its chronology.[56] The choice of the word κατατάσσω ('is...in its due place') may reinforce this idea, since the term implies order. Plutarch would thus have been more interested in Craterus' placement of the Peace in a chronological framework than in his actual citing of the document. At any rate, Callisthenes' denial of the Peace's formal reality places him technically in opposition to the popular chronology, although his *de facto* peace brings him even closer to the popularizers than Ephorus was.[57]

Let us now turn to the ante-Ephorian situation in regard to the chronology of the Eurymedon and the Peace. Since Thucydides failed to mention the Peace, all one can say with certainty is that, first, he seems to have dated the Eurymedon relatively early and, second, he clearly recorded the two major events in the Persian War that Ephorus felt constrained to interpose between the Eurymedon and the Peace.[58] Moreover, Cimon receives very little attention and no praise from Thucydides.[59] This all could lead, of course, to the conclusion that Thucydides was an early representative of a tradition independent of the popular one, but I believe that such a conclusion would be incorrect. My chief reason for so believing is the fact that Thucydides, so far from changing the date of the Peace, deleted it completely from his narrative. It will be argued in Chapter VI that the Peace was an integral part of the tradition before Thucydides and that he was aware of that fact. On the other hand, we noted in Chapter III that Thucydides went to great lengths, even to the point of hypercorrection, to oppose the popular tradition. It is my contention that, in an effort to deflate the popular tradition of the Peace and perhaps also to puncture Cimon's balloon, Thucydides omitted the Peace. It was this omission, rather than any conscious attempt to force the chronology to fit a second and independent tradition, that caused Thucydides inadvertently to supply the germ for the 'Ephorian' version. It matters little for the present discussion whether Thucydides' omission was the result of deceit, hypercorrection, or accurate correction on the basis of a careful analysis of primary, as opposed to popular and oral, sources.

It has been suggested that Thucydides' motive for deflating Cimon's glory could have been a desire to increase by contrast the glories of Themistocles and Pericles.[60] One might be able to derive support for such a thesis from the ambiguity concerning Callias and Pericles in the tradition of the Peace. In fact, it is by no means clear to what extent Pericles was somehow opposed to Cimon in the matter of the Peace, or whether or not Callias was acting as an agent of Pericles' democratic, as opposed to Cimon's conservative, party. The testimony for Callias is too ambiguous for certainty; yet the story that he was fined or rewarded for his part in the negotiations for the Peace could be significant, if we assume that his trial took place after the completion of negotiations and the death of Cimon.[61] As to Pericles' position in the tradition, we will note in Chapter V that Theopompus, at least, viewed Cimon as a democrat and Pericles as a conservative in the 460's.[62] Moreover, we will see in Chapter VI that early in his period of ascendancy Pericles identified himself with panhellenism and the blessings of the Peace,[63] although, as will be brought out in the following pages, the popular tradition considered Cimon to have been the truest proponent of panhellenism and also responsible for the victorious Peace. It seems possible that Cimon and Pericles were not far apart on the issue of peace with Persia in the 460's, and that Thucydides, unhappy with such an interpretation, overemphasized the distinction between democratic and conservative foreign policies which was less striking in the panhellenic 460's than in the 450's and later. If this is true, we are again led to the conclusion that Thucydides attempted to correct the single received tradition on his own initiative, without relying on an independent tradition.

Having examined the evidence of the historians, we must now turn to that of the orators. At first sight the orators do not appear to be very helpful, since they seem to exhibit a chronological vagueness or confusion about the Peace that was noted in Chapter III.⁶⁴ In the *Panegyricus*, for example, Isocrates does not locate his reference to the Peace in the proper place in his narrative of the Persian War.⁶⁵ It stands outside his continuous narrative, and, as we shall see below, its rhetorical purpose was to act as a foil to the Peace of Antalcidas. Isocrates gives absolutely no indication of the Peace's chronology, either relative in terms of the Eurymedon, Egypt, or Cyprus, or exact in terms of the transfer of the hegemony, the Battle of Tanagra, or Cimon's career. Not even the Eurymedon is mentioned by name in the passage that summarizes the period leading up to the Peace.⁶⁶ The accounts of Lysias' *Epitaphios* and the *Menexenus* are essentially the same, although Plato does mention the three major campaigns: ἦσαν δὲ οὗτοι οἵ τε ἐπ' Εὐρυμέδοντι ναυμαχήσαντες καὶ οἱ εἰς Κύπρον στρατεύσαντες καὶ οἱ εἰς Αἴγυπτον πλεύσαντες....⁶⁷ One should note, however, that Plato has produced a faulty chronology, if 'Cyprus' refers to the great expedition after the collapse of the Egyptian rebellion. Moreover, his seeming ignorance of the unique amphibious nature of the Eurymedon victory betrays either a lack of interest in, or confusion about, the details of these campaigns. The same nonchalance about the details of the last phase of the Persian War is evident in the very brief references to it in various Thucydidean speeches:

1. I. 75. 2: the whole period is simply, τὰ ὑπόλοιπα τοῦ βαρβάρου.
2. I. 76. 1: καὶ εἰ τότε ὑπομείναντες διὰ παντὸς ἀπήχθεσθε ἐν τῇ ἡγεμονίᾳ, ὥσπερ ἡμεῖς....
3. III. 10. 2: ἡμῖν δὲ καὶ Ἀθηναίοις ξυμμαχία ἐγένετο πρῶτον ἀπολιπόντων μὲν ὑμῶν ἐκ τοῦ Μηδικοῦ πολέμου. παραμεινάντων δὲ ἐκείνων πρὸς τὰ ὑπόλοιπα τῶν ἔργων.
4. VI. 76. 3: ἡγεμόνες γενόμενοι ἑκόντων τῶν τε Ἰώνων καὶ ὅσοι ἀπὸ σφῶν ἦσαν ξύμμαχοι ὡς ἐπὶ τοῦ Μήδου τιμωρίᾳ....

Presumably Thucydides presented an accurate account of the lack of interest many orators exhibited in the Cimonian campaigns against Persia. A closer examination of Lycurgus and Isocrates, however, will reveal that there was an oratorical, and therefore probably popular, tradition about the Eurymedon.

Lycurgus' testimony is important, because it seems to provide early evidence for juxtaposing the Eurymedon and the Peace (*Leoc.* 72f.):

> It was because they held such beliefs as these that for ninety[68] years they were leaders of the Greeks. They ravaged Phoenicia and Cilicia, triumphed by land and sea at the Eurymedon, captured a hundred barbarian triremes and sailed round the whole of Asia wasting it. And to crown their victory: not content with erecting the trophy in Salamis, they fixed for the Persian the boundaries necessary for Greek freedom and prevented his overstepping them, making an agreement...
> (*Burtt's Loeb translation*)

A standard citation of the terms of the Peace of Callias follows this passage. The first question is, of course, whether or not Lycurgus actually connected the Eurymedon and Peace. If the νίκη in question refers to Cimon's last campaign to Cyprus and if Salamis is equated with the victory off Cyprian Salamis, Lycurgus would seem to be rather close to Ephorus in his chronology. I cannot, however, accept these identifications. The mention of Salamis is surely intended to recall the famous battle of that name and to imply that the present νίκη deserves an equal meed of valor. What, then, is the 'victory' in the present passage? Scholars have suggested either the Eurymedon itself or the cumulative effect of all the eastern campaigns.[69] I maintain that to some extent both answers are correct, and that the famous Cyprus/Eurymedon epigram should serve as the key to our interpretation.

Lycurgus appears to present a contamination of the versions in his account of the Battle of Eurymedon itself. The detail that both the land and naval portions of the battle occurred at the Eurymedon reflects Thucydides and probably also the earlier oral tradition. The capture of a hundred enemy ships, however, must come from Ephorus or the Cyprus epigram.[70] No one can divine Lycurgus' intentions, of course, but it looks as if his eagerness to dramatize the battle led him to ignore the contradictions between the accounts of Ephorus and Thucydides. His primary aim was to recall the famous double victory at the Eurymedon River and to juxtapose it with the Peace, but he wanted to enliven his reference by alluding to the famous epigram. Now if the epigram caused Lycurgus to put the number of captured ships at one hundred, it may also have affected his use of the word νίκη. The expression κράτος πολέμου in the last line of the poem was a ceremonial term for victory.[71] In the narrow sense, the victory was the one at Cyprus, but the description of amphibious warfare in the first quatrain applies equally well to the

Eurymedon, Egypt, even Mycale. As we noted above, the poem actually views the Cyprus campaign as the glorious end of a series of victories.[72] Naturally, anyone who believed that the Peace of Callias signified Athens' ultimate victory would tend to associate the κράτος πολέμου with the Peace. That the epigrammatist and his patron also made this association is perhaps confirmed by the parallel structure of the poem. In the first couplet, Europe and Asia are separated and Ares rules all cities; in the last, Europeans have invaded Asia, and peace has been issued in by victory. Like Ephorus, however, Lycurgus viewed the epigram as a dedication for the Eurymedon. Thus, I submit that Lycurgus created a contamination of the original and the popular interpretations of the epigram: several victories led to the Peace; but the famous epigram really referred to the victory of the Eurymedon alone, and only the Eurymedon deserved to be singled out as being comparable to the Battle of Salamis. By a fallacious but simple enough leap of imagination, Lycurgus applied the term that described a whole series of victories in the original meaning of the poem to the most important specific victory and called the Peace the crown of the Eurymedon.[73]

The problem with the evidence of Lycurgus is that one cannot readily determine whether his emphasis upon the Eurymedon and the Peace derived from a genuine popular tradition or the literary influence of Ephorus. It is interesting to note that Lycurgus' associate, Phanodemus, seems to have narrated a version of the Eurymedon which greatly exaggerated the glory of Athens' achievement in a manner that was not reminiscent of Ephorus.[74] We must look for support in an author who antedates Ephorus, however, before we can say that Lycurgus reflected a true popular tradition. Such support is available in Isocrates.

Our interpretation of the connection between the epigram and the Peace is confirmed by Isocrates, who in fact provides the earliest reference to the poem (*Paneg.* [4], 179):[75]

Οἶμαι δ' ἐκείνως εἰπὼν μᾶλλον δηλώσειν τήν τε περὶ ἡμᾶς ἀτιμίαν γεγενημένην καὶ τὴν τοῦ βασιλέως πλεονεξίαν. τῆς γὰρ γῆς ἁπάσης τῆς ὑπὸ τῷ κόσμῳ κειμένης δίχα τετμημένης, καὶ τῆς μὲν Ἀσίας, τῆς δ' Εὐρώπης καλουμένης, τὴν ἡμίσειαν ἐκ τῶν συνθηκῶν εἴληφεν, ὥσπερ πρὸς τὸν Δία τὴν χώραν νεμόμενος ἀλλ' οὐ πρὸς ἀνθρώπους τὰς συνθήκας ποιούμενος.

I think, however, that I shall show still more clearly both the dishonor which we have suffered, and the advantage which the King has gained by putting the matter in this way: All the

> *world which lies beneath the firmament being divided into two parts, the one called Asia, the other Europe, he has taken half of it by the Treaty, as if he were apportioning the earth with Zeus, and not making compacts with men.* (Norlin's Loeb translation)

To interpret this passage correctly, we need only turn to an earlier one (*Paneg.* [4], 117f.):

> ... *the same barbarians whom we once so chastened for their temerity in crossing over into Europe, and for their overweening pride, that they not only ceased from making expeditions against us, but even endured to see their own territory laid waste;*[76] *and we brought their power so low that....* (Norlin's Loeb translation)

There follow the terms of the Peace. Isocrates explicitly sets up the Peace of Callias and a few words about all the campaigns that led to it as foils for the Peace of Antalcidas. Section 179 accomplishes the same thing implicitly by employing the epigram in a sarcastic manner. On the surface, the reference to the division of earth seems only to solemnize Isocrates' statement. However, the orator certainly intended his audience to recall the epigram as a celebration of all the fifth-century Athenian victories against Persia and their successful conclusion, the Peace of Callias. In a sarcastic way, then, the reference to the epigram fulfills the same rhetorical purpose in section 179 that the explicit reference to the last phase of the Persian War in the other passage did.

After we accept Isocrates' reference to the poem as genuine, further study of its context ought to reveal something more about the history of the epigram. In the two Isocratean passages that we have seen and in their contexts, the orator is at pains to compare the noble Peace of Callias with the infamous Peace of Antalcidas. The same is true of a third passage (*Paneg.* [4], 120):

> *One may best comprehend how great is the reversal in our circumstances if he will read side by side the treaties which were made during our leadership and those which have been published recently....* (Norlin's Loeb translation)

Wade-Gery has suggested that Isocrates' juxtaposition of the two treaties, as though the audience could be expected to read them side by side, may well have had a basis in Athenian topography. As we saw in the previous chapter, the Stoa of Zeus Eleutherios in the Athenian agora stood as a monument to Athens' achievements in the whole Persian War. The significance of the building was not lost on the fourth century, when nostalgic Athenians placed a copy of the decree establishing their second naval confederacy in front of the stoa.[77] This decree directly challenged the Peace of Antalcidas, which possibly was inscribed on a stone erected in the same vicinity.[78] Wade-Gery contends that, shortly before the publication of the *Panegyricus* (ca. 380), a copy or renewal or forgery of the Peace of Callias was erected to disgrace the (?nearby) Spartan treaty.[79] This suggestion would certainly explain how Isocrates could urge his readers to compare the treaties so closely; furthermore, it might also show us why he brought in the Cyprus epigram. Wade-Gery believes that in this same area there were a series of Herms, each of which bore an epigram commemorating one of Cimon's exploits. If one of these Herms bore the Cyprus epigram, one can easily see how the Athenian public could have connected it with the Peace, which came as the culmination of Cimon's campaigns against the Persians.[80]

What we have seen thus far should warrant the conclusions that the early popular version of the chronology of the last phase of the Persian War was ambiguous and confused, but that it exhibited a definite tendency to concentrate on Athens' most glorious battle and to juxtapose that battle with the Peace. This tendency manifests itself particularly in the way the Athenians interpreted the Cyprus epigram as both a dedication for the Eurymedon and a reference to the Peace. We have also seen indications that this popular tradition was identical to the archetypal tradition, which Thucydides, Ephorus, and Callisthenes each received and altered to accommodate the needs of his own historical analysis. It remains only to discuss the position of Cimon in the tradition. Unfortunately, Cimon's importance is not documented in early sources; even the orators concern themselves generally with 'the Athenians' rather than any individual hero. A number of late sources, however, juxtapose the Eurymedon and the Peace in such a way that they must have been relying on the earlier popular tradition; and in these sources Cimon plays a very important role indeed.

We have seen earlier that Callisthenes made Cimon responsible for the Eurymedon and its immediate consequence, the *de facto* Peace. Plutarch went farther by making the Peace *de iure,* and even Ephorus delayed reporting Cimon's death until after his lengthy citation of the Peace's terms. In the *Panathenaicus,* of course, Aristides assumed the epitaphic pose of speaking only about 'the Athenians' or 'the city,' but we have noted that in the *Pro Quattuorviris* his interpretation was similar to Plutarch's. Moreover, in the latter discourse, Aristides cited the Cyprus epigram as a memorial to Cimon's achievement at the Eurymedon, and his reading of the second distich is most interesting (II. 209):

οὐδενί πω κάλλιον ἐπιχθονίων γένετ'ἀνδρῶν
ἔργον ἐν ἠπείρῳ καὶ κατὰ πόντον ὁμοῦ.

Whatever source Aristides employed for the reading οὐδενί—and it may have been quite old[81]—the variant makes Cimon himself a major subject of the poem and serves to unify the connections amongst Cimon, Eurymedon, Peace, and epigram. Moreover, this dwelling on Cimon led Aristides to another amplification: since the Eurymedon was the accomplishment of one man and one force, it was more glorious than the allied and jointly commanded effort at Thermopylae and Artemisium.[82]

Several other late sources confirm the evidence of the preceding paragraph.

1. Trogus, if Justin can be construed to have the Eurymedon and the Peace in mind (II. 15. 20):[83] (Cimon) Xerxen, terrestri navalique bello superatum, trepidum recipere se in regem coegit.
2. Ammianus Marcellinus (XVII. 11. 3): Cimonem ... qui saepe ante et prope Eurymedonta Pamphylium flumen Persarum populum delevit innumerum, coegitque gentem insolentia semper elatam obsecrare suppliciter pacem.
3. Eusebius:
    a. Vers. Arm. Ol. 79.4: Cimon iuxta fluvium Eurymedontem et Persas navali proelio vincebat, et Medicum bellum cessabat.
    b. Jer. Ol. 79. 4: Cimon iuxta Eurymedontem Persas navali pedestrique certamine superat et Medicum bellum conquiescit.
    c. Syn. 470. 7: Κίμων ἐπ'Εὐρυμέδοντι Πέρσας ἐνίκα ναυμαχίᾳ καὶ πεζομαχίᾳ. καὶ ὁ Μηδικὸς πόλεμος ἐπαύσατο.
4. The Souda (s.v. Cimon): Κίμων ... καὶ πλεύσας εἰς Κύπρον καὶ Παμφυλίαν ἐπολέμησε καὶ ἐπ' Εὐρυμέδοντι ποταμῷ ναυσὶ καὶ πεζῷ νικᾷ ἐπὶ τῆς αὐτῆς ἡμέρας. οὗτος ἔταξε καὶ τοὺς ὅρους τοῖς βαρβάροις...

The Souda offers further confirmation in the entry under 'Callias': στρατηγῶν πρὸς Ἀρταξέρξην τοὺς ἐπὶ Κίμωνος τῶν σπονδῶν ἐβεβαίωσεν ὅρους. On the assumption that the author was employing the word βεβαιόω in this passage and τάσσω in the previous one with their normal meanings, the former should imply a legal and formal act and the latter some sort of confirmation. Thus the Souda, just as Plutarch, has no trouble reconciling the popular version, which connects Cimon, the Eurymedon, and the Peace, with the story of Callias' involvement in the negotiations for the latter event.

The preceding discussion has, I hope, determined the content of the archetypal, popular tradition of the Battle of Eurymedon and the Peace of Callias as far as the sources allow. This tradition juxtaposed the Eurymedon and the Peace closely, tended to ignore the other campaigns in the period, and viewed the whole process as Cimon's triumphant achievement. Before closing this chapter, let us consider one further issue: the extent to which we can determine the nature of the popular tradition and the method of its transmission from our analysis of its content. I will maintain that the literary sources indicate that the tradition was originally an oral one and that it survived as such at least down to Aristides' day.

The first indication of the oral nature of the tradition derives from our earlier examination of Isocrates and Lycurgus. Without actually citing the Cyprus epigram, both authors casually refer to it, and they both obviously assume that their audience will know it and its position in the tradition. The evidence of Aristides indicates that the poem continued to be a part of the oral tradition to his day. Aristides, of course, cited the epigram in the *Pro Quattuorviris;* but in the *Panathenaicus* one finds a subtle and seemingly casual allusion to the epigram in a sort of preface which the orator attaches to the earlier account of the Eurymedon in that work (I. 246):

καὶ ἦν αὐτοῖς ἀφορμὴ κατὰ τοῦ βασιλέως τὰ τοῦ βασιλέως πράγματα· καὶ γὰρ ὅρμοι καὶ τείχη καὶ χαρακώματα καὶ πάντα ἐκείνους ἐδέχετο, καὶ ὅπλα καὶ νῆες ἐκείνων ἐγίγνοντο.[84] παρεῖσαν δ'οὐδὲν ἀπείρατον τῆς ἑαυτῶν ἀρετῆς, ὁμοῦ μὲν Φοίνιξι καὶ Κίλιξι καὶ Κυπρίοις ναυμαχοῦντες ἐν μέσῳ τῷ Αἰγυπτίων πελάγει καὶ ναυτικὰ ἀθρόα λαμβάνοντες, ὁμοῦ δὲ πρὸς πᾶσαν τὴν Περσῶν ἀρχὴν διακινδυνεύοντες ἐν τῇ γῇ ἀντ' ἀριθμοῦ σωμάτων ἐθνῶν ἀριθμοὺς διαφθείροντες καὶ λαμβάνοντες.

Out of his own resources the King supplied the Athenians with materiel for the war against himself: his naval bases, fortresses, armed camps, everything went over to them; his arms and ships became theirs.[84] *There was nothing they did not attempt to accomplish with their excellence. They fought naval battles in the middle of the open Egyptian Sea against Phoenicians, Cilicians, and Cyprians, and they captured veritable fleets of ships. At the very same time, they risked dangerous encounters against the whole Persian Empire on land; they killed or captured not just a number of individuals but whole races of people.*

Although this passage purports to be a summary of earlier

campaigns, it consists of material that is appropriate only to the Battle of Eurymedon. The preface actually forms a sort of prolepsis before Aristides' account of the battle itself. For example, Diodorus supports the statement that the Persian fleet at the Eurymedon was manned by 'Phoenicians, Cilicians, and Cyprians.'[85] A complete understanding of the proleptic nature of the preface, however, must depend upon the reader's familiarity with the epigram. Aristides speaks of fighting ἐν μέσῳ τῷ Αἰγυπτίων πελάγει, which clearly recalls ἐν πελάγει in the epigram. The parallel structure introduced by ὁμοῦ μέν ... ὁμοῦ δέ in Aristides, reflects the ὁμοῦ which Aristides read instead of ἅμα in the poem's fourth line. And finally, the poem's ἐν γαίῃ may have inspired Aristides' ἐν τῇ γῇ. If Aristides' assumptions about his Athenian or 'Athenian-educated' audience's grasp of the epigram were well founded, we ought to be able to conclude that the oral tradition of the Eurymedon was as vital in his day as it had been in Isocrates'.

The second indication that the Eurymedon tradition was an oral one comes from its association with the 'theme of fear,' which will receive fuller treatment in Chapter VI.[86] Briefly, it will be maintained that, in the oral, popular tradition, the last phase of the Persian War was viewed as a process whereby the Athenians transferred 'fear' from themselves to the King of Persia; the culmination of this transfer was the Peace. At this point, I should merely like to introduce the evidence that connects this 'theme of fear' with our Eurymedon tradition. The oldest extant witness for this connection is Callisthenes, if he is to be accepted as the source of Plutarch's account of the Eurymedon campaign.[87] In Plutarch's narrative, Cimon planned the whole campaign leading up to the Eurymedon in order to instill fear in the Persians (*Cim.* 12. 2): βουλόμενος αὐτοῖς ἄπλουν καὶ ἀνέμβατον ὅλως ὑπὸ φόβου τὴν ἐντὸς Χελιδονίων ποιήσασθαι θάλατταν. When the battle was over Cimon's plan was fulfilled by the Peace of Callias (13.4): τοῦτο τὸ ἔργον (the battle) οὕτως ἐταπείνωσε τὴν γνώμην τοῦ βασιλέως, ὥστε συνθέσθαι τὴν περιβόητον εἰρήνην. Although Plutarch goes on to discuss the historical problem of the Peace, his rhetoric corresponds exactly to the rhetorical structure of Aristides' account in the *Pro Quattuorviris*. We have seen the end of Aristides' version with its reference to the Peace; some lines earlier the orator introduced the topic of the Eurymedon with an allusion to Cimon's intentions (II. 208):

> *Moreover, Cimon felt that Greece could not be truly guarded if he were to keep the Greeks in their homeland and allow them*

> to rest in security; he knew that security depended on his throwing into the barbarians a fear of ever plotting against Greece again, and that this could only be accomplished if he drove them as far as possible from Greece.

In Chapter VI we will encounter evidence from all the orators and from a Thucydidean speech that the oral tradition of the fifth and fourth centuries made the connection between the 'theme of fear' and the Peace. The preceding analysis of the later sources should allow us to conclude that they are trustworthy witnesses for a further connection amongst 'fear,' Cimon, Eurymedon, and Peace in the old oral tradition.

Our final indication of the oral nature of the tradition derives from the fact that it concentrated so exclusively on the Eurymedon and Cimon. An interesting result of this phenomenon was the tendency to compare Cimon's victory at the Eurymedon with the deeds of the earlier phases of the Persian War. We have seen how Aristides compared the Eurymedon with Thermopylae and Artemisium. A much earlier piece of evidence for the same tendency exists in the one seemingly genuine Athenian Eurymedon epigram in the *Anthology*, which implicitly compares the Eurymedon with Marathon.[88] We have also seen Lycurgus' comparison of Salamis and the Eurymedon, and Plutarch made Cimon's achievement at the Eurymedon the equal of Salamis and Plataea together.[89] In another work, Plutarch mentions the Eurymedon beside Marathon and Plataea as stock themes for orators in his day; and in yet another essay he listed Athens' achievements in the Persian War as, Miltiades' victory at Marathon, Themistocles' at Salamis, and Cimon's capture of one hundred Phoenician ships at the Eurymedon.[90] As these and other sources indicate, the Athenians tended to view the two earlier phases of the war in terms of the greatest battle of each phase, and in the same way the Eurymedon came to epitomize the last phase.[91]

All this is to go beyond our earlier hypothesis that the oral tradition remembered the importance of the Eurymedon and used it in place of several less decisive campaigns. This is in fact to say that the Eurymedon symbolized the whole last phase of the war, which might seem to conflict with our contention that in the popular mind the Cyprus epigram contained a description of the Eurymedon in terms that were apropos to the whole last phase. We are now saying that the popular tradition described the whole last phase of the war in terms that were apropos to the Eurymedon alone. As we saw above, this is precisely what Aristides did in the prolepsis which he appended to his earlier account of the Battle of Eurymedon in the *Panathenaicus*, and it represents the tendency of several of the later sources we have seen. Our apparently contradictory conclusions, however, are what we would expect of an oral tradition. Such traditions tend to compress numerous events that occurred over a long period of time and involved many important people into a briefer, more pointed narrative which centers around a single event and a single person as symbols of the larger context.[92] In the *Iliad*, for example, the story of Achilles' ten-week wrath symbolized the ten-year war at Troy; and yet it is also true that his story was expanded and amplified with stories and themes from all the rest of the war. It is the same with the last phase of the Persian War: the details of the various campaigns and their relative chronology became obscured, and the Athenians concentrated their attention upon elaborating the story of the major personality (Cimon), the most important victory (Eurymedon), and the conclusion of the whole (the Peace).

Undoubtedly, many scholars will accept my argument that the tradition of the Eurymedon exhibits characteristics which insure that it was an oral tradition at least through Lycurgus' time. In spite of Aristides' casual reference to the Cyprus epigram, his use of the theme of fear, and his close juxtaposition of the Eurymedon and the Peace, many will assume that he employed only literary sources. This assumption may facilitate ordinary *Quellenforschung*, but it too often goes hand in hand with a dangerous supposition: most scholars believe that orators, particularly late ones, employed history as mere decoration or justification for the theme of the speech at hand, the only matter of importance for an orator. The problem with this opinion is that it seriously underestimates the historical sense of the Greek rhetorical tradition and of Aristides in particular. If speech-making had been Aristides' only concern, history would have been a dead thing to him. No living tradition could have touched him; he almost certainly would have contented himself with a single, easily available source that reinforced his argument. Ephorus would have supplied the proper version of the Eurymedon for the *Panathenaicus*, and Callisthenes or Plutarch for the *Pro Quattuorviris*. Such a facile explanation, however, cannot account for the complex weaving of traditional material that we have detected in Aristides' versions of the battle. The fact is that no extant literary source can completely and sufficiently explain the text of

Aristides, in which we have nevertheless been able to discover several elements that appear in various different sources for the ancient popular tradition of the Eurymedon. Aristides actually reproduced the ancient oral tradition more fully than his obvious fourth-century oratorical and historical sources, whose concepts of historical truth or rhetorical requirements caused them to take certain liberties with the elder tradition. Aristides, however, had no need to change the received tradition; on the contrary, his aim was to recall to the Greeks the ancient glory of Athens as reflected in the ancient tradition. As a result, Aristides might make use of material from the historians or earlier orators if it suited his purposes, but he knew that no historian or orator had sole claim on the 'real' truth.[93] The raw material from which that truth could be reconstructed was the vast body of oral tradition, which was the common property of historians and orators alike, as well as painters, sculptors, architects, poets, and playwrights.[94] It was the task of each kind of artist to deal as best he could with the tradition, but the tradition itself was sacred.[95]

Whatever Aristides' immediate sources were, his versions of the Battle of Eurymedon and their contexts have, I hope, lent themselves well to the construction of a workable paradigm of my historiographical method as well as to the study of the actual events under consideration. By starting with Aristides and Plutarch, the other late source that presents a full account, we were able to pose the kinds of questions about the earlier tradition that have seemingly led to an increased understanding of both the role played by popular sources in the tradition and the nature of the tradition as a whole. Whereas it has generally been believed that there were two independent traditions about the Eurymedon and all of Athens' campaigns in the East, our inquiries have not revealed any essential contradiction in the various sources that can only be explained by positing different traditions. On the contrary, by explicating the oral characteristics of the version found in popular sources, that version has been shown to have originated in the same tradition that Thucydides, Ephorus, and Callisthenes employed. We can say, therefore, that there were two ancient versions, a popular one and an historical one, of just one ancient tradition of the Eurymedon and other campaigns. While the historians attempted to account for all the elements of the story and to construct a chronological account of the whole period, the popular version stressed the more dramatic sides of the story—Cimon's personality, the famous epigram, the unique Battle of Eurymedon, and the Peace of Callias.

1. Cf. Beecke, *Historischen Angaben,* p. 48f., who accepts Thucydides as the source of the latter passage.
2. 12.1-13.3.
3. Ephorus is cited at *Cim.* 12. 4 (names of Persian commanders) and 12. 5 (size of the Persian fleet); Phanodemus at 12.6 (size of the Persian fleet).
4. Busolt, *Gr. Gesch.*, Vol. III, Part 1, p. 36, n. 1, argues convincingly for the influence of Theopompus on Plutarch. Cf. A.E. Raubitschek, "The Peace Policy of Pericles," *AJA* 70 (1966) 37. For Callisthenes, cf. W. Peek, "Die Kämpfe am Eurymedon," *Athenian Studies Presented to W.S. Ferguson: Harvard Studies in Classical Philology,* Suppl. vol. I (1940), pp. 97-120; J.H. Schreiner, "Anti-Thukydidean Studies in the Pentekontaetia," *SO* 51 (1976) 19-63. Schreiner's important article and its continuation in the next volume of *SO*, pp. 19-38, did not become available to me until this monograph was virtually complete. In some ways his studies have anticipated mine, but in others I either offer independent confirmation of his hypotheses or disagree with him.
5. Most commentators have felt that Callisthenes was attempting to circumvent Theopompus' denial of the authenticity of the Peace; cf. H.T. Wade-Gery, "The Peace of Kallias," *Athenian Studies Presented to W.S. Ferguson: Harvard Studies in Classical Philology,* Suppl. vol. I (1940), p. 122f. However, W.R. Connor, *Theopompus and Fifth-Century Athens* (Harvard, 1968), pp. 84-87, and A.E. Raubitschek, "Treaties between Persia and Athens," *GRBS* 5 (1964) 151-59, have stressed the variety of treaties with Persia and suggested that the one denied by Theopompus (*FGrH* 115 F 153, 154) was not necessarily a simple renewal of the Peace of Callias. Thus, there can be no proof that Callisthenes and Theopompus were talking about the same treaty.
6. The Chelidonians were normally mentioned amongst the terms of the Peace of Callias as the westernmost limit on the range of the Persian fleet: cf. *infra,* Chapter VI.
7. For Ctesias, cf. Schreiner(1976), *supra,* n. 4, p. 39f.; for the oral tradition, cf. *supra,* p. 94 ff.
8. Beecke, *Historischen Angaben,* p. 48f., understood Aristides' debt to Ephorus/Diodorus. And besides presenting a positive statement, Beecke is at pains to refute A. Haas, *Quibus fontibus Aristides in componenda declamatione, quae inscribitur* πρὸς Πλάτωνα ὑπὲρ τῶν τεττάρων, *usus sit* (Diss. Greifswald, 1884), p. 78f., who refuses to accept Ephorus as Aristides' source because of the variation between their versions of the epigram.
9. XI. 60. 3-62. 3.
10. Diodorus introduces the epigram as follows: ὁ δὲ δῆμος τῶν Ἀθηναίων δεκάτην ἐξελόμενος, ἐκ τῶν λαφύρων ἀνέθηκε τῷ θεῷ, καὶ τὴν ἐπιγραφὴν ἐπὶ τὸ κατασκευασθὲν ἀνάθημα ἐνέγραψε τήνδε.... Another version of the epigram appears with minor variants at *Anth. Pal.* VII. 296, with the introduction, εἰς τοὺς μετὰ Κίμωνος στρατευσαμένους ἐν Κύπρῳ Ἀθηναίους, ὅτε τὰς ῥ' ναῦς τῶν Φοινίκων ἔλαβεν. Aristides has preserved a third version at *Pro. Q.* II. 209 and at II. 512: cf. the Scholion on the earlier passage in the *Panath.* (III. 209); Arsen. XXIV. 18; and Apostol. VII. 57a. For these latter authors, cf. E. von Leutsch and F. Schneidewin, eds., *Corpus Paroemiographorum Graecorum,* Vol. II (Göttingen: Libraria Dieterichiana, 1851),

p. 409. Apostolius and his son cite the epigram for grammatical reasons, and their source was almost certainly the Scholion on Aristides. Their comment (Σιμωνίδου ἐλεγεῖα περὶ Ἀθηναίων) reflects the Scholion (εἰς τὰς αὐθημερὸν ταύτας νίκας Σιμωνίδης ὕμνησε, λέγων . . .).

11. Gomme, *HCT* I. 286, n. 2, cannot allow the tactical absurdities of Diodorus' account to be attributed to Ephorus, whom Polybius considered a good naval historian (XII. 25f. 1). Gomme is also troubled by Plutarch's seeming ignorance of an important contradiction between his own account and that of Ephorus. In spite of such caution, however, the *communis opinio* is that, in one form or another, Ephorus was Diodorus' source. Busolt, *Gr. Gesch.*, Vol. III, Part 1, pp. 146ff., n. 5, states the case clearly and summarizes the earlier scholarship. Cf. Beecke, *Historischen Angaben,* p. 48f.; Peek, *supra,* n. 4, p. 97.

12. For a discussion of Ephorus' use of epigrams and an important study of the Eurymedon, cf. Meyer, *Forschungen,* pp. 11ff. For Ephorus' topical arrangement, cf. B. Grenfell and A. Hunt, *The Oxyrhynchus Papyri* (London: Egypt Exploration Fund, 1919), No. 1610, p. 110.

13. Plut. *Cim.* 12. 5 (= *FGrH* 70 F 192).

14. For Tithraustes, cf. XI. 60. 5.

15. Plut. *Cim.* 12.6 (=*FGrH* 70 F 192).

16. XI. 60. 6.

17. Pap. Oxy. XIII. 1610 (*FGrH* 70 F 191). Grenfell and Hunt, cf. *supra,* n. 12, pp. 101f., 124, and 126f., suggest that fr. 48, να?]υς ελ[ον ?/] ανδ[ρων?/ με]γ[α?, represents Ephorus' citation of the poem. Gomme, *HCT* I. 286, n. 2, advises caution in this.

18. Cf. Meiggs, *Athenian Empire,* p. 74f., and Jacoby's note on F 191. Grenfell and Hunt, cf. *supra,* n. 12, pp. 101-08, argue strongly for the identity of Ephorus as the actual author of the papyrus. They dismiss the possibility that the papyrus was written in imitation of Diodorus, and they bring forward numerous arguments for Ephorus. Some of these arguments appear in my text below. Cf. however, C. Rubincam, "A Note on Oxyrhynchus Papyrus 1610," *Phoenix* 30 (1976) 357-366.

19. For the tendency to use Ephorus, at least, in place of his later imitators, cf. Grenfell and Hunt, *supra,* n. 12, p. 105f.; Oliver, *Ruling Power,* p. 895.

20. Numerous details point to the Peace of Callias. First, the 'theme of fear' forms an integral part of the popular tradition about the Peace (cf. *infra,* Chapter VI, p. 151ff.). Second, the terms of the Peace certainly lurk behind Aristides' words about Persians not being allowed to rule Greeks, having to watch out for their own safety, and losing cities (Greek cities, one supposes) and a great amount of land. Third, the oblique comparison with Sparta's infamous Peace of Antalcidas points to the Peace of Callias by way of contrast (cf. Isoc. *Paneg.* [4], 118-21). Fourth, the similarity to Plutarch's account, which is noted just below, points to the Peace of Callias.

21. W. Graf Uxkull-Gyllenband, *Plutarch und die griechische Biographie* (Stuttgart: Kohlhammer, 1927), pp. 50-59, considers Aristides a representative of one tradition of the battle in which the sea-fight preceded the one on land (ναυμαχία πεζομαχία παρισώθη) and Thucydides of a separate independent tradition in which the infantry battle came first (πεζομαχία καὶ ναυμαχία). Peek, cf. *supra,* n. 4, pp. 99-108, has argued convincingly that the order of the words is not significant enough to warrant a differentiation of traditions on such grounds. The order in Thucydides, for example, was probably determined by nothing more meaningful than the conventional expression, κατὰ γῆν καὶ κατὰ θάλασσαν.

22. For the chronology of this period and the unity or disunity of the tradition, cf. C.L. Murison, "The Peace of Callias: Its Historical Context," *Phoenix* 25 (1971) 12-31, and, especially, the articles by Schreiner cited in n. 4. Schreiner attempts to uphold not only the unity of the archetypal tradition (which he identifies with the popular one as written down in Hellanicus) but also its historicity. I agree with a great deal of what Schreiner says, but two points seem troublesome. First, I cannot accept the historicity of his 100-ship battle; and, second, I do not believe that the evidence for the 'popular tradition' supports his hypothesis of a *literary* archetype in the person of Hellanicus, about whom we really know so little.

23. The citation comes in the midst of Aristides' long discussion of the significance of the Eurymedon. I should add that this is the weaker of my points, since it does not in itself imply a major author independent of the one tradition. Aristides could have taken the epigram from a collection in a rhetorical handbook: cf. H.T. Wade-Gery, "Classical Epigrams and Epitaphs," *JHS* 53 (1933) 86, n. 66. M. Jameson, "Waiting for the Barbarian," *Greece and Rome*, Second Series, 8 (1961) 18, suggests that Aristides found a copy of the Themistocles-decree in such rhetorical manuals.

24. *Strat.* II. 9. 10, and *Strat.* I. 34. 1, respectively. Grenfell and Hunt, cf. *supra*, n. 12, pp. 101ff., 111, and 122, point out that the earlier theory that Polyaenus was closer to Ephorus than Frontinus in placing the sea-battle at the Eurymedon and the land encounter at Cyprus (Busolt, cf. *supra*, n. 11) is destroyed by the identification of Pap. Oxy. XIII. 1610, as Ephorus himself.

25. III. 210: Εὐρυμέδων, ποταμὸς Παμφυλίας, ἐν ᾧ ἡ πεζομαχία γέγονεν. For the pairing of the four versions of the Scholia in Dindorf, cf. Lenz, *Aristeidesscholien*, p. 107f., and *Prolegomena*, p. 4f.

26. Besides Callisthenes, Plutarch, and Aristides, these include: Lycurg. *Leoc.* 72f.; Nep. *Cim.* 2. 2-3; Paus. I. 29. 14 (cf. Grenfell and Hunt, *supra*, n. 12, p. 102), X. 15. 4; Amm. Marc. XVII. 11. 3; Euseb. at Jer. *Ol.* 79. 4, and Syn. 470. 7; the Souda, *s.v.* Cimon; Aristodemus, 11. 2-3; Schol. Aristid. (B and D in Dindorf), III. 209; and the epigrams cited in n. 37, *infra*. Several of these passages will be discussed in the following pages.

27. XII. 3. 2-4.

28. Cf. E. Schwartz, "Kallisthenes Hellenika," *Hermes* 35 (1900) 114 and 123. For the whole matter of the Eurymedon and the various expeditions to Cyprus, cf. J. Barns, "Cimon and the First Athenian Expedition to Cyprus," *Hist.* 2 (1953-54) 163-76; M. Sordi, "La vittoria dell' Eurimedonte e le due spedizioni di Cimone a Cipro," *RSA* 1 (1971) 33-48; Schreiner (1976), *supra*, n. 4, who believes that one event, his otherwise unattested 100-ship battle at Cyprus, was described twice by Thucydides; E. Badian and J. Buckler, "The Wrong Salamis," *RhM* 118 (1975) 226-239; S. Parker, "The Objectives of Cimon's Expedition to Cyprus," *AJP* 97 (1976) 30-38.

29. Cf. I. 100. 1, and 112. 4, respectively.

30. Ctesias is the suggestion of Uxkull, cf. *supra*, n. 21, pp. 53-68.

31. Plut. *Cim.* 13. 3. The name Hydrus presents a serious problem: cf. *RE*, Vol. XVII, *s.v.* Hydra. Uxkull, cf. *supra*, n. 21, p. 47, n. 26, would emend Ὕδρῳ to Κύπρῳ, but the reading is unattested. Meiggs, *Athenian Empire*, p. 76, places Hydrus seventy miles east of the Eurymedon.

32. Presumably it was a knowledge of the version used by Thucydides that influenced Ephorus to take liberties with the information he received in the epigram. Although the poem says that 100 enemy ships were captured, Ephorus seems to have

put it thus (Diod. XI. 60. 6): πλείους τῶν ἑκατόν. As for the praise, cf. Diod. XI. 61. 7: νενικηκότες δύο καλλίστας νίκας, τὴν μὲν κατὰ γῆν, τὴν δὲ κατὰ θάλατταν·οὐδέπω γὰρ μνημονεύονται τοιαῦται καὶ τηλικαῦται πράξεις γενέσθαι. P. Friedländer, "Geschichtswende im Gedicht," *Stud. ital. d. filol. cl.* N.S. 15 (1938) 104, n. 2.

33. For a good summary of the older work, cf. Beecke, *Historischen Angaben*, p. 52. The best modern work appears in Wade-Gery, cf. *supra*, n. 23, pp. 82-87; Friedländer, cf. *supra*, n. 32, pp. 102-08; Peek, cf. *supra*, n. 4, pp. 101-08, and *Griechische Vers-Inschriften* (Berlin: Akademie, 1955), no. 16; and D.L. Page, *Epigrammata Graeca* (Oxford, 1975), p. 26; Schreiner (1976), *supra*, n. 4, pp. 19-25.

34. Cf. Gomme, *HCT* I. 288, n. 1. For the general absence of sententious remarks in early epigrams, cf. P. Friedländer, *Epigrammata: Greek Inscriptions in Verse: From the Beginnings to the Persian War* (University of California, 1948), p. 69.

35. Wade-Gery, cf. *supra*, n. 23, p. 85f.

36. For the personification and division of lands, cf. *Pers.* 181f.; for the personification alone, cf. 549. Uxkull, cf. *supra*, n. 21, p. 56, also points out, for the idea of division, Soph. *Trach.* 100; Eurip. *Ion,* 1356, 1585, *Troad.* 927. Friedländer, cf. *supra,* n. 32, p. 106f., adds as well the references to division in Herodotus and Choerilus of Samos. Cf. R. Winnington-Ingram, "Zeus in the *Persae," JHS* 93 (1973) 210-19.

37. There are three such epigrams:

(1) An inscription from a Hellenistic monument found in the Heraeum on Samos; presumably a copy of a genuine dedication for the battle:

[πλεῖστα τρόπαια φέρεν] Μαιάνδριος, εὖτ᾿ ἐπὶ καλῶι
ἐστήσαντο μάχην Εὐρυμέδο[ντι νέες·]
[ὅν δῆμος τίμησεν, ἀριστ]εύσας γὰρ ἐκείνηι
ναυμαχίηι πάντων κλέος ἔθετ᾿ ἀθάν[ατον].
[ὀκτὼ νῆας ἔλεν Μαιάν]δριος, ὧν ἀπ᾿ ἑκάστης
ἀσπίς πρύμναν ἔχει χεῖρ τ᾿ὑποδεξ[αμένη]
[πάσας δ᾿ αὐτάνδρους ἁλ]ὶ τὰς ὑπεδέξατο πόντος
κρυφθείσας, Μήδων συμμαχ[ίην ἄλιον].

Cf. Peek, *supra*, n. 4, pp. 115-20; Wade-Gery, *supra*, n. 23, pp. 97-99; G. Klaffenback, "Samische Inschriften," *Athenische Mittheilung* 51 (1926) 27. One should note the relatively subdued praise in the structurally similar Samian monument for a victory in the Egyptian expedition: cf. W. Peek, "Ein Seegefecht aus den Perserkriegen," *Klio* 32 (1939) 289; *ATL* III. 253, n. 37.

(2) *Anth. Pal.* VII. 258:

Οἵδε παρ᾿ Εὐρυμέδοντά ποτ᾿ ἀγλαὸν ὤλεσαν ἥβην
μαρνάμενοι Μήδων τοξοφόρων προμάχοις
αἰχμηταί, πεζοί τε καὶ ὠκυπόρων ἐπὶ νηῶν·
κάλλιστον δ᾿ ἀρετῆς μνῆμ᾿ ἔλιπον φθίμενοι.

The authenticity of this poem as a contemporary funeral epigram for the Battle of Eurymedon is a vexed question. Meyer, *Forschungen,* p. 20f., accepted the epigram as authentic; B. Keil, "Zu den simonideischen Eurymedon-Epigrammen," *Hermes* 20 (1885) 341, rejects it. For more recent discussion of the topic, cf. Wade-Gery, *supra,* n. 23, p. 79f.; Peek, *supra*, n. 4, p. 100. The similarity between this poem and the one at *IG* I[2] 943, worries P. Waltz et al., *Anthologie Grecque*[2], Vol. IV (Paris: Budé, 1960), p. 167, n. 2, who think our epigram dates from near the end of the fifth century. Others, however, place it with the Samian revolt (440/39) or in 447. For the former, cf. M. Tod, *A Selection of Greek Historical Inscriptions,* Vol. II (Oxford, 1948), no. 48; *SEG* X (1949) 413. For the latter suggestion, cf. *ML*, p. 128.

(3) *Anth. Pal.* VII. 443:
   τῶνδέ ποτ' ἐν στέρνοισι τανυγλώχινας διστοὺς
   λοῦσεν φοινίσσαι θοῦρος Ἄρης ψακάδι·
   ἀντὶ δ' ἀκοντοδόκων ἀνδρῶν μνημεῖα θανόντων
   ἄψυχ' ἐμψύχων ἅδε κέκευθε κόνις.

Wade-Gery, cf. *supra*, n. 23, p. 81, and his predecessors have put forward all the arguments to show that this poem is a 'literary exercise on the Eurymedon theme.'

38. The οἵδε should refer to the dead men: cf. Friedländer, *supra*, n. 34, p. 68. For the expansion of the traditional form, cf. Friedländer, *supra*, n. 32, pp. 105-08.

39. The first line is repeated in a fourth century epigram: cf. G. Kaibel, *Epigrammata Graeca* (Repr. Hildesheim: Olms, 1965), no. 768. The structure and idea reappear in no. 844. Cf. Schwartz, *supra*, n. 28, p. 120, n. 3.

40. Cf. *supra*, n. 28, pp. 118-22.

41. Cf. *supra*, n. 23, pp. 82-87.

42. Cf. *supra*, n. 32, pp. 103-07. Friedländer also upsets Wade-Gery's other arguments.

43. For Peek, cf. *supra*, n. 4, p. 105f.

44. The mention of Cyprus, therefore, could not refer to the detail about a Persian squadron at Cyprus and Hydrus.

45. Beecke, *Historischen Angaben*, p. 50f.; Uxkull, cf. *supra*, n. 21, p. 54f.

46. The other possibility, that the poem is a confused reconstruction of Ephorus and thus a late forgery, was suggested by Waltz, cf. *supra*, n. 37, p. 182, n. 1. This view seems to be precluded by the suggestion that Ephorus himself cited the poem: cf. *supra*, n. 17.

47. Objections to Κύπρῳ include, (1) the notion that ἐν γαίῃ and ἐν πελάγει form a pair of opposites which correspond closely to ἐν ἠπείρῳ and κατὰ πόντον, and (2) the belief that ἤπειρος cannot refer to an island in fifth-century vocabulary. Peek, cf. *supra*, n. 4, p. 106, meets the first objection by pointing out that such artificial parallelism is foreign to the pithy style of epigrams. The second argument ignores the structure of the poem, which moves from a more general idea (ἤπειρος, rather like the conventional κατὰ γῆν: so Gomme, *HCT* I. 288, n. 1) to a more specific explanation of the general term (ἐν Κύπρῳ), not an even more general idea (ἐν γαίῃ): so Meyer, *Forschungen*, p. 10f.; Friedländer, cf. *supra*, n. 32, p. 103; and Peek, *supra*, n. 4, p. 107.

48. Meyer, *Forschungen*, p. 10f., and Peek, cf. *supra*, n. 4, p. 107. Friedländer, cf. *supra*, n. 32, p. 107, connects the epigram with Pausanias' notice of those who died, πλεύσαντες ἐς Κύπρον ὁμοῦ Κίμωνι, and had a monument in the Cerameicus (I. 29. 13). J. Schreiner, "The 100-ship battle at Kyprus and the land-battle in Phoenicia about 460 B.C., omitted by Thucydides and forgotten by scholars," *Akten des vi. internat. Kongr. für griech. & latein. Epigraphik*, 1972, p. 426f., is not content with Cimon's last campaign to Cyprus and assigns the epigram to an earlier expedition to Cyprus connected with the Egyptian expedition. Barns, cf. *supra*, n. 28, pp. 163-76, argues more convincingly and thoroughly for an earlier expedition, but neither he nor Schreiner, it seems to me, answers the problem raised by the excessive level of praise in the poem.

49. Cf. *supra*, n. 41.

50. Isoc. *De pace* (8), 86. The most striking similarity amongst the epigrams derives from their evaluation of the deed: ἐπὶ καλῶι ... Εὐρυμέδοντι, in the Maiandrios

epigram; κάλλιστον δ' ἀρετῆς μνῆμα, in *Anth. Pal.* VII. 258; οὐδέν πω κάλλιον, in the present epigram. For the reading κάλλιον, instead of Diodorus' τοιοῦτον, cf. Friedländer, *supra,* n. 32, p. 104f.

51. For the popular tradition as represented in the orators, cf. M. Cary, "The Peace of Callias," *CQ* 39 (1945) 89.

52. The exact dates are, of course, problematic. The confused Diodorus puts the end of the Egyptian affair in 460, but Diodorus is at his worst in matters of exact chronology. It may not be too far amiss to maintain that Ephorus' chronology was closer to that suggested by Thuc. I. 110. 2, 112. 3; Diod. XII. 3. 1; and Plut. *Cim.* 18. 7f. As Raubitschek has noted, cf. *supra,* n. 4, p. 38, these passages show that Cimon's last campaign in Cyprus and the end of the Egyptian affair were closely linked. The end of the Cyprus campaign, then, provided the earliest date for the Peace, and Ephorus enhanced the credibility of this date by making that campaign the equal of the Eurymedon as a great victory. For a possible fragment of the Peace that mentions Egypt, cf. Wade-Gery, *supra,* n. 5, p. 155f. Cf. now, Schreiner (1976), *supra,* n. 4.

53. For the discomfiture of the Athenians and Cimon's death, cf. Thuc. I. 112. 4, and Plut. *Cim.* 19. 1f. For Diodorus' footnote on Cimon's death, cf. XII. 4. 6. For the more 'historical' account, in which Cimon dies *before* Callias negotiates the Peace, cf. Aristodemus, 13. 1f.

54. The passage cited, *supra,* p. 77 (Plut. *Cim.* 13. 4). It should also be noted that a scholarly problem has arisen over Plutarch's citation of Callisthenes. Meyer, *Forschungen,* p. 4f., suggested that Plutarch was wrong and Callisthenes indeed believed in a formal Peace, but 'did not mention' it after the Eurymedon. Wade-Gery, cf. *supra,* n. 5, p. 123, is probably correct in opposing Meyer and translating οὔ φησι as 'deny,' i.e., *negat.* Murison, cf. *supra,* n. 22, p. 15, raises a more serious problem by translating 'denied the existence of a treaty *in these terms.'* This is possible but not as certain as Murison believes. Surely it is a matter of emphasis: Murison translates ταῦτα συνθέσθαι, but ταῦτα συνθέσθαι would mean 'made this treaty.'

55. Cf. Connor, *supra,* n. 5, pp. 84-87; Murison, *supra,* n. 22, p. 16.

56. *Athenian Empire,* p. 130.

57. Of the two major sources which eschew the popular tradition, Nepos (*Cim.* 2. 2-3) fails to mention the Peace altogether, and Aristodemus (13. 1f.) follows Ephorus in substantially separating the Eurymedon from the Peace.

58. For Thucydides' early date for the Eurymedon, cf. Schreiner (1976), *supra,* n. 4.

59. *Ibid.,* p. 44 *et passim.*

60. *Ibid.*

61. Callias' position in the tradition is not entirely clear. The earliest reference to him as an ambassador to Persia is in Herodotus (VII. 151); but his first unambiguous connection with the Peace is in Demosthenes (*Fals. leg.* (19), 273), where he is said to have been fined for his behavior on the embassy: cf. K. Kraft, "Bemerkungen zu den Perserkriegen," *Hermes* 92 (1964) 168. Plutarch (*Cim.* 13. 5) and Pausanias (I. 8. 2) represent a tradition in which Callias was rewarded for his part in the peace with Persia, although Pausanias leaves open the possibility that not everyone agreed with that tradition: cf. Meiggs, *Athenian Empire,* p. 130. M. Sordi, "La propaganda del mondo greco," *RSA* 1 (1971) 210, wonders why Callias' descendant fails to mention the Peace at Xen. *Hell.* VI. 3. 4-6. Moreover, there is some problem with the identity of the Callias in question: cf. H.G. Mattingly, "The Peace of Kallias," *Hist.* 14 (1965) 276. For a discussion of Callias' family and party, cf. *ATL* III. 275ff. Cf. also, D. Mosley, "Callias' Fine," *Mnemosyne* 26 (1973) 57f.

62. Cf. *infra,* Chapter V, p. 112ff.
63. Cf. the discussion of the debate on Pericles' building program, *infra,* Chapter VI, p.158f.
64. Cf. *supra,* Chapter III, p. 62.
65. Cf. Schwartz, *supra,* n.28, p. 116.
66. Cf. *Paneg.* (4), 117f., cited*supra,* p. 91.
67. Lys. *Ep.* (2), 55-57; Pl. *Menex.* 241d-242a.
68. Thus the Loeb edition. Conomis' more recent (1970) Teubner text reads 'seventy'.
69. For the former opinion, cf. Schwartz, *supra,* n. 28, p. 111, n. 2. For the latter, cf. Wade-Gery, *supra,* n. 5, p. 125.
70. That Lycurgus was not relying only on the epigram is made clear by his use of the term translated by Burtt as 'captured' (αἰχμαλώτους). The same term appears in Diodorus (XI. 62. 1) and Plutarch (*Cim.* 12. 8). Ephorus may have inspired the later uses of the word, but one should not overlook the possibility that it formed a part of the oral tradition. In this regard, it is interesting to note that the epigram at *Anth. Pal.* VII. 258, honors the Athenian αἰχμηταί: cf. B.D. Meritt, "Epigrams from the Battle of Marathon," in S. Weinberg (ed.), *The Aegean and the Near East* (Locust Valley, New York: Augustin, 1956), pp. 271-73.
71. Friedländer, cf. *supra,* n. 32, p. 107.
72. Cf. *supra,* p. 83.
73. This is certainly how Aristides understood Lycurgus in the *Panathenaicus* (I. 250); ὥστ' εἶναι τὸν κύκλον τοῦτον ἀντ' ἄλλου τινὸς στεφάνου τοῖς Ἕλλησιν ὑπὲρ κεφαλῆς καὶ τὴν φρουρὰν ἐξ αὐτῆς τῆς χώρας τοῦ βασιλέως.
74. Plut. *Cim.* 12.6; cf. Schwartz, *supra,* n. 28, p. 126; Jacoby, *FGrH,* III B (Sup. I), p. 191.
75. So Schwartz, *ibid.,* p. 120; Meyer, *Forschungen,* p. 11; Wade-Gery, cf. *supra,* n. 23, pp. 85 and 92, n. 89.
76. I would point out the parallelism between Isocrates' 'laid waste' (πορθουμένην) and Lycurgus' 'ravaged' (ἐπόρθησαν) at *Leoc.* 72.
77. *IG* II² 43.
78. Perhaps implied by Wade-Gery, cf. *supra,* n. 23, p. 92, n. 89.
79. Cf. *supra,* n. 5, p. 127. This would explain Theopompus' denial of the Peace on epigraphic grounds, since the lettering in this case would certainly be Ionic. Moreover, if the copy were of the renewal with Darius rather than the original with Artaxerxes I, one could more easily understand the tradition's difficulty about dating the Peace by archon years. C. Schrader, *La Paz de Calias: Testimonios e Interpretación* (Barcelona: Universidad de Barcelona, Instituto de Estudios Helenicos, 1976), *passim,* denies that the stele with the Peace of Callias was erected before the late 350's.
80.This is to salvage the still possible and interesting suggestions from the wreck of Wade-Gery's main arguments: cf. *supra,* n. 23, pp. 87-93. Wade-Gery made two mistakes: (1) he identified the 'Herm-stoa' with the Stoa of Zeus, and (2) he split up the Cyprus epigram. The Herm in question might well have been not in the 'Herm-stoa,' as Wade-Gery supposed, but in the general area known as 'Hermai,' whose border ran right up to the Stoa of Zeus.
81. Wade-Gery, cf. *supra,* n. 23, p. 88f., suggests the epigram was one of several for Cimon's exploits in which, according to Aeschines, the Demos would not let the general's name appear in print: ἐπὶ τῷ Στρυμόνι ποταμῷ ἐνίκων μαχόμενοι Μήδους· οὗτοι δεῦρο ἀφικόμενοι τὸν δῆμον ᾔτησαν δωρεὰν καὶ ἔδωκεν αὐτοῖς ὁ δῆμος τιμὰς

μεγάλας, ὡς τότ'ἐδόκει, τρεῖς λιθίνους Ἑρμᾶς στῆσαι ἐν τῇ στοᾷ τῇ τῶν Ἑρμῶν, ἐφ' ᾧτε μὴ ἐπιγράφειν τὸ ὄνομα τὸ ἑαυτῶν, ἵνα μὴ τῶν στρατηγῶν, ἀλλὰ τοῦ δήμου δοκῇ εἶναι τὸ ἐπίγραμμα. ὅτι δ'ἀληθῆ λέγω, ἐξ αὐτῶν τῶν ποιημάτων γνώσεσθε (*Ctes.* (3), 183; cf. Demosth. *Lept.* (20), 112). One imagines a symposium of Cimon's friends or admirers in which one gentleman, called on for his share of the entertainment, substitutes for a scolion the Cyprus epigram with one variation, οὐδενί. It would combine a compliment to Cimon and a comical slap at the jealous Demos.

82. II. 209f.

83. Grenfell and Hunt, cf. *supra*, n. 12, p. 102, see an echo of Ephorus in this passage.

84. Oliver, *Civilizing Power*, p. 70, joins this sentence with what follows about the Eurymedon. In this case the sentence reflects the context of the battle as reported by Plutarch (*Cim.* 12. 1-5) and Diodorus (XI. 60. 4-5). On the other hand, Behr in the *Loeb Aristides*, p. 152, joins the sentence with what precedes: such would recall the earlier operations of the Delian League.

85. Diod. XI. 60. 5; cf. Schreiner (1976), *supra*, n. 4, pp. 22-25. It should be noted that Aristides inserted a similar prolepsis (called 'Zusammenfassung und Vorwegnahme,' by Beecke, *Historischen Angaben*, p. 48f.) between his rhetorical introduction and actual account of the battle in *Pro Quattuorviris* (II. 208f.):

διὰ ταῦτα εἰς τὴν ἐκείνων ἐξῆγε τὸν πόλεμον καὶ περιέπλει μὲν Κύπρον, παρέπλει δὲ Παμφυλίαν, ἐναυμάχει δὲ Φοίνιξι καὶ Κυπρίοις καὶ οἷστισι προσμίξαιεν αὐτῶν. ἐπὶ δὲ Εὐρυμέδοντι...

For this reason Cimon brought the war into the territory of the barbarians by circumnavigating Cyprus and coasting along Pamphylia. He fought naval battles with Phoenicians, Cyprians, and whatever barbarian contingents he could engage. At the Eurymedon....

86. Cf. *infra*, Chapter VI, p. 151f.; *supra*, Chapter III, p. 43f.

87. Cf. Peek, *supra*, n. 4, pp. 97-120; Schreiner (1976), *supra*, n. 4, pp. 46-49.

88. For the epigram, cf. *supra*, n. 37, no. 2. The implied comparison relies on the poet's citation of πεζοί τε καὶ ὠκυπόρων ἐπὶ νηῶν from one of the Marathon epigrams: cf. the article by Meritt mentioned in n. 70, *supra*.

89. *Cim.* 13. 3.

90. Cf. Plut. *Praec. ger. reip.* 17 (= *Mor.* 814c); *De glor. Ath.* 7 (= *Mor.* 349d).

91. Cf. the conclusions of F.W. Schlatter, S.J., *Salamis and Plataea in the Tradition of the Attic Orators* (Diss. Princeton, 1960). For possible early evidence for the importance of the Eurymedon, cf. A.E. Raubitschek and G.P. Stevens, "The Pedestal of the Athena Promachos," *Hesp.* 15 (1946) 107-114; Raubitschek, *Dedications from the Athenian Akropolis* (Cambridge: Archaeol. Inst. of America, 1949), no. 172.

92. Cf. N. Austin, *The Greek Historians* (New York: Van Nostrand—Reinhold, 1969), p. 3; J. Vansina, *Oral Tradition: A Study in Historical Methodology*, trans. by H. Wright (Chicago: Aldine, 1965), p. 102, for oral traditions of history in general. Without dealing with the general principles behind oral traditions, Schwartz, cf. *supra*, n. 28, p. 115, explicated the compressed nature of the tradition of the period from the Eurymedon to the Peace: in der panegyrischen Tradition die attischen Eroberungskriege gegen Persien zu einem verschwommenen Ganzen zusammengelaufen waren.

93. Ἀκρίβεια: cf. *supra*, Chapter I.

94. This is the meaning of Isocrates' comment at *Paneg.* (4), 9: cf. *supra*, Chapter I, p. 8f.

95. Aristid. I. 225.

CHAPTER V
THE ATHENIAN INTERVENTION IN THE REVOLT OF EGYPT

We saw in the preceding chapter that later authors popularized the version of Athens' eastern ventures which juxtaposed the Battle of Eurymedon and Peace of Callias more closely than the chronology of the historians would allow. In the *Panathenaicus*, however, Aristides interrupts the popular chronology by separating his accounts of the Eurymedon and the Peace with a certain amount of rhetorical expansion, and, more importantly, by interposing between them the story of the Egyptian revolt from Artaxerxes I and the Athenian intervention on behalf of the rebels. In this chapter, I will attempt to explicate Aristides' reasons for composing a narrative that appears to owe more to the historical than the popular understanding of the sequence of events, and I will suggest that in fact Aristides has resurrected a long-ignored popular tradition about the revolt of Egypt.

Aristides alludes to the Egyptian affair just once, where he elaborates on it considerably in the regular narrative section of the *Panathenaicus* (I. 247f.):

> In this way the Athenians laid open the whole Persian Empire and shook it to its foundations. Those who owed their allegiance to Persia could only feel contemptible, but Athens encouraged everyone by her own example. As a result, the Libyans near Pharus revolted, and the Egyptians joined in the rebellion. Although later on, it seems, the King reimposed his domination over some of the rebels, he lost the marsh district, a very large portion of Egypt. He may have conquered the whole of Egypt twice before, but this time the triremes from Athens were like lightning bolts from the sky. The Athenians were the only leading participants in international politics who thought of their own city as if it belonged to others; they also, however, considered foreign countries to be their own rather than the property of the natives, if the latter governed badly. Those Athenians lived the lives of guards; yet they were not stationary guards, nor were

their protective patrols confined to one area. We have to say that they were roving sentries for Greeks all over the world.[1]

The grand literary themes of the popular tradition of the Persian War are paraded throughout the passage and integrate it completely with the surrounding portions of the story. The panhellenic virtue of the Athenians in Egypt as elsewhere continues to effect the reversal of the Persian king's fortune, which will lead in a few lines to his total collapse and the Peace of Callias. Rather interestingly, however, Aristides seems to exhibit as much care in recording the history of the event as in exploiting its literary value, an unusual phenomenon in a popularizing text.

Apart from the reference to Egypt's earlier relations with Persia, the passage recalls three historical incidents, the three stages of the revolt: the secession of the Libyans and Egyptians, the success of the rebellion in the marsh district, and the Athenian intervention. Although I have followed Aristides' order in reporting these three events, he was clearly writing for rhetorical effect and would have reversed the order of the last two events in a strictly chronological narrative. The winning of the swamps contrasts sharply with the two previous conquests of Egypt, in which the Persians took the whole country; yet Aristides surely implies that the reason for the difference was the swift and effective intervention of the Athenian triremes *before* the conclusion of the third conquest.[2] That is to say, Aristides adopts in detail the chronological as well as the factual framework of the historical version as found in Thucydides, Ctesias, Diodorus, and Aristodemus. They unanimously divide the revolt into the three stages of native rebellion, Athenian intervention, and at least partially unsuccessful conclusion.[3] Moreover, they arrange the stages in that very order and place the whole affair between the Eurymedon and the Peace.[4]

For all his care in matters of fact and chronology, however, Aristides hardly describes the Egyptian expedition with the accuracy of the historians. In fact, we must call his account misleading in its patriotic optimism about the efficacy and success of the Athenian intervention. Aristides' victorious boasting might be applicable to the first actions fought by the Athenians and their allies, during which they won at least one naval battle and aided the rebel leader Inaros in besieging the remaining Persians in the White Fortress.[5] The end of the expedition, however, was a great disaster for the Athenians, and the only serious disagreement among the standard literary sources is over the magnitude of the loss. Some evidence points to a staggering disaster comparable to that of the Sicilian expedition; other sources allow that the losses were severe but mitigate them to a certain extent. Thucydides, of course, leads the list of those who stress the severity of Athens' defeat.[6] He must be understood to have believed in the destruction of nearly the whole allied armament of two hundred ships along with a relieving squadron of fifty ships, despite the effort of some modern critics to read him otherwise.[7] Even in an oratorical context, Isocrates and a speaker in Diodorus can point to the full magnitude of the Egyptian disaster as a paradigm of the democracy's self-inflicted wounds.[8] Aristodemus' somewhat confused narrative ignores the loss of the crews of the original fleet but follows Thucydides in reporting the destruction of the relieving force.[9] Of those who lessen the Athenian loss, Ctesias maintains that only forty Athenian ships were sent to Egypt in the first place, and he narrates a romantic tale about their crews' adventures after surrendering to the Persians.[10] Diodorus certainly follows Ephorus in telling about the Athenians' heroic stand and eventual return home after the destruction of their ships.[11] Finally there is Justin, whose epitome of Trogus has been used by some to correct Thucydides. Justin implies that a substantial portion of the Athenian fleet was recalled after its initial intervention in support of Inaros' revolt.[12]

Even though these last three sources may evidence a tradition independent of Thucydides and more sympathetic to Athens' efforts,[13] the version is still not sufficiently optimistic to account for Aristides' estimation of the Egyptian affair. For Aristides, Egypt ranks with the Eurymedon as one of the great, panhellenic exploits of the Persian War, a forerunner of the triumphant Peace. We find a similar judgment expressed about Egypt only in the *Menexenus* (241d-e):

> We really must call to mind also those men who put the finishing touches of salvation on the labors of their predecessors by sweeping away every trace of the barbarian and driving it from the sea. These were the ones who fought the naval engagement at the Eurymedon, who campaigned towards Cyprus, and who sailed to Egypt and to many other places. We should remember these men and give them thanks, since they caused the King to fear for, indeed to concentrate his attention upon, his own safety, rather than to plot the ruin of the Greeks.

Without any independent confirmation, however, this passage can only serve to exemplify the stage in the tradition where all of Athens' achievements in the Eastern Mediterranean were compressed in the popular imagination and no event except the Peace and the Eurymedon was described in detail.[14] We have seen how to some extent Cimon's last expedition to Cyprus was rescued from this obscurity in the fourth and later centuries. The historiography of the affair in Egypt, however, remains quite different from that of the other events, since even fourth-century Athenian apologists could not reverse the negative verdict of Thucydides.[15] Something other than the influence of Ephorus or the orators is needed to explain the text of Aristides.

Some might say, of course, that Aristides merely employed his considerable literary license to rewrite the history of Athens' Egyptian venture in a more chauvinistic and optimistic vein than his predecessors. If such a statement were to be left unqualified, however, it would result in an underestimation of the historiographical value of an author who seldom constructed historical narratives without care and precedents. Aristides probably rewrote his sources' accounts rather often, but his method of composition can usually tell us a great deal about those sources. To be sure, applying this generalization to the Egyptian affair will be an important goal in this chapter, in which I will contend that Aristides consciously worked out his account of Egypt as a correction of the pessimistic versions of Thucydides and Theopompus. Moreover, I will maintain that in order to correct those sources Aristides uncovered and employed an older version, perhaps the original popular one which the cautious Thucydides and the caustic Theopompus felt themselves constrained to criticize and correct.

The first step in explicating Aristides' correction of any extant source must be to demonstrate his thorough familiarity with that source. This is not a difficult task in the case of Thucydides, who seems to have inspired at least four close imitations in Aristides' version of the Egyptian affair. In the first place, Aristides' account of the original revolt amongst the natives probably recalls Thucydides' introduction to the whole affair (I. 104. 1):

> *Inaros, the son of Psammetichus, was a Libyan and king of the Libyans to the west of Egypt. He rose up from Marea, a city south of Pharus, and caused the majority of Egypt to revolt from King Artaxerxes. When he thus became the leader of the revolt, he called in the Athenians for help.*

The mention of Pharus and the importance of the Libyans are details that appear only in Thucydides and Aristides.[16] Second, Aristides' use of the word συναπέστησαν for the action of the Egyptians may reflect Thucydides' description of the Egyptians who did not revolt as οἱ μὴ ξυναποστάντες (I. 104. 2). Third, Aristides and Thucydides are the only narrators of the affair who even mention the swamp, much less comment on the extent of the marshland.[17] A final and more subtle echo of Thucydides appears in Aristides' epilogue to the Athenian intervention (I. 248): μόνοι γὰρ ἀνθρώπων τῶν εἰς κοινὸν πολιτευσαμένων τὴν μὲν οἰκείαν ὥσπερ ἀλλοτρίαν ἐνόμισαν, τὴν δὲ ἀλλοτρίαν οὐχ αὑτῶν ἀλλοτρίαν. ... This passage clearly reflects Thucydides' version of a comment made by the Corinthians about the character of the Athenians (I. 70. 6): ἔτι δὲ τοῖς μὲν σώμασιν ἀλλοτριωτάτοις ὑπὲρ τῆς πόλεως χρῶνται, τῇ δὲ γνώμῃ οἰκειοτάτῃ ἐς τὸ πράσσειν τι ὑπὲρ αὐτῆς.

All these similarities led Beecke to believe that Thucydides was Aristides' main source.[18] What Beecke failed to notice, however, was that Aristides corrected the details from Thucydides just as carefully as he imitated them. To begin with, the whole tone of Aristides' narrative differs from that of Thucydides, but the difference surely implies a conscious correction rather than simply a different point of view. The beginning of Thucydides' narration of the Egyptian revolt follows a long discussion of purely Hellenic affairs,[19] and it does not connect Egypt with Athens' earlier Eastern campaigns. Thucydides, true to his intention of depicting the growth of Athenian power and aggression and ruthlessly pruning away extraneous material, expresses little interest in the Egyptian revolution insofar as it relates to Persian or Egyptian internal matters. He does not, in fact, present a narrative of the Egyptian revolt, but of the Athenian expedition to Egypt and its relation to the growth of Athenian power and aggression.[20] He commences with a statement of persons, places, and events, which is just enough to introduce the Athenians. He closes with a brief statement of the results: the death of Inaros and the success of Amyrtaeus, which prepares the way for the second Athenian intervention. Aristides, on the other hand, conceived of the revolt as a symptom of the disintegration of the Persian Empire caused by Athens' growing interference. He felt that the Egyptian campaign should not be viewed in Thucydides' manner as an isolated lesson in Athenian power politics, but as a chapter in the story of Athens' salvation of Hellenism.[21] This difference between the two accounts can be seen in the way Aristides distinguishes carefully between the origin of the revolt amongst the Libyans and its continuation with the Egyptians, where Thucydides only gives an uninformative hint of a larger issue.[22] As we shall see in detail below, the distinction was made to enhance the panhellenic quality of Athens' intervention.[23]

As for the other similarities between the two authors, Aristides naturally corrects Thucydides' version of the outcome of the revolt. For the historian, Amyrtaeus' control of mere marshland is small consolation for the Athenian losses. Aristides ignores the Athenian disaster and implies that the swamps constituted a large and important part of Egypt. Moreover, in his interpretation of the whole affair, Aristides corrects the negative implication of Thucydides' speech of the Corinthians. For them, the Athenian quality of patriotic selflessness was merely a symptom of international restlessness (I. 70. 9): ὥστε εἴ τις αὐτοὺς ξυνελὼν φαίη πεφυκέναι ἐπὶ τῷ μήτε αὐτοὺς ἔχειν ἡσυχίαν μήτε τοὺς ἄλλους ἀνθρώπους ἐᾶν, ὀρθῶς ἂν εἴποι. Although the words are not used, the tendency towards πλεονεξία and πολυπραγμοσύνη is clearly present.[24] Aristides corrects Thucydides' Corinthians by interpreting their insight into Athenian selflessness as a symptom of panhellenism rather than imperialism. The Athenians not only treated their own bodies as if they belonged to others, they also acted on the assumption that no country belongs to its ruler if it is ruled badly. In other words, they protected Hellenic interests against the misgovernment of the Persian king.

The attempt to explicate Aristides' correction of Theopompus presents a serious problem not found in dealing with Thucydides. Inasmuch as the Chian historian's account of the Egyptian affair has not come down to us in continuous form, our first step must be to discover just what that account contained. This necessarily involves an examination of possible borrowings from Theopompus in the biographies of Plutarch, rare and brief as such imitations may be. We can, however, compare the results of that study with indications in other authors in order to expand our knowledge of Theopompus' version of the Egyptian revolt. Only then can we press our search for Aristides' correction of Theopompus.

Plutarch does not tell the story of Athens' intervention on behalf of Inaros in his *Cimon* or any of the other *Lives*. Presumably we are to infer from this omission that the biographer followed Thucydides and other historians in failing to assign that first expedition to the command of Cimon.²⁵ This should not, however, be considered a conclusive argument against the possibility that one of Plutarch's important sources understood Cimon as the motivating force behind both the original intervention and the later expedition sent to aid Amyrtaeus soon after the defeat of the first.²⁶ Such an inconsistency in Plutarch, who narrated in some detail Cimon's command of the campaign of which the second expedition was a part, should not startle the reader of the *Lives*. ²⁷ Moreover, careful study of various passages from the *Lives* will indicate that Theopompus was a major source for Plutarch's conception of Athenian dealings with Egypt and did indeed believe that Cimon commanded, or rather acted as commander-in-chief for, both expeditions with his period of ostracism coming between the two commands.²⁸ In fact, Plutarch's account of Cimon's last expedition to Egypt and Cyprus will form the basis of the following argument. I will maintain that in the *Philippica* Theopompus spoke of this campaign and the original Athenian intervention in Egypt in practically the same breath and in such similar terms, that Plutarch himself or some intermediary source confused the two expeditions.²⁹ Thus, what Plutarch says about the second of the expeditions was probably applied to both in Theopompus' compact and bitterly anti-Athenian comments.

Plutarch opens his account of the second expedition with a statement about Cimon's motives for initiating the campaign (*Cim.* 18. 1):

> Well then, as soon as Cimon returned from exile he stopped the war and reconciled the rival cities. After peace³⁰ was made, since he saw that the Athenians were unable to keep quiet, but wished to be on the move and to wax great by means of military expeditions; also because he wished that they should not exasperate the Hellenes generally, nor by hovering around the islands and the Peloponnesus with a large fleet bring down upon the city charges of intestine war, and initial complaints from the allies, he manned two hundred triremes. His design was to make another expedition with them against Egypt and Cyprus. He wished to keep the Athenians in constant training by their struggles with Barbarians, and to give them the legitimate benefits of importing into Hellas the wealth taken from their natural foes. (Perrin's Loeb translation)

After discussing some omens of Cimon's death, Plutarch continues his account of the expedition (*Cim.* 18. 5-7):

> But since he could not get out of the expedition, he set sail, and

> *after detailing sixty of his ships to go to Egypt, with the rest he made again for Cyprus. After defeating at sea the royal armament of Phoenician and Cilician ships, he won over the cities round about, and then lay threatening the royal enterprise in Egypt, and not in any trifling fashion,—nay, he had in mind the dissolution of the King's entire supremacy, and all the more because he learned that the reputation and power of Themistocles were great among the Barbarians, who had promised the King that when the Hellenic war was set on foot he would take command of it. At any rate, it is said that it was most of all due to Themistocles' despair of his Hellenic undertakings, since he could not eclipse the good fortune and valor of Cimon, that he took his own life. (Perrin's Loeb trans.)*

Later, just before his death, Cimon sent an embassy to the shrine of Zeus Ammon in search of oracles. Upon their return to the coast, the ambassadors reached a Greek camp, ὃ τότε περὶ Αἴγυπτον ἦν (18.8).[31] By that time, however, Cimon was dead, and so the Athenians sailed home.

Uxkull discovered that Cimon's generosity and kindness constitute major motifs which give the *Life of Cimon* a considerable degree of thematic unity.[32] The son of Miltiades won over his fellow citizens with his generosity,[33] and out of kindness he kept the Athenians from bothering their allies.[34] Quite significantly, both motifs can be explicitly linked with Theopompus' digression on the Demagogues in the tenth book of the *Philippica*. The stories of Cimon opening his garden and making other gestures to the Athenian populace are found in Plutarch and Nepos, and are attributed to Theopompus by Athenaeus.[35] On the side of kindness, Theopompus told about Cimon's return from exile to arrange the peace between Athens and Sparta.[36] Chapter 18 of the *Cimon* contains both themes: the new expedition to Egypt is aimed at obtaining wealth for the Athenians, keeping them busy in training, and preventing them from disturbing their fellow Greeks. Moreover, Cimon's return from exile and his peace are specifically mentioned at the beginning of the chapter.[37] It seems reasonable to conclude that Theopompus was a major source for Plutarch's comments about part of Cimon's political and military career, especially the last expedition to Egypt and Cyprus. Precisely what Theopompus said is another question. According to Uxkull, Theopompus was certainly hostile towards Athens but friendly to Cimon, the panhellenic hero who struggled to keep the ambitious Athenians from disturbing their allies. Most recent scholarship has pointed out that Uxkull's estimation corresponds rather more closely to Plutarch's adaptation of Theopompus than to the original version of the latter author himself.[38] In fact, Theopompus viewed Cimon as a democrat and a demagogue, the type of φιλότιμος which is so often criticized in the *Philippica*.[39] For example, when Theopompus repeated the story of Cimon's generosity with the masses, he was portraying Cimon as a politician seeking to curry popular favor at the expense of his enemy, Pericles.[40] It was a story of base party politics with Cimon the *radical* opposed to Pericles the *conservative*.[41] We are interested at present, however, in Cimon's military rather than political career. We must therefore attempt to revise our understanding of Theopompus' views on Cimon's foreign policy just as his domestic policy has been re-interpreted.

In Chapter 6 of the *Cimon*, we find Cimon's gentleness towards the Greeks contrasted with Pausanias' wanton attitude. Plutarch capitalized on the story's obvious moral, but a more sinister political interpretation lurks beneath the surface (6. 2): (Cimon) ὑπολαμβάνων πρᾴως τοὺς ἀδικουμένους (by Pausanias) καὶ φιλανθρώπως ἐξομιλῶν, ἔλαθεν οὐ δι' ὅπλων τὴν τῆς Ἑλλάδος ἡγεμονίαν, ἀλλὰ λόγῳ καὶ ἤθει.[42] Cimon's kindness only served to gain the hegemony for Athens. Likewise, in Chapter 11, the other Athenian generals are said to have made themselves unpopular with the allies by exacting from them the full quota of infantry and manned ships, but Cimon won a reputation for gentleness by allowing the allies to supply money and empty hulls in lieu of their quotas. This policy, however, made the Athenians into the hardened δεσπόται of their empire (11.3):

> For those who did no military service became used to fearing and flattering those who were continually voyaging, and for ever under arms and training, and practicing, and so, before they knew it, they were tributary subjects instead of allies. (Perrin's Loeb translation)

The cynicism inherent in this interpretation appears in Thucydides,[43] but *a priori* we should have no trouble in believing that Plutarch learned from Theopompus to apply it specifically to Cimon. Confirmation of this hypothesis can be found in Chapter 18, which, as we have seen, definitely derives from Theopompus. Plutarch adds his own moralizing, of course, but it does not completely obscure Theopompus' Machiavellian interpretation of Cimon's last campaign to Cyprus and Egypt. Theopompus surely stressed the degree to which Cimon capitulated to the mob's restlessness in agreeing to lead the expedition. Cimon's aims were to avoid irritating the Spartans, but also to harden the Athenians as the taskmasters of their empire, and to lead them in an imperialistic venture motivated by πλεονεξία. It is even possible that the Athenian restlessness at this point is that which Pericles once attempted to restrain (Plut. *Per.* 20. 3): the Athenians were eager to Αἰγύπτου τε πάλιν ἀντιλαμβάνεσθαι καὶ κινεῖν τῆς βασιλέως ἀρχῆς τὰ πρὸς θαλάσσῃ.[44] In this case, Pericles would be opposing Cimon, an imperialist as well as a democrat. This passage from the *Pericles*, like the ones from the *Cimon*, certainly reflects Theopompus' bias against Cimon.

Having now dealt with Theopompus' account of the second Athenian expedition to Egypt and Cyprus, we must now try to determine what he said about the initial intervention on behalf of Inaros. Plutarch does not consciously report the earlier campaign, but Chapter 31 of his *Themistocles* certainly reveals the influence of Theopompus' account of Inaros' revolt (31. 4-6):

> *But when Egypt revolted with Athenian aid, and Hellenic triremes sailed up as far as Cyprus and Cilicia, and Cimon's mastery of the sea forced the King to resist the efforts of the Hellenes and to hinder their hostile growth; and when at last forces began to be moved, and generals were despatched hither and thither, and messages came down to Themistocles saying that the King commanded him to make good his promises by applying himself to the Hellenic problem, then, neither embittered by anything like anger against his former fellow-citizens, nor lifted up by the great honor and power he was to have in the war, but possibly thinking his task not even approachable, both because Hellas had other great generals at the time, and especially because Cimon was so marvellously successful in his campaigns; yet most of all out of regard for the reputation of his own achievements and the trophies of those early days; having decided that his best course was to put a fitting end to his life, he made a sacrifice to the gods, then called his friends together, gave them a farewell clasp of his hand, and, as the current story goes, drank bull's blood, or as some say, took a quick poison, and so died in Magnesia. (Perrin's Loeb trans.).*

Surely this account of Themistocles' suicide and that in *Cimon* 18 reflect the same source. Both oppose the version of Ephorus, who praises the suicide as a panhellenic deed,[45] and of Thucydides, who rejects the popular story altogether and maintains that Themistocles died a natural death.[46] Theopompus, the source of Plutarch's version, accepted the popular story of suicide by drinking bull's blood, but he subverted Ephorus' generous interpretation by pointing to Themistocles' fear of Cimon's achievements. There is no question that in Chapter 18 of the *Cimon* the second expedition to Cyprus and Egypt and Cimon's successes there form the background for Themistocles' death. In Chapter 31 of the *Themistocles*, however, we encounter a serious chronological confusion which, if my understanding is correct, will lead us to some knowledge of Theopompus' views on the initial expedition to Egypt. The mention of Greek triremes sailing to Cyprus and Cilicia is probably too general to pinpoint, but one passage leaves no room for doubt: Αἴγυπτος τ' ἀφισταμένη βοηθούντων Ἀθηναίων. This can refer only to Inaros' rebellion.[47] It appears that in the tradition of Theopompus a confusion arose between the intervention to aid Inaros and the later expedition of Cimon, so that Plutarch, or some intermediary, was led to connect Themistocles' death with each expedition in turn. One should be able to conclude from this confusion that a reader of the *Philippica* would have found the two campaigns handled in very similar ways. It remains only to show, as best we can, how the two events came to be treated so closely by Theopompus.

Theopompus, of course, does not deserve all the blame for confusing the tradition of the Egyptian affair. As we noted in the previous chapter, there had always been a problem with the chronology of Athens' eastern campaigns, and this is particularly true of the expeditions to Cyprus.[48] Thucydides clearly distinguishes two such campaigns: the first was in progress when all the forces were sent off to aid Inaros, and the second was decreased by a detachment of sixty ships for Amyrtaeus.[49] These distinctions, however, were lost on the popular tradition of the fourth century. Plato and Isocrates mentioned one expedition to Cyprus and one to Egypt but failed to notice that both campaigns involved both places.[50] Ephorus, if Diodorus is a reliable indication, ignored Cyprus in his narration of Inaros' revolution and did not mention Egypt in connection with Cimon's last campaign to Cyprus.[51] If, however, the parallelism between *Themistocles* 31 and *Cimon* 18 indicates the confusion which I have suggested it does, Theopompus may have resurrected Thucydides' connection between Cyprus and Egypt in *both* campaigns. This similarity, then, would have contributed to the confusion of the two campaigns in later sources.

To be sure, the digression on the demagogues in *Philippica* X shows Theopompus at his moralizing worst, more interested in accusing individuals of φιλοτιμία and Athens of πλεονεξία than in clarifying historical details.[52] Our particular concern is the chronology of the section on Cimon, which was extremely compressed. In fact, Theopompus has Cimon's ostracism, recall, and his peace negotiations with Sparta taking place within a period of five years.[53] The story of Tanagra was probably added to explain the recall, and Cimon's last expedition to Cyprus and Egypt followed shortly.[54] By this chronology, Cimon was ostracized not much more than five years before the Five Year Truce, which is generally dated between 454 and 451, usually towards the latter.[55] This would have made Cimon both active in Athenian politics at the time of Inaros' revolt and the obvious man to lead, or at least exercise general control over, any expedition to Egypt. This severe compression in Theopompus' chronology, taken together with Plutarch's confusion between the two expeditions to Cyprus and Egypt, leads me finally to three conclusions about Theopompus' narrative. (1) Theopompus included a brief section on the original Athenian intervention in Egypt before Cimon's ostracism. (2) Cimon commanded, or rather acted as overall commander of, both the earlier and later expeditions. (3) His motives for both were purely imperialistic. One more passage in Plutarch would serve to confirm these suggestions, if indeed Theopompus is the source (*Cim.* 15. 2):

> But when he sailed away again on military service, the populace got completely beyond control. They confounded the established political order of things and the ancestral practices which they had formerly observed, and under the lead of Ephialtes they robbed the Council of the Areopagus of all but a few of the cases in its jurisdiction. (Perrin's Loeb translation)

The reforms of Ephialtes are generally placed around 462. We have evidence of only one naval expedition that Cimon could have commanded in that year, the original expedition to Cyprus and Egypt.[56]

Theopompus was not treading on new ground when he condemned the Egyptian expedition to aid Inaros as an imperialistic adventure.[57] Thucydides himself may have contributed to this interpretation by describing the final disaster in Egypt in terms which are parallel to those he used for the conclusion of the great Sicilian expedition.[58] Moreover, this similarity to the Sicilian disaster was not lost on the 'Old Oligarch,' Isocrates, and the speaker in Diodorus XIII, and indeed Theopompus used it if Plutarch is again representative of him (*Per.* 20. 3):[59]

In other matters he did not accede to the vain impulses of the citizens, nor was he swept along with the tide when they were eager, from a sense of their great power and good fortune, to lay hands again upon Egypt and molest the realms of the King which lay along the sea. Many also were possessed already with that inordinate and inauspicious passion for Sicily. (Perrin's Loeb translation)

A fragment of Cratinus might be a condemnation of Athenian imperialism in Egypt,[60] and even Diodorus could not completely exclude the unsympathetic version from his otherwise phil-Athenian account.[61] Beside his talk of Athenian panhellenism, Diodorus has preserved some comments on Athenian motives that could bear a very negative interpretation. Before the Athenians sent aid, according to Diodorus, they considered their own future security and what they could get out of Egypt.[62] Theopompus, then, accepted the official judgment about Egypt, but, in his normal manner, he dramatized the affair by connecting it with a specific individual, Cimon in this case.[63] Moreover, it is likely that Theopompus' account of the Egyptian affair would have impressed later antiquity as being the most eloquent condemnation of the Athenian adventure.

We now come to the goal of our digression on Theopompus, a full explication of Aristides' relationship to Theopompus in the matter of the Egyptian affair. The ancient commentators on Aristides were fully aware of Theopompus' importance for their studies, and so they may have believed that the orator himself had borrowed from the historian. The hypothesis of the *Panathenaicus* contains the statement that Theopompus' *Philippica* was one of the standard sources for the period covered by Aristides' narrative.[64] More important for our purposes, however, the Scholion BD on the *Pro Quattuorviris* relies on Theopompus' compact section about Cimon, which we have been examining. Fr. 88 is in fact the Scholion on Aristides' allusion to Cimon's recall, and Connor believes that a similar reference in the hypothesis of the *Pro Quattuorviris* may reflect the same source.[65] The Scholion BD also tells the story of Cimon's generosity in a way that surely recalls Theopompus, fr. 89.[66] We are, however, most interested in evidence that Aristides himself employed Theopompus. Connor has pointed out that the orator may have quoted Theopompus in describing the eventual reaction of the Athenians from their ostracism of Cimon (*Pro Quatt.* II. 212):

πάλιν γε κατήγαγον πρὶν τὰ δέκα ἐξήκειν ἔτη, ἵν' αὐτοῦ τῆς φωνῆς ἀκούσειαν·οὕτως ἐπόθησαν. The last word reflects the use of πόθος by Plutarch and *desiderium* by Nepos in the same context, one which certainly derived from Theopompus.[67] If Aristides once delved into the *Philippica* for the story of Cimon's recall, the same source might have inspired some of his remarks about the Egyptian affair in the *Panathenaicus*. Indeed, I believe this to be the case, and I put forward two reasons in support of my conclusion. First, Aristides' use of the term ἐκινήθησαν (revolted) for the rebellious Libyans closely resembles Plutarch's use of the same word in a passage cited earlier.[68] I think both authors borrowed the word from Theopompus' narrative of the Egyptian affair, although only Plutarch kept the connotation of imperialism in the passage. My second reason, though less concrete than the first, could have rather wider implications.

I suggest that the influence of Theopompus can be detected in Aristides' comparison of the arrival of the Athenians to a bolt of lightning. The scholiast, apparently trying to explain the connotation of unexpectedness in the simile, gives an interesting version of the event (III. 210):

Inaros, the son of Psammitichus, was king of the Libyans. He was astonished at the Athenian invasion, and then he rebelled from the King and went over to the Athenians.

The surprise of Inaros, however, not only explains the comparison to lightning, it also implies an interpretation of the cause of the revolt not found in any extant source. Unless the scholiast was simply confused, the notion that a surprise Athenian invasion instigated Inaros' rebellion might well derive from Theopompus. As we have seen, his account stressed Athenian imperialism and the ambition of Cimon in both Egyptian expeditions. If my suggestion is correct, Aristides borrowed the concept of unexpectedness from Theopompus, and the scholiast, recognizing Aristides' source, presented a closer version of Theopompus' text in his note.

It is my belief that Aristides intended his borrowings from Theopompus concerning the Egyptian affair to underscore his attempt to correct that historian's account. To begin with a topic touched upon above, when Aristides corrected the opinion about the Athenians that Thucydides put into the mouths of their Corinthian critics, he may also have been correcting Theopompus.[69] The Corinthians accused the Athenians of being incapable of ἡσυχία, but the same term reappears in Plutarch's account of the second expedition to Egypt (*Cim.* 18. 1): τοὺς Ἀθηναίους ἡσυχίαν ἄγειν μὴ δυναμένους, ἀλλὰ κινεῖσθαι καὶ αὐξάνεσθαι ταῖς στρατείαις βουλομένους.[70] If, as seems likely, the phraseology comes from Theopompus, then the whole section of the *Panathenaicus* with which we have been dealing must be considered a correction of both Theopompus and Thucydides. Aristides meets the criticism of both authors by introducing the last phase of the war with some interesting remarks on the nature of ἡσυχία (I. 244):

> *An honorable and real peace* (ἡσυχίαν) *could be had by all only if the Greeks pushed the barbarians as far as possible from Greece. ... The only people who are truly at peace* (ἡσυχάζουσιν) *are those who show that they do not always insist on living in peace.*

In this passage and throughout the section, Aristides is at pains to demonstrate that Athens' aims were selfless and panhellenic. It is by examining this insistence on the nobility of Athenian motives in the matter of Egypt that we can most clearly uncover Aristides' attack on Theopompus.

Where Theopompus used the verb κινεῖν in the sense of imperialistic aggression similar to the invasion of Sicily, Aristides employs it in the passive in such a way as to imply that the Libyans rose up of their own accord.[71] The Athenians inspired the revolt only indirectly, to the extent that they weakened the authority of the Persian government enough to cause the type of native revolt that had occurred previously in Egypt. The Athenians actually intervened in the rebellion quite hurriedly only to prevent it from being crushed. Thus, Aristides bowed to Theopompus' concept of a speedy Athenian intervention, but for the orator the speed does not imply the unexpectedness that it seems to in the historian. As Aristides goes on to say, the speed was not unexpected but totally consistent with Athens' constant role as guardian of the Hellenic world. It was not the Athenians' aim indiscriminately to κινεῖν τῆς βασιλέως ἀρχῆς τὰ πρὸς θαλάσσῃ (Plut. *Per.* 20. 3), but to protect Hellenic interests everywhere. All of this corrects Theopompus' use of κινεῖν and refutes his imputing base motives to the Athenians; yet it raises a serious question about Aristides' interpretation of the Egyptian affair. How could Aristides imply that Libyans and Egyptians were Hellenes? We will return to this question below, and the answer to it will, I believe, aid us in understanding the traditional sources that Aristides reflected in correcting Theopompus' attitude to the Egyptian rebellion.

If Aristides corrected Thucydides and Theopompus, as I have suggested, then we should have to assume that he either corrected them on the basis of his own imagination or set them against an account that was more sympathetic to Athens. Furthermore, if no major historical sources support Aristides' version, as seems to be the case, we must presume that either he had no sources or his sources are essentially lost to us. To reject the former alternative in each case and contend that Aristides employed lost patriotic Athenian sources might seem to be an exercise in scholarly futility, were it not for what we have learned about Aristides in the earlier chapters. Although he was all too capable of rhetorical expansion on a historical event, he did not create events out of nothing. Throughout Aristides' narrative of the Persian War, one can find precedents for every factual statement and many thematic ones, and those sources generally follow a single line which we have called the Athenian popular tradition. This was, of course, the very tradition that Thucydides and Theopompus criticized, and thus Aristides' correction of those authors should come as no surprise. Moreover, it will not be excessively artificial to argue that, in correcting the historians, Aristides returned to the very tradition that they in their turn had corrected. The next stage in my argument, therefore, must be to ferret out those few ancient references that support Aristides but stand outside of, and possibly predate, the critical historical version of the Egyptian revolution.

Aristides begins his account of the Egyptian affair with a chauvinistic concept at least as old as Aeschylus' *Persae*. The two authors comment in much the same way on the adverse effect of Athenian victories on the stability of the Persian Empire, and in fact Aeschylus seems to have written his play in the belief that the empire was about to collapse as a result of Salamis. In a particularly telling passage, the chorus of Persians envisions a personified Asia lamenting the cost of Xerxes' war (548-553):

> Now the whole of Asia, emptied of its men, groans (στένει). Xerxes led, alas; Xerxes destroyed, alas; Xerxes wrongly set everything in ocean boats.

The first two lines are clearly reflected in the last distich of the Cyprus epigram:[72]

> ... μέγα δ' ἔστενεν Ἀσὶς ὑπ' αὐτῶν
> πληγεῖσ' ἀμφοτέραις χερσὶ κράτει πολέμου.

The epigrammatist and those familiar with his poem probably

believed that the Persian chorus was fearing future losses as much as lamenting past ones, and indeed Aeschylus lent himself to this interpretation by going on a few lines later to discuss the future perils of the empire (584-594):

> *Those in the Asian land are not going to be ruled by Persians for long; they are not going to be subject to tribute payable to their arbitrary rulers; and they are not going to fall down on the ground in reverence. For the King's strength is completely ruined. Men's tongues will no longer be held in check, since the people have been freed to speak openly and the yoke of power has been cut loose.*

The Persians are afraid that refusal to pay tribute, disrespect for Persia, and talk of freedom will replace their domination and, as Atossa puts it, διαπεπόρϑηται τὰ Περσῶν πράγματα (714).

It was maintained in Chapter III that the *Persae* contained an accurate gauge of the early popular tradition at Athens. This seems to hold true also in the present case, where we can see that Aeschylus shared the popular view in suggesting that the Persian Empire was in decay.[73] Reports of various court intrigues concerning Xerxes[74] and Artaxerxes[75] and the rebellions of Babylonia,[76] Bactria,[77] Egypt, and Syria[78] must have begun reaching Greek ears not long before the production of the *Persae*. Various motives are mentioned for these disturbances: love, revenge, thirst for power, on the individual level, and, on the national level, the desire for liberty and hatred of paying tribute.[79] An Athenian reader, however, noting that these incidents followed on Xerxes' disaster and Cimon's eastern campaigns, would have felt that somehow the forces of the Delian League were responsible. A rather extreme example of this chauvinism is to be found in Ctesias' strange tale about the part that the Athenian survivors of the Egyptian debacle played in the revolt of Syria.[80] Other, more conventional references to Persia's instability, however, seem to constitute a real motif in the popular tradition of Athens' eastern campaigns. Herodotus was naturally quite interested in Persia's domestic problems in themselves, but, in a typical bow to Athenian tradition,[81] he also put an echo of Aeschylus' Atossa into the mouth of one of Xerxes' advisers. In a speech couched in the platitudes of Attic tragedy, Artabanus warns Xerxes that, if he invades Greece, he may invite the same fate that Darius nearly suffered: διέργαστο ἂν τὰ Περσέων πρήγματα (VII. 10. γ. 2). Accounts of the period in Attic orators point to the conclusion that the

Epitaphios and other popular oratory retained the tragic façade but merged the motif of Persia's decline with the wider 'theme of fear,' which will be examined in greater detail in Chapter VI.[82] This oratorical tradition viewed the cumulative effect of Athenian victories as a profound reversal in the King's fortune: previously he had been the terrifying aggressor, now he was fearfully witnessing the collapse of his own empire. One even finds the motif of Persia's decline linked specifically with Cimon in a source friendly to Athens. Diodorus says that Cimon pressed the siege of Salamis during his final expedition against Cyprus for a definite reason: to demonstrate how Athenian sea power could embarrass Persia and weaken her prestige.[83] Diodorus used the same word, καταφρονέω, for Persia's decline in prestige that Aristides does in his introduction to the Egyptian affair. If the two had a common literary source, it was presumably Ephorus who would normally repeat popular Athenian ideas in such matters.

Unfortunately, one is hard pressed to find examples of the motif of Persia's internal decline connected directly with the Egyptian revolution. For the only clear instance, we must turn to Diodorus' account of the rebellion's beginning (XI. 71.3):

> When the inhabitants of Egypt learned of the death of Xerxes and of the general attempt upon the throne and the disorder in the Persian kingdom, they decided to strike for their liberty. At once, then, mustering an army, they revolted from the Persians, and after expelling the Persians whose duty it was to collect the tribute from Egypt, they set up as king a man named Inaros. (*Oldfather's Loeb translation*)

Quite significantly, Diodorus repeats two of the motives which Aeschylus associated with native revolts in general: talk of ἐλευθερία and hatred of the Persian tribute.[84] However, in the light of the bad press the Egyptian affair received from Thucydides and Theopompus as well as the disastrous conclusion of the Athenian intervention, it is small wonder that no other examples are forthcoming. As we noted earlier, Theopompus seems to have agreed that Cimon aimed at ὅλης τῆς βασιλέως ἡγεμονίας κατάλυσιν (Plut. *Cim.* 18.6), but he twisted the Athenian motives into unabashed imperialism.[85] Later writers would naturally avoid such an unpleasant topic; yet there might have been a stronger reason for the failure to connect Egypt with the domestic troubles of the Persian Empire. It is quite possible that in the Athenian popular tradition the Egyptian affair was not normally conceived of as a native revolt within the empire, but a secession of Greeks from their Persian despot. The Athenian intervention, therefore, would have been an act of panhellenic liberation.

Most Athenians certainly believed that their city carried on the war against Persia after Plataea as a panhellenic crusade. As we saw in Chapter III, vengeance may have been a motive in fact, but in literature, public buildings, and men's minds the liberation of fellow Greeks was the major concern.[86] Naturally, therefore, the popular media were most interested in the separation of *Hellenic* states from Persia in the period from the revolt of Potidaea in 480 to the ratification of the Peace of Callias with its guarantee of autonomy for Greek cities.[87] For example, when Aeschylus in the *Persae* lists the states that were likely to rebel after Xerxes' disaster, all the cities are Greek ones that Darius had conquered or ruled securely. Historians can of course find exceptions, such as the case where Cimon coaxed or forced Carians and Lycians to revolt from Persia;[88] yet both peoples were indispensable to Cimon's strategy before the Eurymedon, and the Carians were so thoroughly Hellenized that their cities may have claimed Greek origin through some god or hero.[89] Meiggs has even deduced from the tribute lists that Athens generally sought to bring into her league only those cities in the distant East that somehow could be considered Greek.[90] Moreover, the Athenians wished it to be known that their subjects were in some sense their children (their colonists), a concept publicized by the empire's gifts to Athena and the Eleusinian deities and the designation of Athens as 'mother-city of crops.'[91] If the Athenians, then, tended to advertise their activities in the eastern Mediterranean as a form of panhellenism, one must interpret a public document such as the casualty-list of the Erechtheid tribe with great care.[92] Members of the tribe were honored for actions in Greece and three areas of the East: Cyprus, Egypt, and Phoenicia. The cities of Cyprus certainly claimed Greek origin, and fighting in Phoenicia could have had something to do with Dorus under Mt. Carmel, which had ancient connections with Greece and does appear on the tribute lists.[93] Could it be publicly claimed that Athenians fell for the cause of Hellenic freedom in Egypt?

For Diodorus, one motive of the Egyptian insurgents was freedom, a term usually confined to the aspirations of Greek states in the context of the Persian War;[94] the author of the *Menexenus* connected the Athenian intervention with the other exploits in the panhellenic war of liberation.⁹⁵ These authors may preserve a faint echo of a tradition which treated the Egyptian affair as a Greek revolt, but we can perhaps witness the tradition at or near its birth in Aeschylus' *Supplices*. The play was probably produced sometime between the native revolt and the Athenian intervention, and so allusions to Athens' involvement in Egypt should come as no surprise.⁹⁶ It is of course dangerous to search for such correlations between historical events and mythical tragedies of similar date; yet we cannot overlook the possibility that, in the matter of Egypt, Aeschylus reflected, or perhaps helped create, a popular interpretation of a political issue.⁹⁷

The plot of the *Supplices* undeniably corresponds to the situation that must have prevailed while the Athenians were deciding whether to honor Inaros' request for aid. Individuals from Egypt seek aid from a Greek state against a barbarian race that would oppress them at home.⁹⁸ The Danaids come in the guise of Greek suppliants to make their appeal to Zeus Soter, the traditional god of suppliants.⁹⁹ This god, however, was regularly honored at the time of the play's production as the aggressive symbol of panhellenism under his new title, Zeus Eleutherios, in whose name Inaros may well have appealed to Athens.¹⁰⁰ The Athenian Assembly granted Inaros' request with a formal resolution (ἐψηφίσαντο).¹⁰¹ Similarly, the Danaids must go before the Demos of Argos, and the result of the Assembly meeting appears in the form of an official document: ἔδοξεν ... ἡμᾶς μετοικεῖν τῆσδε γῆς ἐλευθέρους (605ff.). In fact, the political machinery of the state in the play, supposedly Pelasgian Argos, reflects fifth-century democracy rather than heroic monarchy.¹⁰² Moreover, the play is permeated by the feeling that war is about to break out between Argos and the sons of Aegyptus.¹⁰³ If the mythical situation has an analogue in the historical, the imminent war would be the upcoming one between Athens and Persia over Egypt. The most significant correlation between the *Supplices* and the Egyptian affair, however, may be found in the racial distinctions central to the play. The sons of Aegyptus have reverted to barbarism,¹⁰⁴ but the Danaids have maintained an essential Hellenism and put forward a claim of Greek ancestry as the basis of their request for aid from a Greek city against barbarians. The suppliants' claim requires some proof, since their outlandish appearance deceives Pelasgus into thinking they are Libyans, children of the Nile, or some other kind of barbarians.¹⁰⁵ The

Danaids prove their claim by recalling the story of Argive Io, who fled to Egypt and gave birth to Epaphus there. Epaphus in turn fathered Libya, the grandmother of Danaus and Aegyptus.[106] This carefully defined contrast between Hellenism and barbarism provides the key to understanding the intended emotional impact of the play on Athenian attitudes towards the Egyptian affair. Aeschylus did not explicitly provide a racial parallelism between the Danaids and Inaros' rebels on the one hand and the Egyptians and Persians on the other; yet his audience probably knew enough about northeastern Africa to make the connection by itself.

Presumably the Athenians conceived of Aegyptus' sphere as Egypt proper, an area that most Greeks believed to have been thoroughly barbaric from mythical to their own times.[107] This would leave for Danaus the neighboring territory of Libya. Although the Greeks in the fifth century had no exact concept of the boundaries of Libya, there is ample evidence to suggest that in the context of Inaros' revolt they would have applied the name of Libya to the western part of the Nile's delta.[108] From at least the third century, this area was known as the Kingdom of Libya, and fifth-century Greeks knew that local dynasts there were Libyans like Inaros.[109] What is more important for our purposes, the Greeks knew that these Libyans were descended from the Saite kings of Egypt, who had fostered the myth of Io and made much of their connections with Hellenism.[110] The Saites greatly revered the Apis bull, Epaphus of Greek myth, whose birth Aeschylus locates at Canobus near Sais.[111] Amasis, the Saite who died facing Cambyses' invasion, set up a monument on Lindus to commemorate the stop made there by the Danaids on their flight to Greece.[112] The Saite line had long employed Greek mercenaries and finally granted Greek merchants the privilege of founding Naucratis.[113] Since this colonial foundation might have been popularly connected with Io's wanderings, the myth should perhaps be viewed as a symbol of the bond between Saites and Greeks.[114]

The Egyptian revolt, of course, arose from the Libyan-Saite area of the delta, which offered the Persians far stiffer resistance than the territory south of Memphis.[115] The unique spirit of the original Libyan rebels no doubt enabled them to hold out in their own territory, to retain a certain degree of autonomy, and to maintain good relations with Athens long after the revolt's collapse amongst ordinary Egyptians.[116] Thucydides was perfectly well aware of the important racial distinction in the Egyptian revolt (I. 104. 1): Ἰνάρως δὲ ὁ Ψαμμητίχου, Λίβυς βασιλεὺς Λιβύων τῶν πρὸς Αἰγύπτῳ, ὁρμώμενος ἐκ Μαρείας τῆς ὑπὲρ Φάρου πόλεως ἀπέστησεν Αἰγύπτου τὰ πλείω.[117] The Egyptians who rebelled are merely called, ξυναποστάντες. It should come as no surprise, however, to learn that Thucydides ignored the emotional appeal inherent in the racial distinction. Nevertheless, we should not forget this form of appeal, nor, I suspect, did Inaros, when he sent to Athens for aid against the barbarians. His ambassadors must have paraded his family's ancient ties with Hellenism, perhaps mentioning Io, the Danaids, and Naucratis. Since the *Supplices* falls into this historical context, it strains the imagination to believe that the similarities between Inaros' Libyans and Aeschylus' Danaids were fortuitous. Whatever the strategic or economic reasons for the Athenian intervention in Egypt were, the official, popular, and emotional issue must have been panhellenism, the liberation of a people with sacred ties to Greece. This is precisely the issue to which the *Supplices* addresses itself, and for this reason in particular I believe the play was at least partially intended as a public declaration of the poet's support for the Athenian intervention in Egypt.

The awareness of the part played by the racial question in the Egyptian affair underwent a nearly complete eclipse in the tradition after Aeschylus. In the fifth century, Herodotus and Thucydides were aware of the distinction between Libyans and the others; but Herodotus noticed it only in the casual manner of a sightseer in Egypt, and, as we have seen, Thucydides probably considered the racial issue little more than Athenian jingoism.[118] Only faint traces of this important matter survive from the fourth century, when the interpretation of the ill-fated Egyptian expedition as an imperialistic adventure all but superseded the view of it as part of the panhellenic crusade.[119] We have seen hints of the Aeschylean view in the *Menexenus* and Diodorus, and another appears in Ctesias, who knows that Inaros was a Libyan whose success was most evident in the western delta.[120] Ctesias, however, begins his account with the simple declaration, ἀφίσταται Αἴγυπτος. Likewise Diodorus shows that he misses the point of the racial question, when he says that *Egyptians* started the revolt for purely Egyptian reasons and then proceeded to make Inaros their king.[121] For centuries almost no one wrote about the Egyptian affair except to lament the Athenian losses or moralize about imperialism, until the racial distinction with its full Aeschylean implication emerged from obscurity in Aristides'

Panathenaicus (I. 247): ἐκινήθησαν μὲν οἱ πρὸς Φάρῳ Λίβυες, συναπέστησαν δὲ Αἰγύπτιοι. One might argue that Thucydides inspired this sentence, but he could not have been responsible for the interpretative epilogue which Aristides appended to his account of the Athenian intervention in Egypt. The orator sees the Athenian expedition as epitomizing the Athenians in their role as guardians of Hellenic territory: τοῦ διὰ πάσης γῆς Ἑλληνικοῦ περιπόλους ἐκείνους χρὴ καλεῖν. Aristides thus reproduces the ancient tradition that the rebels were Hellenes and that the intervention was a matter of panhellenism. It remains only to suggest the specific channels through which the old tradition made its way down to Aristides.

So far in this chapter we have been concerned with showing how Aristides corrected Thucydides and Theopompus by returning to a genuine popular version of the Egyptian affair that was current in fifth-century Athens. Our comments about this popular tradition have been confined to a comparison between the earliest and latest of its sources and an examination of the few unconscious or hostile references to it in intermediary sources. The scarcity of exact evidence from Aeschylus to Aristides prevents us from pinpointing the latter's source by means of verbal parallels or other more exact methods.[122] We are thus left with the rather more conjectural method of induction from the tradition we have discovered. Our knowledge of the characteristics of this tradition should enable us to formulate generalizations about the nature of a source that could convey such material. When these generalizations are juxtaposed with a list of the types of sources Aristides is known to have used, we ought to be able to make a specific suggestion about his source for the revolt of Egypt. Let us begin with a brief review of our remarks about the tradition.

Aristides drew upon a tradition of the Egyptian affair that preserved the potent emotional climate of the *Persae* and *Supplices*. Aeschylus and Aristides share two of the major themes surrounding the event: the impact of Athens' victories on the Persian Empire and the primacy of the issue of panhellenic liberation. If Herodotus is any indication, these old themes with their inherent Athenian bias remained unchallenged for many years. With Thucydides, however, the old tradition went underground, as it were, and our only knowledge of it in his day derives from inferences made on the basis of his attack upon it. That is to say, one can probably deduce from Thucydides' use of the Egyptian affair as an example of Athenian imperialism, that he was correcting the old tradition with its exclusive interest in Athenian panhellenism. The same method of reasoning can be applied to Theopompus. If he saw the Athenian intervention as an imperialistic adventure consistent with Cimon's policy of enslaving Greece, the tradition he was challenging probably saw it as an act of Athenian and Cimonian panhellenism. Finally, we have noted that from the fourth century the old tradition practically disappeared. This is rather unusual in view of the fact that the tradition of other events such as the Peace of Callias was challenged by the sceptical historians but still reappeared in the popular media after them. If Isocrates is typical, the older version of the Egyptian expedition gave way to Thucydides' gloomy interpretation.

These conclusions about the nature of the old tradition seem to support at least two generalizations about the type of source that could have transmitted such material down to Aristides. First, our source, quite unlike Thucydides or Theopompus, was concerned only with Athens' conduct of the Persian War. Athenian panhellenism overseas was the theme; relations between Athens and the rest of mainland Greece did not enter the picture. Presumably this source relied on the tradition that separated the fifth century into two chronological and thematic entities, the Persian War and the Peloponnesian War.[123] My second point stems from the nearly complete eclipse of the old tradition from Thucydides to Aristides. Although we must not let the great loss of ancient literature deceive us into constructing fallacious arguments *ex silentio,* it does look as if the authority of Thucydides and Theopompus all but drove the sympathetic version of the Egyptian affair out of the written tradition. This would seem to suggest the startling conclusion that the old tradition was transmitted orally from the fifth century B.C. to the second of our era. Although the oral transmission of a tradition over so long a period might seem highly unlikely at first, I devote the concluding chapter to a brief suggestion of how a continuous tradition of Athenian history could have survived in oral form down to Aristides' day. It will be seen that this tradition is essentially that of the *Epitaphios,* which certainly fits the requirement that Aristides' source for the Egyptian affair divide the fifth century into Persian and Greek halves.[124]

1. The unity of the passage around the topic of the Egyptian revolt has apparently not gone unchallenged. G.F. Hill, *Sources for Greek History*[1] (Oxford, 1907), p. 118, quotes Aristides as a source for the revolt only up to the mention of the loss of the swamp. Behr, in his Loeb edition of the *Panathenaicus*, is not entirely clear; but, by placing the sentence about the triremes at the beginning of a new section, he may imply that they should not be connected with the Egyptian affair. Oliver, *Civilizing Power*, p. 130, clearly believes that the triremes belong to the Egyptian revolt.

2. Presumably this is the understanding of the scholiast, who seems to be explaining the reason for the loss of the swamps (III. 211): ἀπόλλυσιν Αἰγύπτου μοῖραν οὐκ ὀλίγην, τὸ"Ἕλος] μέρος τι τῆς Αἰγύπτου Ἕλος καλεῖται, ὁ πρὸς Ἀθηναίους ἐχώρησεν.

3. This is not to say that the continuous accounts agree in all details of fact and chronology. Their accounts are in fact often at variance with each other, but one can always pick out the three main stages of revolt. For the native revolt, cf. Thuc. I. 104. 1; Cts. 63; Diod. XI. 71. 3-4; Aristod. 11. 3. For the Athenian intervention, cf. Thuc. I. 104. 2; 109; 112. 3; Cts. 63f.; Diod XI. 71. 5-75; Aristod. 11. 3-4. Only Thuc. I. 110, mentions the loss of the swamps, but Diod. XI. 77.1-5, and Aristod. 11. 4, record an unsuccessful end, and Cts. 65, has the rebels holding out for a while in the town of Byblos. For the scholarship on the location of Byblos (and the history of the revolt in general), cf. P. Salmon, *La Politique égyptienne d'Athènes* (Bruxelles: Académie Royale de Belgique, 1965), pp. 172-74, who identifies it as a place in Prosopitis, where the Athenians made their last stand in Thucydides, Diodorus, and Aristodemus. One should also note that Herodotus, as well as Thucydides (I. 110. 2), knew that a leader by the name of Amyrtaeus survived in the swamps. Herodotus locates Amyrtaeus' refuge at a place called Elbo (II. 140. 2).

4. A most serious chronological problem amongst the historical sources is one which Aristides conveniently ignores: the circumstances of the actual beginning of armed conflict in Egypt. The first combat in the revolt seems to have occurred at Papremis (Hdt. III. 12. 4, and VII. 7; for its location in the northeastern part of the delta, cf. Salmon, *ibid.*, pp. 144-46). Ctesias (63) and Diodorus (XI. 74. 2-4) both describe this same initial battle, in spite of their variation in certain details (cf. Salmon, p. 143f., and Meiggs, *Athenian Empire*, p. 474). The problem is whether this battle occurred before the Athenians arrived, as Ctesias seems to imply and Meiggs, p. 93, states (for other scholars as well, cf. Salmon, p. 146, n. 7), or, as Diodorus puts it, the Athenians took part in the battle.

5. For possible Athenian participation in the land battle, cf. the previous note and Diod. XI. 74. 2-4. The naval battle is better known. Not only is there Ctesias' detailed account (63) and Thucydides' brief hint (I. 104. 2: καὶ ἀναπλεύσαντες ἀπὸ θαλάσσης ἐς τὸν Νεῖλον τοῦ τε ποταμοῦ κρατοῦντες καὶ τῆς Μέμφιδος τῶν δύο μερῶν πρὸς τὸ τρίτον μέρος ὃ καλεῖται Λευκὸν τεῖχος ἐπολέμουν), but we have the Samian epigram which probably commemorates this battle: cf. W. Peek, "Ein Seegefecht aus den Perserkriegen," *Klio* 32 (1939) 289-306. However, Salmon, *ibid.*, pp. 148-50, and F.K. Kienitz, *Die politische Geschichte Aegyptens vom 7. bis zum 4. Jahrhundert vor der Zeitwende* (Berlin: Akademie, 1953), p. 72, doubt Peek's indentification of this battle as the subject of the epigram. H.D. Westlake, "Thucydides and the Athenian Disaster in Egypt," *CP* 45 (1950) 209-11, accepts the identification.

6. Meiggs, *Athenian Empire*, p. 106, speaks of this as "the official version in the fourth century."

7. For the loss of the original force, cf. I. 110. 1. For the loss of the relieving force, cf.

I. 110. 4. For the attempt to mitigate Thucydides' statements, cf. Westlake, *supra*, n. 5, p. 209f., and 215, n. 10. For the ongoing modern debate on the extent of Athens' losses, cf. Salmon, *supra*, n. 3, pp. 181-89; J. Libourel, "The Athenian Disaster in Egypt," *AJP* 92 (1971) 605-15; Meiggs, *Athenian Empire*, pp. 104-28; J. Bigwood, "Ctesias' Account of the Revolt of Inaros," *Phoenix* 30 (1976) 1-25.

8. Isocrates may well have had Thucydides in mind at *De pace* (8), 86: cf. Westlake, *ibid.*, p. 215, n. 6. Diodorus' evidence appears in a speech of a Syracusan delivered in 413 (XIII. 25. 1f.). In addition, a comment by Aelian probably reflects Isocrates' statement in the *De pace* (*V.H.* V. 10).

9. Aristodemus, 11. 4.

10. Cts. 63ff. Cf. Bigwood, *supra*, n. 7.

11. Diod. XI. 77. 4f.

12. Justin, III. 6. 6f.:
    parvae tunc temporis classe in Aegyptum missa vires Atheniensibus erant. itaque navali proelio dimicantes facile superantur. interiecto deinde tempore post reditum suorum aucti et classis et militum robore proelium reparant.

Westlake, cf. *supra*, n. 5, p. 215, n. 23, suggests that Trogus may have derived his information from Ctesias.

13. Meiggs, *Athenian Empire*, pp. 473-75, suggests Hellanicus as an ultimate source behind some of these comments.

14. Cf. *supra*, Chapter IV. p. 96f.

15. By the word 'negative,' I refer not only to Thucydides' opinion of the magnitude of the Athenian losses, but also to his views on the motive of the expedition, for which, cf. *supra*, pp. 111ff.

16. Cf. *supra*, p. 128, and n. 117.

17. Cf. Thuc. I. 110. 2: Αἴγυπτος δὲ πάλιν ὑπὸ βασιλέα ἐγένετο πλὴν Ἀμυρταίου τοῦ ἐν τοῖς ἕλεσι βασιλέως·τοῦτον δὲ διὰ μέγεϑός τε τοῦ ἕλους οὐκ ἐδύναντο ἑλεῖν. ...

18. *Historischen Angaben*, p. 53, where, quite interestingly, he suggests the possibility of another, pro-Athenian source but does not pursue the matter.

19. I. 100. 2-103. 4.

20. Various scholars point this out in various ways. Salmon, cf. *supra*, n. 3, p. 124f., stresses the fullness of Diodorus' account and its use of sources avoided by Thucydides: cf. Meiggs, *Athenian Empire*, p. 474. It is often noted that Thucydides' whole account is remarkably brief and omits much: cf. Westlake, *supra*, n. 5, p. 209f. The reason for this, according to J. Barns, "Cimon and the First Athenian Expedition to Cyprus," *Hist.* 2 (1953) 174, is that Thucydides "is interested in the Egyptian affair only when it begins to affect Athens."

21. For the important matter of the motive of the Athenian intervention, cf. *supra*, pp. 125ff.

22. Cf. *infra*, n. 117. Aristides would relish the opportunity to borrow a word (συναπέστησαν) from Thucydides while correcting his source's use of the term. The same phenomenon occurs in the orator's use of the speech of the Corinthians at Sparta.

23. Cf. *supra*, pp. 125ff.

24. In this speech, Athenian traits are ὕβρις (68.2), the enslaving of others (68. 3), gradual encroaching on others (69. 3), αὔξησις (69.4), innovation and daring (70.2f.), seeking more (70. 4: οἴονται τῇ ἀπουσίᾳ ἄν τ: κτᾶσϑαι; cf. also, 70. 7: κτήσωνται, and

70.8: κτᾶσθαι), and finally their restlessness. The theme of ἡσυχία is repeated five times in the speech: of the Spartans at 69. 4, 71. 1, 71. 3 (by implication); a lack of it in the Athenians at 70. 8 and 9. Aristides borrows from the following speech, that of the Athenians with its panhellenic sentiments, to correct the Corinthians: cf. 74. 4, where it is said that the Spartan ἡσυχία would have made it easy for Xerxes to conquer Greece.

25. Cf. Gomme, *HCT* I. 306f. Ctesias names an Athenian commander, a Charitimides, who later loses his life in conflict with the Persians in Egypt (64).

26. This is the expedition of sixty ships detached from the two-hundred sent to Cyprus under Cimon (Thuc. I. 112. 3) very soon after the defeat of the first expedition (cf. Diod. XII. 3. 1).

27. For an omission that is quite similar and will indeed be discussed later (cf. *supra*, p. 115), see Gomme, *HCT* I. 285.

28. For this chronology, cf. A.E. Raubitschek, "The Peace Policy of Pericles," *AJA* 70 (1966) 37f., and "Kimons Zurückberufung," *Hist.* 3 (1955) 379-80. Cf. W. Connor, *Theopompus and Fifth-Century Athens* (Washington: Center for Hellenic Studies and Harvard, 1968), p. 149f., n. 17. Cf. however, J. Schreiner, "More Anti-Thukydidean Studies in the Pentekontaetia," *SO* 52 (1977) 21-29, where Callisthenes is very strongly put forward as Plutarch's source.

29. For the possibility of such an intermediary source, cf. Connor, *ibid.*, p. 153, n. 37.

30. Almost certainly this is Cimon's Peace, the Five Years Truce, which Thucydides (I. 112. 1) places just before the expedition to Cyprus and Egypt.

31. Raubitschek, cf. *supra*, n. 28, "Peace Policy," p. 38, believes that this was the camp of the survivors of the final disaster of the expedition originally sent to aid Inaros.

32. W. Graf Uxkull-Gyllenband, *Plutarch und die griechische Biographie* (Stuttgart: Kohlhammer, 1927), pp. 76-82.

33. For his πραότης and ἀφέλεια, cf. *Cim.* 5.5. Chapter 10 contains the traditional story of Cimon's generosity to the Athenian populace. The same principle is implied by his statement about taking pride in enriching his city with the spoils of her enemies: cf. 14.4; 18. 1.

34. Chapter 6 describes how Cimon's troops were disciplined with kindness. In Chapter 11, Cimon lets the allies contribute money, as they wish, instead of ships and men.

35. Plut. *Cim.* 10; *Per.* 9; Nepos, *Cim.* 4; Theopompus, fr. 89; cf. Schol. Aristid. III. 517, and especially III. 446, where Cimon is described as a democrat. Cf. A.E. Raubitschek, "Damon," *Cl Med* 16 (1955) 82, and Connor, cf. *supra*, n. 28, pp. 31-37, 153, n. 37.

36. Fr. 88, which, interestingly, is from the BD Scholion on Aristides' *Pro Quattuorviris:* cf. III. 528. Cf. also, the passage for which fr. 88 serves as a note, II. 212, and the hypothesis of the speech, III. 515. Nepos, *Cim.* 3. 2, borrowed this story from Theopompus. Connor, cf. *supra*, n. 28, pp. 26-28, discusses the passage in detail, and at p. 151, n. 22, suggests that all extant references to Cimon's recall may derive from Theopompus.

37. Cf. *supra*, n. 30, and Connor, *ibid.*, p. 28, who notices the similarity in language found in *Cim.* 18. 1 (ἔλυσε τὸν πόλεμον), *Per.* 10. 4 (εἰρήνην ἐποίησε), and fr. 88 (εἰρήνην ποιήσασθαι and τὸν πόλεμον κατέλυσε).

38. H.T. Wade-Gery, "Two Notes on Theopompus," *AJP* 59 (1938) 129f.; A.E. Raubitschek, "Theopompus on Thucydides the Son of Melesias," *Phoenix* 14 (1960) 86; Connor, cf. *supra*, n. 28, pp. 24ff. At p. 35, Connor suggests a similar adaptation of Theopompus by Nepos.

39. Connor, *ibid.*, p. 33, and by the same author, *The New Politicians of Fifth-Century Athens* (Princeton, 1971), pp. 20f., 37, 140.

40. Beside fr. 89, the story of Cimon's generosity, one should place Scholion BD on Aristides, III. 446, where Cimon is described as a democrat who advanced his career by making generous gestures. The passage betrays much Theopompan influence: cf. Connor, *ibid.*, *Theopompus*, p. 37. Cf. also Theopompus, fr. 90, in which Cimon is roundly criticized for theft and bribery.

41. Raubitschek, cf. *supra*, n. 38, p. 86, believes that all the references to Cimon as a democrat (see previous note: Nepos, *Cim.* 2.1; Plut. *Cim.* 5.4; 10. 1-5) and Pericles as an aristocrat (Schol. BD on Aristides, III. 446; Plut. *Per.* 7; 9. 2-3) derive from Theopompus. Connor, who once agreed (*GRBS* 4 [1963] 113), now casts doubt on the identification of Theopompus as the source of *Per.* 7 (cf. *supra*, n. 28, p. 154, n. 44).

42. One can visualize Theopompus taking particular delight in bursting a typical Athenian balloon with his use of the word φιλανθρώπως.

43. Thuc. I. 99. The similarity between Thucydides and Plutarch is clear: cf. Plutarch's λυπηρὰν ἀρχήν (11.1) and Thucydides' λυπηροί (99. 1), terms which applied to Athens because of her imperial exactions. Gomme, *HCT* I. 284f., notes how Plutarch has adapted his source in the present passage. Gomme also suggests the interesting possibility that Stesimbrotus was behind Theopompus as the original source: cf. Meiggs, *Athenian Empire*, p. 16.

44. In this interpretation, the πάλιν would refer to the expedition to aid Inaros: cf. A. Weizsäcker, *Untersuchungen über Plutarchs biographische Technik* (Berlin: Weidmann, 1931), pp. 50ff. Gomme, *HCT* I. 379, n. 2, finds the assumption unlikely.

45. Diod. XI. 58. 2-3: cf. B. Perrin, *Plutarch's Themistocles and Aristides* (New York: Scribners, 1901), p. 257, who traces the popular version of Themistocles' death; A. Podlecki, *The Life of Themistocles* (Montreal and London: McGill—Queens, 1975), pp. 43, 59, 105.

46. I. 138. 4, where the historian not only reports Themistocles' death by disease but explicitly rejects the story of suicide.

47. Gomme, *HCT* I. 444, notices this confusion and points out that E. Langlotz, *Zur Zeitbestimmung der strengrotfigurigen Vasenmalerei* (Leipzig: E.A Seemann, 1920), p. 49, considers the reference to be to the Egyptian rebellion of Inaros. Cf. Perrin, *supra*, n. 45, p. 255.

48. Ephorus, of course, confused the second campaign to Cyprus with the Eurymedon, and Thucydides lent himself to the confusion by describing the Eurymedon and the battle of Cyprus in similar terms. On the synchronism of Themistocles' death and Cimon's campaigns, cf. Podlecki, *supra*, n. 45, pp. 114 and 195; R.J. Lenardon, *The Saga of Themistocles* (London: Thames and Hudson, 1978), p. 199f. Cf., also, the twentieth Epistle of Themistocles, *To Polygnotus*, where the events surrounding the end of his life are dealt with.

49. I. 104. 2; 112. 2f.

50. Cf. *supra*, p. 109, and Isoc. *De pace* (8), 86.

51. For Egypt, cf. XI. 71ff. For Cyprus, cf. XII. 3ff.

52. Connor, cf. *supra*, n. 28, p. 30.

53. *Ibid.*, pp. 27-29, 105f. Cf. Raubitschek, *supra*, n. 28, "Peace Policy," p. 37f. The relevant passage is Theopompus, *FGrH* 115 F 88.

54. For Tanagra, cf. Connor, *supra*, n. 28, p. 29f. For Egypt, cf., of course, the connection with Plut. *Cim.* 18. 1. Another relevant passage is Nepos, *Cim.* 3. 3f., almost certainly inspired by Theopompus.

55. Connor, *ibid.*, pp. 27-30, and *supra*, n. 39, pp. 17, 58-62.

56. Raubitschek, cf. *supra*, n. 28, "Peace Policy," p. 38. This, of course, raises an interesting question about Pericles' position in Athenian politics in 462 B.C., if, as we have suggested, cf. *supra*, p. 116, he opposed Cimon's later campaign to Egypt as an imperialistic and democratic adventure.

57. One should note that this opinion has many adherents amongst modern scholars: Meiggs, *Athenian Empire*, p. 95; F.M. Cornford, *Thucydides Mythistoricus* (London: E. Arnold, 1907), p. 37; Salmon, cf. *supra*, n. 3, pp. 90, 121, 128f., who recognizes the importance of economic motives, but disagrees with those who interpret the expedition as a mad, imperialistic adventure (for whom, cf. Salmon, p. 128, n. 1) or as motivated primarily for economic reasons (cf. G.B. Grundy, *Thucydides and the History of His Age*, Vol. I [Oxford, 1948], pp. 185ff.).

58. Cf. L. Pearson, "Thucydides as Reporter and Critic," *TAPA* 78 (1947) 48, n. 24, and Westlake, cf. *supra*, n. 5, p. 212, who compares Thuc. I. 110. 1 (καὶ ὀλίγοι ἀπὸ πολλῶν πορευόμενοι διὰ τῆς Λιβύης ἐς Κυρήνην ἐσώθησαν, οἱ δὲ πλεῖστοι ἀπώλοντο) with VII. 87.6 (καὶ ὀλίγοι ἀπὸ πολλῶν ἐπ' οἴκου ἀπενόστησαν). Cf. *supra*, n. 6.

59. Isocrates and the speaker mention the two expeditions in the same breath, cf. *supra*, n. 8. For the 'Old Oligarch,' cf. (Xen.) *Ath. Pol.* 2.7: διὰ τὴν ἀρχὴν τῆς θαλάττης πρῶτον μὲν τρόπους εὐωχιῶν ἐξηῦρον ἐπιμισγόμενοι ἄλλῃ ἄλλοις· ⟨ὥστε⟩ ὅ τι ἐν Σικελίᾳ ἡδὺ ἢ ἐν Ἰταλίᾳ ἢ ἐν Κύπρῳ ἢ ἐν Αἰγύπτῳ ἢ ἐν Λυδίᾳ ἢ ἐν τῷ Πόντῳ ἢ ἐν Πελοποννήσῳ ἢ ἄλλοθί που, ταῦτα πάντα εἰς ἓν ἤθροισαι διὰ τὴν ἀρχὴν τῆς θαλάττης. If my interpretation of the mention of Sicily as a reference to the great expedition is correct, it could have a serious effect on the argument over the dating of this work.

60. Fr. 73, Kock (Pollux, *Onomasticon*, IX. 91): ὅτι τοὺς κόρακας τἀξ Αἰγύπτου χρυσία κλέπτοντας ἔπαυσαν.

61. Diod. XI. 71. 4-5. Here and in the mouth of the Syracusan speaker, Diodorus speaks of 300 Athenian ships involved in Egypt. At XI. 74.3, only 200 ships arrive to aid Inaros. Meiggs, *Athenian Empire*, p. 474, suggests that this inconsistency could represent reliance on two independent sources. I note with interest that the figure 200 appears in a battle-narrative sympathetic to Athens, whereas the other passages are hardly connected with Athenian philanthropy or panhellenism. The text of Plutarch at *Cim.* 18. 1, is problematic: the better manuscripts read 300 ships, the variant is 200. Cf. the apparatus in Cl. Lindskog and K. Ziegler, *Plutarchi: Vitae Parallelae*, Vol. I (Leipzig: Teubner, 1960). One wonders whether Theopompus was responsible for the number 300 and the negative implications in both Diodorus and Plutarch.

62. The one benefit the Athenians did derive from Egypt was the gift of grain sent to Athens by a Psammetichus in 445/4: cf. Schol. Aristoph. *Vesp.* 718 (Philochorus, fr. 119) and Plut. *Per.* 37. 3-4. The accounts vary considerably but probably represent two versions of the same tradition: cf. *FGrH*, III, Suppl. B, Notes, p. 374, n. 5. Jacoby believes that Psammetichus was Inaros' son and successor.

63. Connor, cf. *supra*, n. 28, p. 106, notes how Theopompus often borrowed from, but exaggerated, Thucydides. This may be the case with the Egyptian affair, for which these two authors agree on the Athenian motive and the conjunction of Cyprus and Egypt: cf. *supra*, p. 117. Theopompus, however, might have found a similar malignant attitude to Cimon in Stesimbrotus; cf. *supra*, n. 43, and Connor, p. 103.

64. Lenz, *Prolegomena*, p. 115.

65. Cf. Connor, *supra*, n. 28, p. 151, n. 22. Fr. 88 appears at Aristid. III. 528, and the reference for the hypothesis is III. 515.

66. III. 446. Cf. Connor, *ibid.*, p. 36f.; Raubitschek, *supra*, n. 38, p. 86.

67. Plut. *Cim*. 17. 7 (πολὺν αὐτῶν πόνον); *Per*. 10. 3 (καὶ πόθος ἔσχε τοῦ Κίμωνος); Nepos, *Cim*. 3. 2 (eius virtutis desiderium). Cf. Connor, *ibid.*, p. 151, n. 19.

68. Cf. *supra*, p. 116f. (*Per.* 20.3).

69. Cf. *supra*, p. 112.

70. I find the repetition of the word κινέω significant, even though its meaning is not precisely the same at *Per.* 20. 3, or in Aristides.

71. Rather than repeat the long passage, I refer the reader to the translation on p. 107. It is interesting to note that Plutarch uses κινεῖν in rather the classical sense, to move or stir up. Aristides' use of the word to mean revolt, on the other hand, was a normal later usage, first found in Dio Cassius (cf. XXXIX. 54; XL. 15). The Scholion BD on our passage of the *Panath*. implies that ἐκινήθησαν and ἀπέστησαν are completely interchangeable (III. 210): ἐκινήθησαν, ἀντὶ τοῦ ἀπέστησαν. λέγει γὰρ καὶ Θουκυδίδης "Ἰναρως δὲ... ἀπέστη. Aristides himself used the words interchangeably in the *Panath.*: cf. I. 160; 251 compared with 258.

72. Cf. *supra*, Chapter IV, p. 78.

73. Cf. *supra*, Chapter III, pp. 52f. For the sad status of the Persian Empire early in the Pentecontaetia, cf. Salmon, *supra*, n. 3, p. 91, and H. Bengtson, *Griechische Geschichte* (München: Beck, 1969), p. 209. Plutarch mentions that, before the Athenian intervention in Egypt, the King was inactive towards Greeks owing to his preoccupation with the affairs of his own country (*Them.* 31. 3).

74. For Xerxes' affair concerning Masistes, cf. Hdt. IX. 108ff.

75. For the plot of Artabanus, the death of Xerxes, and the rise of Artaxerxes, cf. Cts. 60f.; Diod. XI. 69; 71. 1-2.

76. Hdt. I. 183; Strabo, XVI. 738; Arrian, VII. 17. As in the case of Egypt, there had been an earlier revolt, for which cf. Bengtson, *supra*, n. 73, pp. 168, 176.

77. Hdt. IX. 113; Cts. 62.

78. Cts. 67ff.

79. For the two national motives, cf. *supra*. p. 124.

80. Cts. 67ff.

81. Cf. *supra*, Chapter III, p. 47.

82. Cf. *supra*, Chapter III, p. 43f.; *infra*, Chapter VI, pp. 151f.

83. Diod. XII. 4. 2. Earlier in this same campaign, Cimon took the cities of Citium and Marium, whose inhabitants he is said to have treated φιλανθρώπως (Diod. XII. 3. 3). One wonders whether his true motive was to foment rebellion amongst Persia's subject states. J. Wells, "The Persian Friends of Herodotus," *JHS* 27 (1907) 37f., suggests that the leader of the 'peace-party' at the Persian court, Megabyzus, carried

on the revolt of Syria (Cts. 67ff.) in connection with Cimon.

84. *Persae*, 589-97. Just a few lines below the present passage, Diodorus notes that Inaros tried to convince the Athenians to *liberate* Egypt.

85. Note also the interesting remark of Plutarch that Cimon's untimely death afforded a respite τοῖς βασιλέως πράγμασι (*Cim.* 19. 3).

86. Cf. *supra*, Chapter III, pp. 49f.

87. For Potidaea, cf. Hdt. VIII. 126. 3. For the autonomy clause, cf. Chapter VI, pp. 148f. For Aeschylus' comment on the states likely to rebel from Persia, cf. *Persae*, 864-95.

88. Cf. Plut. *Cim.* 12. 3-4.

89. For the Carians, cf. Strabo, XIV. 2. 27; for the Lycians, cf. Strabo, XIV. 3. 10. Minos, Apollo, and Glaucus figure in the legends about these peoples.

90. *Athenian Empire*, pp. 58, 102.

91. Cf. *supra*, Chapter II, p. 23f.

92. *IG* I² 929 = *ML* 33.

93. Since the action in Phoenicia is not recorded by literary sources, it is difficult to say what the expedition involved. It is interesting to note, however, that the inscription probably belongs to the early years, perhaps the first year, of the Athenian intervention in Egypt: cf. *ATL* III.174f.; Salmon, cf. *supra*, n. 3, pp. 156ff. This would be the very period in which, according to Meiggs, *Athenian Empire*, p. 420f., Dorus first appeared on the tribute lists. Cf. J. Schreiner, *SO* 51 (1976) 19ff.

94. XI. 71. 3; cf. *supra*, p. 124.

95. 241e; cf. *supra*, p. 109.

96. For the date of the play, E. Luppino, "L'intervento ateniese in Egitto nelle tragedie eschilee," *Aegyptus* 47 (1967) 209-11, discusses the sources, scans the modern scholarship, and suggests 462/1 as the date. Among the various discussions of the date of the revolt, J. Scharf, "Die erste ägyptische Expedition der Athener," *Hist.* 3 (1954) 308-18, most clearly discusses the delay between the beginning of the revolt (? 463/2) and the Athenian intervention (?462/1).

97. Luppino, *ibid.*, pp. 197-212, adduces numerous similarities between the *Prometheus Vinctus* and the *Supplices* to suggest that the former anticipated the other in the matter of Egypt; both plays were part of Aeschylus' program to persuade the Athenians to intervene in Egypt. A. Garvie, *Aeschylus' Supplices: Play and Trilogy* (Cambridge Univ., 1969), p. 156, refuses to accept this political explanation of the play and mentions other scholars who are equally unconvinced by arguments such as those of Luppino. Garvie, pp. 141-62, also mentions the various attempts to interpret the *Supplices* along other political lines. Cf. A.J. Podlecki, "Politics in Aeschylus' *Supplices,*" *Class. Folia* 26 (1972) 64-71, who supports the connection between the play and Inaros' revolt.

98. Although the sons of Aegyptus were descended from the same stock as the family of Danaus, they display a barbaric and hybristic character and are called ἐχϑροί (225): cf. Luppino, *ibid.*, p. 205f. This is why many scholars refuse to see the play as favoring the *Egyptian* revolt: cf. Garvie, *ibid.*, p. 156, n. 2.

99. They come with boughs of supplication (22, 241f., 334). For Zeus Soter, cf. 26, 347, 385.

100. Inaros clearly made a request for protection, but what he promised in return is by no means clear. Our only indication is in Diod. XI. 71. 4f.: Inaros promises joint rule (κοινὴν τὴν βασιλείαν) and gifts to Athens. The Athenians, for their part, expect to, τοὺς δὲ Αἰγυπτίους ἰδίους ἑαυτοῖς παρασκευάσαι πρὸς τὰ παράλογα τῆς τύχης. If all of this amounts to membership in the Athenian Empire as a tribute-paying subject, then two conclusions should follow: (1) Inaros' people wished themselves to be considered Greek (cf. *supra*, p. 125f.); (2) their supplication was made in proper Hellenic style as a request to join the League. To be sure, their request was for liberation (Diod. XI. 71. 4: ἔπεμψε δὲ καὶ πρὸς Ἀθηναίους ... ἐὰν ἐλευθερώσωσι ...), and to the Athenian in the early Pentecontaetia, this should have been tantamount to a request to enter the Delian League. Zeus Eleutherios, as we have seen (cf. *supra*, Chapter III, p. 50f.), symbolized the goal of the League to liberate all Greeks from barbarian domination.

101. Diod. XI. 71. 5.

102. *Suppl.* 338ff.; cf. Luppino, *supra*, n. 96, p. 208f.; Garvie, *supra*, n. 97, pp. 150-54.

103. For the passages, cf. Luppino, p. 204, n. 2: 342; 357f.; 400f.; 412; 439; 476; 1044.

104. Cf. *supra*, n. 98.

105. For their appearance, cf. 234-37. For Pelasgus' mistaken beliefs, cf. 277-89.

106. *Suppl.* 291-324. Pelasgus' earlier fear that the Danaids might have been Libyans becomes ironic, in the sense that they, as true Libyans, are also Greeks.

107. For mythical times, cf. the myth of Busiris. For historical times, cf. Anaxandrides, *Poleis*, fr. 39 (Athen. *Deipnos.* VII. 299f.), for which cf. J. Edmonds, *The Fragments of Attic Comedy*, Vol. II (Leiden: Brill, 1959), p. 61.

108. For the meaning of Libya in the fifth century, cf. Luppino, *supra*, n. 96, p. 202, n. 3.

109. Cf. Salmon, *supra*, n. 3, p. 93, who cites the relevant information.

110. Salmon, *ibid.*, points out that the name of Inaros' father, Psammetichus (Thuc. I. 104. 1), probably connects him with the 26th dynasty. Amyrtaeus in our sources is probably akin to the Saite mentioned by Manetho (*Aegyptiaca* [*Epitome*], fr. 72).

111. For the Apis, cf. Hdt. II. 153; III. 28f. In a sense, the Apis became a symbol of Saite resistance to Persian rule: cf. A. Olmstead, *History of the Persian Empire* (Univ. of Chicago, 1948), pp. 227, 236. For the birth of Epaphus, cf. *Prom.vinc.* 813, 846.

112. Hdt. II. 182.

113. For the general relations between Saites and Greeks, cf. the last third of Hdt. II. For Naucratis, cf. Hdt. II. 154; 178.

114. Cf. Luppino, *supra*, n. 96, pp. 198, 203f.

115. So Kienitz, cf. *supra*, n. 5, p. 68f.

116. For their holding out, cf. Amyrtaeus' control of the swamps (Thuc. I. 110. 2). This is where a Psammetichus raised a revolt and held out: cf. Hdt.II.152. The question of the degree of their autonomy is more difficult. Herodotus, III. 15. 3, tells us that after the revolt the Persians allowed the sons of Inaros and Amyrtaeus to rule their fathers' estates. Moreover, Herodotus knew that in his day Marea was so secure that it did not require a Persian garrison (II. 30). Nevertheless, we cannot ignore the

famous gift of grain, which seems to have been given to Athens by a successor of Inaros: cf. *supra,* n. 62.

117. It is, of course, difficult to decide whether Thucydides believed that the popular revolt or merely the revolutionary leader himself rose up in Libya. Some hint of Thucydides' intention might be found in his use of the word ὁρμώμενος. Thuc. often uses the word in the middle with the military idea of rising up with a force from a certain base of operations: cf. I. 64, 74, 90; II. 69 (twice); III. 31, 85, 95, 98; IV. 1, 3, 8, 52, 61, 102; V. 6; VI. 34, 50; VII. 18; VIII. 24, 76. Sometimes the subject is plural, sometimes it is singular and agrees with the army's leader. On the other hand, ὁρμάω in the middle frequently means simply "start" or "move" from a place: cf. II. 96; IV. 52, 125; V. 1; VI. 3, 31; VII. 2, 33; VIII. 3. Thus, although Thuc. may have meant to indicate by his use of the verb that the popular revolt began in Marea, we cannot be certain.

118. Herodotus knew of the Libyan area around Marea (II. 30), he called Inaros a Libyan (III. 12. 4; 15. 3; VII. 7), and spoke of Inaros and Amyrtaeus as local dynasts in the western delta (III. 15). For Thucydides, cf. the preceding paragraph.

119. Cf. *supra,* p. 126.

120. Cts. 64f., where Inaros holds out for a while in Byblus: cf. Luppino, *supra,* n. 96, p. 205, n. 2.

121. XI. 71. 3. Diodorus does, however, report that there were Libyans in the rebel army (XI. 74. 2), and that the *Egyptians* proved to be rather spiritless soldiers in the final battle (77. 3). One wonders whether the latter statement were made as a contrast to a more complimentary one about the Libyans in Diodorus' source.

122. The fact that Aristides cites the *Persae* a few lines earlier (cf. Oliver, *Civilizing Power,* p. 130, *s.v.* section 152), cannot allow us to suppose that Aeschylus himself was Aristides' source for the Egyptian revolt. Aristides recognized a similarity in tone between the *Persae* and the tradition he was following, but it seems highly unlikely that he borrowed his version of the Egyptian affair from an understanding of the political implications of the *Supplices.*

123. Cf. *supra,* Chapter III, pp. 62 ff.

124. *Ibid.*

CHAPTER VI

THE PEACE OF CALLIAS

The popular media of ancient Athens lavished more praise on the victories of Marathon and Salamis than on any other deeds of the Persian War. The Athenian tradition offered third prize, however, to the peace that marked victory and the end of the war. This event is now commonly referred to by the name of Callias, the only Athenian diplomat connected with it in the sources.[1] The abundance of evidence for this peace surprises us, and even the ancients commented on its popularity as a topic of Athenian chauvinism.[2] Chauvinism and popularity, however, are not the stuff of history, and the Peace has had a checkered career in the pages of historical scholarship.

The major historical problem has long been the very existence of the Peace. The fullest extant accounts, those in Diodorus and Plutarch, maintain that Athens and Persia negotiated and promulgated a treaty in specific terms towards the middle of the fifth century.[3] Callisthenes and perhaps Theopompus, on the other hand, denied or at least questioned the formal status of the Peace.[4] Their criticisms and, more especially, the failure of Herodotus and Thucydides to refer unambiguously to the Peace have led some modern scholars to reject the concept of a *de iure* treaty and instead speak merely of an informal cessation of hostilities and a recognition of the military and political *status quo* in the Aegean.[5] In addition, a troublesome lack of consistency in the various citations of the treaty's terms and the chronological problem with which we dealt in Chapter IV compound the issue of the Peace's formal existence. Moreover, the student must be aware that the sources might have mistakenly applied to our peace details that properly belong to the so-called Peace of Epilycus, the Peace of Antalcidas, or other treaties with the Persians.[6] Unfortunately, there is no decisive epigraphical or other documentary evidence with which we might address these historical problems, and so our solutions must derive in the first place from an understanding of the literary sources.[7] It is my purpose, then, to examine primarily the literary tradition of the Peace in this Chapter, and I will be satisfied if a small contribution is made to our knowledge of the origin and transmission of the tradition upon which the literary references are based.[8]

Since many of the extant references to the Peace of Callias either derive from or occur in popular Athenian media, this event would seem to be an excellent paradigm for a study of the popular tradition. Unfortunately, the Peace does not lend itself easily to the type of analysis which we have conducted in the previous chapters, where we have attempted to trace a continuous popular version of events well into the fifth century. The major problem stems from our seeming inability to discover any reference to the Peace older than Isocrates' *Panegyricus*, which was published in 380.[9] Scholars generally posit one of two hypotheses to explain this late date in the light of the rest of the literary tradition. According to some, the Peace was purely an invention of fourth-century propaganda, perhaps of Isocrates himself as a foil to the Peace of Antalcidas.[10] Others suggest that there had been some kind of peace in the mid-fifth century, but for some reason it remained unimportant in the tradition until Isocrates awakened popular interest in it.[11] In either case, two facts must be taken into account: first, Isocrates seems to have cited the Peace directly from a document, and, second, Craterus certainly knew of a document that bore the text of the Peace of Callias.[12] Scholars have proposed several ingenious theories to account for a fourth-century copy of the true Peace or a counterfeit document set up for propagandistic purposes. The monument was probably erected in the eighties, between Antalcidas' treaty and the publication of the *Panegyricus*, although some scholars argue for a date in the forties, when numerous forged stelae seem to have been put up.[13]

Despite the interesting results of much of the modern scholarship on the Peace, it has had the unfortunate effect of fragmenting the tradition. This division results primarily from the variation that our sources show in the matter of the Peace's chronology and terms. As we saw in Chapter IV, some sources date the Peace relatively late, after the end of the Egyptian and Cyprian expeditions, while others connect it rather more directly with Cimon and the climax of his achievements, the Battle of Eurymedon. Scholars have attempted to explain this variation by postulating the existence of two or more independent ancient traditions about the fifth-century Peace.[14] The citations of the treaty's terms seem to exhibit even more variety than the chronology. Some sources only allude vaguely to what might be called terms; in others, lists of stipulations appear to reflect an actual document, but even amongst these lists the sources frequently disagree on the specific terms. Predictably, then, scholars attempt to discover independent traditions by finding patterns in the various citations of terms.[15] The unity of the tradition of the Peace, however, has not been completely stripped of its defenses. Murison employed a very able review of the literary sources in a way that opposes the general tendency towards multiplying the tradition. He maintained that just one tradition of the terms of the fifth-century Peace existed in the fourth century, but that at least two versions of the tradition came about from the inability of fourth-century authors to date the Peace to the circumstances resulting from the Eurymedon or to those following Cimon's last expedition to Cyprus.[16] In Chapter IV, we arrived at the same conclusion by analyzing the chronology of the Eurymedon in a manner quite unlike that of Murison, and now I should like to apply this new method directly to the Peace itself. Murison, like most other scholars, explained the transmission of the tradition by concentrating on the matter of immediate historical interest, that is, the extant literary references to the terms and chronology of the Peace.[17] I propose, on the contrary, to give special consideration to the influence of the tradition's essentially rhetorical and even oral nature upon our literary sources. I hope that this approach will broaden the prespective of our investigation by taking into account the contexts of the various literary sources and thereby discovering otherwise unnoticed references to the Peace.

Aristides' account of the period before the Peace is, as we have seen, thoroughly saturated with the rhetorical tradition and may even have been influenced by a living tradition of Athenian history which was orally transmitted to his own day. It might be well, then, to imitate the procedure of the previous chapters and begin with his version of the Peace. In the *Panathenaicus,* Aristides waxes eloquent on the Athenian treaty that he sees as the culminating achievement of the last phase of the Persian War. He begins, rather in the manner of Isocrates, with a vague allusion to the Peace (I. 249):[18]

    A. The King gave way before Athens so great a distance

on land and sea that you could not call his action merely back-
watering or a tactical retreat. He actually abandoned the entire
coastal region, tens of thousands of stadia of Asia—no less than
the whole territory of a huge empire. As a result, not only did
the islands and all of the various Greeks in them become free,
but even the Greeks who inhabited his own country found
themselves as far from his domination and empire as old Greece
had previously been.

A few lines later, Aristides speaks of the terms of the Peace in
greater detail (I. 249f.):

B. Thanks to Athens' struggles and expeditions, the King was
so weakened[19] that he agreed, first, never to sail west of two
boundaries stipulated as the Chelidonians in the south and the
Cyaneans in the north and, second, to keep fully five hundred
stadia away from the sea in all directions. The perimeter
created by this second term stood rather like another victory-
crown[20] on the heads of the Greeks—a guard-post in the heart
of the King's own country.

Such was the war that Athens prosecuted against the barbarians both in Greece and in their own country; but such also
was the Peace that she made. In both she showed that she did
not march out in pursuit of wealth nor even for the pleasure of
gain, but with this one goal in mind: to secure the freedom of
the Greeks from the barbarians. And yet who could name a
nobler crowning act of war or peace with Greeks or with barbarians than that by which Athens concluded her business
in those days?

Later in the oration, when Aristides is comparing the Athenian
empire with that of Sparta, he returns to the Peace (I. 277):

C. (You have seen that Athens surpassed Sparta in war against
the barbarians,) but you will now see an even greater difference
in the matter of peace. Athens' Peace dictates terms to the King
and says that he must do only what she tells him. In the first
place, Athens does not allow him to send his ships west of the
Chelidonians and Cyaneans. (But the treaty continues): "If,
however, you take pride in your cavalry, you shall no longer
send it near the sea, but shall stay away from the sea the distance that this cavalry of yours can ride in one day. Moreover,
you are to obey with regard to the Greeks in your own territory
as well as those in Greece." This is what Athens' Peace says;
Sparta's, however, ...

Finally, we should take note of a passage from the *Ad Romam* where
Aristides contrasts the infinity of Rome's empire with the

restrictions placed on that of Persia (I. 325f.):

> D. No crags in the sea such as the Chelidonians or the Cyaneans limit your empire, Romans, nor does the distance of one day's horse-ride to the sea. Your dominion is not fixed to stipulated boundaries; no one else publicly declares the point beyond which your power may not extend.

This clearly constitutes an allusion to the Peace of Callias, the only unambiguous one outside the *Panathenaicus*.

Historians of the Peace of Callias might at first hope to find valuable evidence in the preceding passages, but Aristides' text soon appears to raise more problems than it solves. The orator leaves no doubt about accepting the existence of a formal treaty. In passage B, the King agrees to specific terms which are quoted indirectly and then cited directly in C. Moreover, Aristides refers to the Peace as the culminating act of the Persian War and compares it with the Peace of Antalcidas, the existence of which is not doubted. As to the terms of the Peace, what we may call the naval limits and the autonomy clause present no difficulty. Passages B, C, and D agree that the King's navy was not allowed to penetrate west of the Cyaneans and Chelidonians. Passages A and C show that the Peace guaranteed the freedom of Ionia and the islands.[21] A third term, however, the limit placed on the King's westward expansion on land, does not fare as well as the others in Aristides. The large area of stadia in passage A and the limit of five hundred stadia from the sea in B are compatible,[22] but the daylong ride by horse in C and D seems to reflect a different document or an independent tradition. The texts in the *Panathenaicus* exhibit a similar inconsistency concerning the chronology of the Peace. In passages A and B, Aristides apparently imitated Ephorus in placing the Peace after the end of the Egyptian affair.[23] Passage C, on the other hand, does not so easily admit of chronological analysis, but, in the section immediately preceding it, a description of the Battle of Eurymedon serves as Aristides' account of the whole last phase of the war.[24] It seems that in C, then, Aristides reflected the same tradition as Plutarch did in linking the Eurymedon and the Peace rather closely as cause and effect.

The apparent contradictions in Aristides' versions of the Peace of Callias have serious implications for our understanding of the tradition. In fact, these contradictions ought to admit of only one of two possible explanations, both of which will have a bearing on the question of the tradition's unity. According to one explanation, Aristides drew at random from the literary sources which he knew so well and was trying to surpass rhetorically; historical contradictions were small fry in the construction of a literary tour de force. This was essentially the conclusion of Beecke, who looked only at Aristides' version of the treaty's terms and deduced from them that the territorial limits come directly from Demosthenes or Plutarch and the autonomy clause from Lycurgus.[25] This interpretation may not entail a conclusive argument in favor of a multiplicity of fully independent traditions about the Peace, but it implies at least that Aristides was unaware of any overwhelming unity in the tradition. Furthermore, it suggests that the history of the Peace was a dead issue for Aristides, not a matter of a compelling, living tradition but of citations gleaned for rhetorical rather than historical purposes from the 'ancients.' The alternative explanation, on the contrary, would be that a vital tradition exerted considerable influence upon Aristides' historiography. The impact of this tradition would have convinced the orator that this was the only tradition of the Peace and that apparent contradictions in literary sources were no more than minor variations or the results of differing versions of the single tradition. Again, this is not absolute proof that there was never more than one tradition, but one should not lightly dismiss Aristides' testimony in such a matter. I believe that this second explanation is essentially true. To prove it, however, we must examine the unity of the tradition from the viewpoint of the Peace's chronology, its terms, and especially its rhetorical context in our sources and at the same time demonstrate Aristides' knowledge of that unity.

Since the unity of the received tradition in the matter of chronology was discussed in Chapter IV, it might be well to review the conclusions reached there before approaching the other topics.[26] We discovered that oratory and other popular media transmitted a version of the Peace's chronology that was probably the only version until the middle of the fourth century. This version upset Thucydides' chronology of the last phase of the Persian War by so exaggerating the importance of the Battle of Eurymedon that other campaigns were cast into relative oblivion and the date of the Peace was moved closer to that of the battle.[27] Ephorus and Callisthenes certainly joined the popular media in recognizing that without the Eurymedon there could have been no peace, and they bowed to the common tradition as much as they dared, but their research revealed that the popular chronology was impossible. As a result, Ephorus placed the Peace after the end of Athens' involvement in Egypt, and Callisthenes denied the *de iure* existence of the Peace. We concluded that whatever ambiguity the sources show for the chronology of the Peace does not derive from a multiplicity of traditions but only from the very difficulty in dating the Peace that troubled Ephorus and Callisthenes. Furthermore, in discussing Aristides' attitude towards the chronology, we noted that he did not simply follow a popular tradition in the context surrounding passage C and a historical tradition before the version in A and B. In fact, the account of the Eurymedon before C follows that of Ephorus, and the one accompanying A and B is closer to Plutarch.[28] Aristides probably preferred the rhetorically more pleasing chronology of the popular version;[29] yet, when he wanted to include the Egyptian affair in his narrative, he accepted the logic that demanded a clear separation between the Eurymedon and the Peace. All this surely indicates that Aristides, like Ephorus and Callisthenes, wrote under the influence of an overwhelmingly unified tradition of the Peace. Nevertheless, Aristides' tradition, like that of Ephorus and Callisthenes, was vital and flexible enough to recognize details about chronology and other matters from unaided reasoning or independent sources and to accept them naturally, without becoming, as it were, a scissors and paste job.

A study of the terms of the Peace will offer less difficulty than one might be inclined to think; it will in fact support the conclusions which we derived from our study of the chronology. Wade-Gery developed perhaps the most ingenious of the numerous attempts to identify a unity beneath the varied citations of the terms. He wove every extant reference to a stipulation into a complex set of regulations governing relations between Athens and Persia in the Aegean.[30] Subsequent scholarship has necessitated modification of many of Wade-Gery's hypotheses, especially his interpretation of Isocrates' tribute clause and the concept of a demilitarized zone bounded by Phaselis, the Chelidonians, and the southern Cyaneans.[31] Aristides himself provides the evidence that destroys the latter theory.[32] The orator designates the Cyaneans as the boundary in the north and thus proves that the ancient tradition had in mind the northern Cyaneans, to which the name was usually applied in Greek literature.[33] More successful attempts than Wade-Gery's to discover unity amongst the terms have been made by those who accept some stipulations as variants for others and try to explain how they could have originated from a common source.³⁴ Let us apply this method, first, to the land limits, then the naval ones, and finally to the autonomy and non-aggression clauses.

Isocrates alone says that the Athenians established the Halys River as the limit west of which the King's army could not come.³⁵ Although some scholars interpret this stipulation literally, as though Isocrates had independent information about the Peace, Sordi is probably closer to the truth in maintaining that its use was dictated by the exigencies of fourth-century propaganda.³⁶ Even in the fifth century, the Halys had been popularly considered the proper boundary between Hellenes and Persians, so that Isocrates would naturally mention it when attempting to define geographically Athens' act of panhellenic liberation.³⁷ The other sources give a land limit in terms of various distances east of the Aegean: one day's ride by horse,³⁸ three days' march on foot,³⁹ four hundred stadia,⁴⁰ and, of course, Aristides' five hundred stadia. These citations would seem at first to contradict each other, but in fact they are probably only variations on the same theme: a longitudinal line drawn through Asia Minor at approximately the latitude of Sardis. Herodotus reports that Sardis was three days' walk from Ephesus at a rate of one hundred eighty stadia a day,⁴¹ and presumably a horse could travel three times faster than a man. Since measuring by horse-rides was consistent with Persian practice, we may assume that a day's ride was the original form of citation and that other forms represent attempts to put the distance into Greek formulae.⁴² Aristides was certainly not aware of any dichotomy in the tradition of the land limits, and in fact he seems to have had a remarkable grasp of the traditional point of view. He felt that the standard form was a day's horse-ride and he also knew that this form of expression was used because of its special meaning in respect to Persians.⁴³ Nevertheless, Aristides did not feel any compunction about varying the 'standard' form of the term in a manner that is not recorded in other extant sources.⁴⁴ All this seems to me to suggest that there was one essential conception of the land limit in the received tradition at least down to Aristides' time and that it had a standard form of expression in literature. As happens with living traditions, however, the form could undergo change for rhetorical purposes while the historical essence remained the same.⁴⁵

The various citations of the limits that the Peace put upon the

King's movement by sea exhibit the same dichotomy as the land limits. Demosthenes and Plutarch, possibly following the document copied by Craterus, stipulate the Cyaneans and Chelidonians.[46] Isocrates mentions only one limit, the city of Phaselis, and Ephorus was probably imitating his teacher when he noted the name of the same city.[47] The historian, however, added the Cyaneans, and Lycurgus used the same pair of limits.[48] Isocrates probably introduced Phaselis for propagandistic purposes, and, if so, that city should be considered a variant for the Chelidonians.[49] Aristides seems to have accepted the version of Demosthenes and Plutarch without reservation. Still, it is interesting to note that in passage B he directs the reader's attention to the essence of the matter, a limit to the north and one to the south; he does not solely rely on a quotation from a written source. Moreover, Aristides presents a substantially different version from that of the later sources. The Souda, Aristodemus, and, probably dependent on him, a Scholion on Hermogenes, agree on three limits: the Cyaneans, Phaselis, and the Chelidonians.[50] Aristodemus and the scholiast add the otherwise unattested Nessus River.[51] Presumably these three, or four, locations appeared together in the rhetorical handbooks and represent the final, frozen version of the ancient tradition. Aristides, by contrast, shows a stage of the tradition that is considerably more vital.

The remaining two stipulations should be considered together, since they appear to form a reciprocal agreement between the treaty's signatories. In the fullest citation of the Peace's terms, that of Ephorus as found in Diodorus, the first of three clauses directed towards the King guarantees the autonomy of Asiatic Greek cities.[52] In the last clause, however, the Athenians promise not to attack the King's land, provided that he abides by the other stipulations.[53] For obvious reasons, the non-aggression clause dropped out of the tradition, which was primarily concerned to show how Athens forced the King into accepting a one-sided Peace.[54] The autonomy clause, on the other hand, reappears in Lycurgus and the Souda;[55] yet we soon encounter the same dichotomy that appeared in the citations of the territorial limits, since Demosthenes and Plutarch fail to mention autonomy.[56] Schrader concludes that Ephorus and his imitators represent a panegyric tradition which invented the autonomy and non-aggression clauses and that the other authors reflect the independent tradition of the stele, which did not bear these two clauses.[57] I cannot accept this conclusion for reasons which, when taken together, will suggest again that there was only one ancient tradition of the Peace.

Unlike Schrader, I believe that Isocrates' testimony guarantees that the copy of the Peace was published between the dates of the Peace of Antalcidas and the composition of the *Panegyricus*.[58] It is therefore likely that Ephorus saw the stele, and in fact, the similarity between his account and that of Isocrates almost assures us of their common reliance on the published copy.[59] Moreover, we should not accept Plutarch's omission of the non-aggression and autonomy clauses as evidence for their absence from Craterus' copy of the Peace.[60] Plutarch does not purport to cite Craterus' entire copy, or even to quote from it at all; he only uses its presence in Craterus' collection to refute Callisthenes' theory of a purely *de facto* Peace. It is more natural to assume that Plutarch took his territorial limits from Callisthenes, whose account can be fully reconciled with that of the panegyric tradition.[61] If, then, we can say that Ephorus took the autonomy and non-aggression clauses from the stele, Lysias' testimony, which certainly antedates the publication of the stele, will have serious implications for our argument. Lysias does not mention a peace or quote specific terms in his *Epitaphios*, but, in the very context in which other authors refer to the Peace, he gives what amounts to concrete definitions of the four clauses of the treaty.[62] I quote only the relevant portion: οὔτε τύραννος ἐν τοῖς Ἕλλησι κατέστη, οὔτε Ἑλληνὶς πόλις ὑπὸ τῶν βαρβάρων ἠνδραποδίσθη. This whole passage defines autonomy, and the word πόλις could recall the distinction between cities and country that is inherent to the reciprocality of the non-aggression and autonomy clauses. If Lysias' remarks are faithful to the wording of the epitaphic tradition, it would seem that these two clauses had their origin in the fifth century. To be sure, such clauses would not be out of place in a fifth-century treaty. Autonomy was a common enough stipulation in Greek treaties, and they were normally cast in bilateral formulae.[63] Moreover, the cities/country formula appears in the Spartan-Persian treaties that amounted to an ignominious repeal of the Peace of Callias.[64]

Perhaps the most interesting aspect of the autonomy clause for our investigation, however, is the definition of autonomy that it implies.[65] Although Lysias defined the word narrowly in the sentence cited above, his introduction to the whole passage illustrates the situation in the popular tradition (*Ep.* [2], 55): μετὰ πλείστων γὰρ πόνων καὶ φανερωτάτων ἀγώνων καὶ καλλίστων κινδύνων ἐλευθέραν μὲν ἐποίησαν τὴν Ἑλλάδα. Whatever significance 'autonomy' was meant to have in the original draft of the Peace, the Athenian tradition never distinguished it from 'freedom.' Freeing the Greeks constituted the goal of the Delian League, and the Peace signalled the fulfillment of that goal. In three references to the Peace, all of which reflect Ephorus, Diodorus could speak of an autonomy clause in two and a freedom clause in the other.[66] Lycurgus also used both words, autonomy as the actual term and freedom in his introduction.[67] The latter is particularly interesting, since Lycurgus joins it to the territorial limits: ὅρους τοῖς βαρβάροις πήξαντες τοὺς εἰς τὴν ἐλευθερίαν τῆς Ἑλλάδος. For Lycurgus, then, setting limits upon Persian suzerainty was tantamount to insuring Greek freedom and autonomy. This was precisely Aristides' understanding of the meaning of the territorial limits (passage A): (ὁ βασιλεὺς) ἀφῆκε πάντα μὲν τὸν κάτω τόπον... ὥστε μὴ μόνον τὰς νήσους καὶ τοὺς ἐν ταύταις παντοδαποὺς Ἕλληνας ἐλευθέρους εἶναι....[68] This testimony of someone so familiar with the tradition as Aristides was, strongly supports Murison's belief that the bald citation of the Peace's territorial limits implies the freedom and autonomy of the Asiatic Greeks.[69] Thus, if Demosthenes and Plutarch omit the autonomy clause, their omission can hardly be used as evidence of an alternative tradition.[70] I would even suggest that the presence or absence of the autonomy clause in fourth-century versions of the Peace was dictated by the authors' attitudes to the Peace of Antalcidas with its insincere guarantee of autonomy to mainland Greece and its repeal of autonomy for the Ionian cities.[71] Where the author was not interested in comparing the two treaties, as in the case of Demosthenes in the *De Falsa Legatione,* the territorial limits sufficed. Ephorus, however, was interested in the comparison and in this he probably took his cue from Isocrates. In the *Panegyricus,* the orator contrasts the two treaties and condemns as hypocritical the freedom and autonomy of Antalcidas' treaty.[72] Although Isocrates does not mention a similar clause in the earlier peace, he strongly implies its existence by stating that Athens set limits upon the King's power.[73]

The effect of our discussion so far has been primarily negative: although we have seen indications that there was only one tradition of the Peace in antiquity, the main thrust of our argument has been towards disproving the notion that variation in chronology and terms necessarily implies the existence of two or more independent traditions. A persuasive and more positive argument for the unity of the tradition can be found by examining the rhetorical context of our sources for the Peace. A single theme, which I call the theme of fear, permeates the entire ancient tradition and persistently receives more attention in our sources than details about chronology and stipulations do. This topos constitutes the rhetorical essence of the tradition of the Peace and, very much in the manner of pervasive themes in living, oral traditions, it assumes a number of different forms in various sources. Late as Aristides was, he fully appreciated the unity behind this variety and, in fact, he lavished more care on drawing together the permutations of the theme of fear than on all the actual details about events in the last phase of the war. Once again, then, we find in Aristides a clue to the unity of the living ancient tradition and perhaps a key to understanding otherwise unnoticed allusions to the Peace.

Aristides interprets the last phase of the war as a process whereby Athens fought to reverse the terror that the King had instilled in the Greeks and to change it into a Persian fear of the Hellenes. He opens his account with a statement of Athens' intention (I. 243): τοὺς φόβους καὶ τοὺς κινδύνους εἰς τὴν ἐκείνων μεταστῆσαι.[74] This theme reappears in the *Pro Quattuorviris*, where Aristides enhances his account of Cimon's achievement at the Eurymedon by framing it with dual references to a transfer of fear to the barbarians:[75]

1. Cimon's intention before the battle (II. 208):
... εἰ τοῖς βαρβάροις φόβον ἐμβάλοι.

2. The result of the battle (II. 210): ... ὥστε ἕως ἔξη Κίμων τεθνάναι περιῆν τοῖς βαρβάροις τῷ φόβῳ τοὺς Ἕλληνας. ...

The latter passage is particularly interesting because it leads directly into a reference to the Peace which is not as obvious as the other four in Aristides (II. 210):

E. *It was not up to the barbarians to determine which Hellenic cities should be under their sway, but only to look out for their own safety. The Athenians set free all the cities from such a fate and caused the greater part of Ionia to revolt, the very opposite of what the Spartans did later.*

One could pick out an allusion to the autonomy clause, a clear parallel to passage A (*he abandoned the coastal region*), and the familiar contrast with the Peace of Antalcidas; yet the theme of fear is the important point, and the Peace functions only as a symbol for the completion of Cimon's transfer of fear to the barbarians.

Aristides follows an essentially similar, although greatly expanded, pattern in the *Panathenaicus*. He again employs the theme of fear as a framing device, whose opening element was cited just above. This time, however, the frame encompasses the entire offensive camgaign from Mycale to the Peace, and, more important for our purposes, Aristides does not close it by simply mentioning the King's fear. Much as historians tend to concentrate on Aristides' literal statements about the Peace in passages A and B, the orator himself concentrated more attention upon presenting a virtual compendium of the various traditional permutations of the fear-theme as an introduction to his version of the terms of the Peace. Let us begin with the two variations on the theme that we have noted in earlier chapters.

In the first of the comments that Aristides inserts between his accounts of the Egyptian expedition and the Peace, the orator praises the Athenians as guardians of Greece (I. 248): φυλάκων δ' ἐβίωσαν βίον. Aristides then expands upon this thought and points out that Athens' guardianship consisted in forestalling another Persian attack by completely reversing the fortune previously enjoyed by the King.[76] The reversal of fortune implies a transfer of fear, and, in the framing device of the *Pro Quattuorviris*, Aristides explicates the affinity between the theme of fear and what we might call the guardian motif:

1. Before the Battle of Eurymedon (II. 208): (Κίμων) τῆς Ἑλλάδος φυλακὴν ἀληθεστάτην ἡγεῖτο... εἰ τοῖς βαρβάροις φόβον ἐμβάλοι.... [77]

2. After the battle and leading into the Peace (II. 210): ... ἐκεῖνος φύλαξ ἦν τῆς Ἑλλάδος, οὐ μόνον τῆς ἑαυτοῦ πόλεως, καὶ τοιούτους ἐπικούρους τοῖς Ἕλλησι παρέσχετο, ὥστε ἕως ἔξη... [78]

The use of the guardian motif as a corollary of the theme of fear reflects the thematic structure of the relevant portion of Plato's *Menexenus*. Since the King was contemplating further action against Greece after Plataea, the Athenians carried the war to the Eurymedon, Cyprus, and Egypt.[79] As a result, the King was reduced to fear for his personal safety and sue for peace.[80]

If ancient authors naturally connected the reversal of the King's fortune with a transfer of fear to him, one can easily see how the motif of taming the King's excessive hybris could also be considered a corollary of the theme of fear. We noted in Chapter III that the view of Xerxes as a man of hybris, whose peripeteia the Athenians caused, goes back to the fifth-century tradition as found in Aeschylus and Herodotus.[81] Moreover, we saw that Aristides viewed the Peace as the culmination of this process of humbling the King.[82] Isocrates provides the oldest extant evidence for this tendency to link the Peace with the taming of the King's pride (*Paneg.* [4], 117): (βαρβάρους) ἡμεῖς διαβῆναι τολμήσαντας εἰς τὴν Εὐρώπην καὶ μεῖζον ἢ προσῆκεν αὐτοῖς φρονήσαντας οὕτω διέθεμεν, ὥστε... εἰς τοσαύτην ταπεινότητα.... Isocrates' version of the Peace follows this statement.[83] Ephorus exploited the same theme, if Diodorus is a reliable indication (T27): τὴν περιβόητον Περσῶν ἡγεμονίαν ἐπὶ τοσοῦτον ἐταπείνωσαν....[84] Plutarch, in turn, employed this wording for a framing device around his account of the Eurymedon and the Peace:

1. Before the battle (*Cim.* 12. 1): τοῦ μεγάλου βασιλέως οὐδεὶς ἐταπείνωσε καὶ συνέστειλε τὸ φρόνημα μᾶλλον ἢ Κίμων.

2. After the battle (*Cim.* 13. 4 = T35a): τοῦτο τὸ ἔργον οὕτως ἐταπείνωσε τὴν γνώμην τοῦ βασιλέως, ὥστε συνθέσθαι τὴν περιβόητον εἰρήνην.

Plutarch may have borrowed Ephorus' words, but he associated them very closely with a direct version of the theme of fear which he took from Callisthenes.[85] The latter framed his account of the Eurymedon with dual references to the theme of fear in very much the same way as Aristides in the *Pro Quattuorviris*:

1. Before the battle (*Cim.* 12. 2): (Κίμων) βουλόμενος αὐτοῖς ἄπλουν καὶ ἀνέμβατον ὅλως ὑπὸ φόβου τὴν ἐντὸς Χελιδονίων ποιήσασθαι θάλατταν.

2. After the battle (*Cim.* 13. 4 = T35b): ...ἔργῳ δὲ ποιεῖν διὰ φόβον τῆς ἥττης ἐκείνης....

These remarks of Plutarch, which in fact constitute Callisthenes' version of the Peace, have a serious implication for our understanding of the tradition. Callisthenes' historical sense may have prevented him from accepting the *de iure* existence of the Peace because of the impossible consequences of the traditional chronology; yet he still bowed to the old tradition as much as he could by making its chief rhetorical feature, the theme of fear, the very heart of his *de facto* Peace. The implication ought to be, not that Callisthenes was writing under the influence of an independent tradition which destroyed the credibility of the popular tradition, but that he knew of only one tradition of the Peace and aligned his version as closely with it as his own research allowed him.

When Aristides comes to the climax of his introductory remarks on the Peace in the *Panathenaicus,* he employs an even more allusive form of the theme of fear than Plutarch did. The orator implies that the transfer of fear to Persia corresponds to three successive stages in the King's policy towards Greece, the third of which constitutes his acceptance of the Peace (I. 248f.):

> *The King finally advanced to the point of realizing that his third policy was better, or rather more unavoidable, than his initial one. At first, you see, he intended to annex Greece and the rest of Europe to his empire; but he became aware that he was desiring impossibilities.*[86] *His second policy was to preserve the empire he already had, but Athens would not even tolerate that. Finally, he attached greater significance to his personal safety ... (passage A).*

The reversals in the King's policy appear as a version of the theme of fear throughout the fourth-century panegyric tradition. Lysias presents perhaps the most interesting evidence, since it is the oldest and very clearly demonstrates the importance of the theme of fear in the tradition of the Peace (T13): ὁ μέγας βασιλεὺς οὐκέτι τῶν ἀλλοτρίων ἐπεθύμει, ἀλλ' ἐδίδου τῶν ἑαυτοῦ καὶ περὶ τῶν λοιπῶν ἐφοβεῖτο.... These remarks occur in the context of only the vaguest chronology and a few hints at the terms of the Peace.[87] For Lysias, then, as for Callisthenes, the tradition of the Peace consisted primarily in the moral issue, the theme of fear. This theme could practically stand by itself as a reference to the Peace. Isocrates, of course, offers more details concerning the terms of the Peace but interprets the event just as Lysias does: he contrasts the original Persian intention of invading Greece with the later situation in which the Persians watched their own territory plundered and accepted the Peace.[88] Ephorus may have offered a similar contrast between the King's hostile intentions and eventual loss of hope.[89] Finally, the *Menexenus* also contains the contrast between the King's original plotting against the Greeks and his subsequent fear for his own safety.[90] Plato refers to this situation as a peace, εἰρήνη, but gives no other details. Even more than in Lysias' case, then, the theme of fear does service as an author's complete reference to the Peace.

Various scholars have condemned the versions of Lysias, Isocrates, and Plato as too untrustworthy to be seriously considered in an investigation of the Peace.[91] We noted earlier that scholars have also divided the sources into two or more groups, each of which supposedly reflects an independent tradition. Modern historians, however, have based their interpretations on literary analyses of various historical details concerning the Peace, particularly the terms and chronology. In an earlier part of this chapter, we saw that seemingly divergent details in literature can be reconciled with the concept of a single, living tradition of the Peace that survived virtually intact down to Aristides' day. Now we can confidently add that Aristides and his predecessors in the tradition were not primarily interested in these details at all, except as they had a bearing on the author's larger panegyric or historical context.[92] Ancient authors concentrated on the rhetorical essence, the moral meaning, of the last phase of the war; they viewed that conflict as a process whereby the Athenians transferred fear from the Greeks to the King, and they knew that there was a specific point where this conflict and this process came to a climax and ended. This theme of fear appears in such variety and in so many seemingly contradictory literary sources of the Peace, that it does not lend itself well to standard *Quellenforschung*. These difficult literary characteristics, however, lead me to suggest first, that at least until Aristides' time the theme of fear constituted a living, orally transmitted popular tradition of the Peace and, secondly, that the theme's universal appeal strongly implies that it was an integral part of the only true tradition of the Peace ever known to the ancient sources.

Anyone attempting to prove these suggestions must deal, in the first place, with a problem raised by the *Atthis*. Presumably the Atthidographers wrote a version of history that was very close to that of the fifth-century popular tradition.[93] This raises the possibility that what I have called evidence of an oral, unified, and universal tradition was, after Hellanicus, in fact merely one literary tradition amongst many. We have seen, however, that fourth-century orators give some indication of having written under the influence of a strong, oral tradition. Moreover, it is the contention of this chapter that Aristides provides evidence that an oral version of the tradition continued to exist, perhaps beside a similar written one, well into the second century of our era. We have already noted that Aristides' accounts of the details of the Peace show signs of the influence of a living tradition;[94] the evidence is stronger in the case of the theme of fear. The orator selected quite freely from the various versions of the terms and chronology of the Peace, but some overriding influence compelled him to construct a virtual compendium of testimonia for the theme of fear. There can be no question of borrowing from a single literary source, even an *Atthis*. In his unrelenting search for ἀκρίβεια, Aristides discovered the essence of the popular tradition of the Peace, which, I believe, could only have been brought home to him by the unified, oral tradition that was so clearly reflected in all the literary sources. In Chapter VII, I will suggest how the oral tradition of the Persian War could have been preserved down to Aristides' time.

The other problem obstructing our interpretation of the tradition is a familiar one to the students of the Peace: lack of fifth-century evidence. If Lysias and Plato wrote accurate versions of the traditional Epitaphios, it is possible to suggest that the later rhetorical tradition of the Peace as the completion of the transfer of fear to the King had its roots in the oral tradition of the Epitaphios in the fifth century. In addition to this conjecture, however, I should like to examine four sources of information that supply firmer evidence for the continuity of the popular tradition from the fifth to later centuries. My sources are Thucydides, Plutarch, certain Athenian monuments, and the Cyprus epigram.

We have seen that Thucydides gives a faithful version of the popular tradition of the Persian War in the speech that he put into the mouths of Athenian diplomats visiting Sparta in 432.[95] After discussing the war of freedom in Greece, the Athenians go on to defend their city against charges of aggression. They begin by pointing out three circumstances that forced them to maintain and even expand an empire: first there was fear, then honor, and finally profit.[96] Raubitschek has argued convincingly that these three circumstances represent the Athenians' conception of three chronological periods in the Pentecontaetia.[97] In the first period, the Athenians retained the empire because of their fear of a Persian counterattack.[98] In the second period, they received the honor of being the mistress of a great empire. Finally, they derived considerable financial profit from their holdings. The most serious objection to such an interpretation is Thucydides' failure to note in the Pentecontaetia two internal divisions that are required to make up the three periods. A divergence between speech and analysis in Thucydides, however, should not necessarily be viewed as an inconsistency. In the present case, Thucydides' own division of the fifth century into chronological units does not agree with that of the popular tradition; yet the historian correctly attributes to his

Athenian characters the common Attic view of chronology, which sharply differentiated the period of the Persian War from periods during which Hellenic interrelations were most important.[99] The second chronological period in the Athenian speech apparently extended to the transfer of the treasury of the League from Delos to Athens, after which the Athenians greatly profited from their collection of tribute.[100] The first period presumably included the time from 479 until some point at which the Greeks no longer needed to fear the King. Greeks of a later generation certainly knew that this point was the Peace of Callias. I have discussed the unity of the rhetorical tradition about the Peace, which was conceived of as the culmination of the process whereby the Greeks transferred fear to the King. This tradition extended from Lysias and Isocrates to Aristides. Moreover, it was accompanied by a tendency to date the Peace as soon as possible after the Battle of Eurymedon. Thucydides' Athenians clearly had in mind the same chronology, since, on the assumption that each of their three periods lasted at least a decade, the transfer of fear would have been completed ten years before the transfer of the treasury, i.e., not long after the Eurymedon.[101] From all this, I conclude that Thucydides consciously included in the Athenian speech a reference to the popular tradition of the Peace. Whether Thucydides knew of an actual document or simply reflected a popular opinion about Persia's essential capitulation to the Athenian offensive, his allusion to the Peace is just as decisive as that of the *Menexenus,* in which the theme of fear stands alone as a reference to the treaty. The fact that Thucydides did not include the Peace in his Pentecontaetia proves only that he did not attach enough significance to the phenomenon to give it a place in his compact narrative.

To support the conclusion of the preceding paragraph, I should like to discuss briefly the context that surrounds our supposed reference to the Peace. The Athenians divide the speech into two parts, each of which deals with one major theme.[102] In the first part, the speakers propound the thesis that Athens deserves her empire as a reasonable reward for her victories at Marathon and Salamis; in the second, they defend their city's imperial policies against charges of injustice. They allude to the Peace, as one would expect, when they begin their treatment of the second theme. Both themes were very much part of the rhetorical and popular tradition of the fifth and fourth centuries and almost certainly played a major role in the epitaphic tradition.[103] Herodotus and Thucydides himself, in the speech of Euphemus in Book VI, attest to the antiquity and popularity of the first theme.[104] So also, in a way, do Lysias and Isocrates, who employ their accounts of the Persian War to justify a second Athenian hegemony.[105] Defenses of Athenian imperialism appear in nearly every extant *Epitaphios* and many speeches that reflect the epitaphic tradition, but the most interesting for our purposes are those of Isocrates in the *Panegyricus* and Aristides in the *Panathenaicus*.[106] These defenses follow the lines dictated by the tradition in general, but they also reflect Thucydides' speech of the Athenians in particular.[107] Both later authors include in their defenses a comparison between the conduct of Athens and Sparta during the periods of their respective empires. So also, in Thucydides, the Athenians compare their empire with a hypothetical Spartan one, based on the supposition that Sparta had not abdicated her position as leader in 478. When Isocrates and Aristides come around to the question of foreign policy in their comparative defenses, they create a dramatic contrast between the treaties of Callias and Antalcidas. Clearly, then, fourth-century propaganda had something to do with their mentioning the Peace; yet the allusion to the theme of fear in the Athenians' speech corresponds structurally to the clear references to the Peace in Isocrates and Aristides. I would conclude from this that a reference to the Peace, particularly in its aspect of completing the transfer of fear to the King, was already a rhetorical formula for use in popular Athenian defenses of the empire by the time Thucydides wrote and perhaps by 432.[108] The connection between the Peace and the empire, however, is probably even older.

Whether or not there was a Peace of Callias, Pericles clearly revised Athens' position within the Delian League and her relationship with the allies near the middle of the fifth century.[109] Pericles attempted to transform the fighting alliance, which the Oath and Covenant of Plataea and other agreements had established, into what Raubitschek calls an Athenian Amphictyony. Although Thucydides ignores any such purposeful transition, the popular tradition and inscriptional evidence prove its existence by preserving, among other things, the Congress Decree, the transfer of the treasury, and Pericles' building program.[110] These events seem to make most sense in the context of a peace with Persia,[111] but Plutarch's report of a public Athenian debate on Pericles' building policy could prove to be a stumbling block to such an interpretation.¹¹² Pericles' opponents on this issue argue that Demos will suffer damage to its reputation for transferring the treasury from Delos to Athens. They say that Pericles himself has destroyed the only acceptable excuse for the transfer, namely, that fear of the barbarians impelled Athens to move the treasury in order to protect it. The allies will consider themselves tyrannized, if they see the money that is extracted from them 'for the war' put to work on buildings in Athens. Pericles replies that no accounting is owed to the allies as long as the Athenians are doing their duty, προπολεμοῦντες αὐτῶν καὶ τοὺς βαρβάρους ἀνείργοντες. Scholars normally interpret the passage as strong evidence against the Peace: Pericles destroyed the excuse for transferring the treasury simply by using the money for his building program, and his reply to his opponents implies that the war was still in progress.¹¹³ Against this view, however, I should like to suggest that, especially if the passage has been garbled in transmission, another interpretation is possible. As to Pericles' reply, no one claims that a Peace of Callias, much less a *de facto* cessation of hostilities, issued in a period of mutual disarmament and complete trust between Athens and Persia.¹¹⁴ Whatever balance existed was a balance of power, so that, in a sense, Pericles could still describe the Athenians as προπολεμοῦντες even after hostilities had stopped. In fact, ἀνείργοντες aptly describes Athens' imposition of naval and territorial limits on Persia. Furthermore, I note with interest that the opposing party says that fear of Persia *is* the only honorable excuse; they do not say it *was* the excuse that was made. Thus, I believe it is possible that Pericles' opponents were saying that he had destroyed the excuse, perhaps even before the transfer of the treasury, by destroying the fear, that is, by making peace with Persia. If this is true, we have found another example of the theme of fear used as a reference to the Peace. Moreover, this passage may be a very early example, since there is nothing to suggest that Plutarch's story does not reflect a real event.¹¹⁵

Tenuous as the foregoing conclusion might seem to be, one can add considerable support to it by reviewing the nature of several of the monuments that Pericles actually sponsored. The statue of Athena Promachos symbolized Athens' position in the forefront of the war for freedom.¹¹⁶ The stoa of Zeus Eleutherios was erected to enhance the Persian War monument that had grown up around an old sanctuary of Zeus.¹¹⁷ The building of the Telesterion at Eleusis reflected the importance of the cult of Demeter, Persephone, and Triptolemus in Pericles' newly organized and religiously oriented Athenian Amphictyony.[118] Similarly, the Parthenon's frieze would point up the importance of the *Panathenaea* in the new alliance, and the metopes, of course, symbolized the Persian War.[119] Finally, there was the Temple of Athena Nike, which bore a frieze depicting Greeks fighting barbarians.[120] Although the Spartans thwarted the full application of the proposals of the Congress Decree throughout Greece, these monuments show that Pericles implemented at least its first two proposals within the Athenian league.[121] The first proposal would have abrogated the prohibition in the Oath of Plataea against rebuilding temples destroyed by the Persians; the forerunners of the Telesterion, Parthenon, and Temple of Nike had been destroyed by Xerxes.[122] The second clause concerned offerings to the gods in fulfillment of vows made during the war; all the monuments and the religious practices they symbolized fall into the category of such offerings. All of this means that these monuments symbolized, not simply Athens' glorious conduct of the Persian War, but the *end* of that war, the fulfillment of the purpose of the wartime alliance, the beginning of a new period of peace. In a very real sense, then, these monuments are testimonia for the Peace, *de facto* if not *de iure*.[123] And it was a peace with victory, as we can see in the significance of the Temple of Nike and also the statue of Athena, which Demosthenes called a victory-prize of the war against the barbarians.[124]

The theme of victory leads nicely into my final testimonium, the Cyprus epigram. In Chapter IV, we concluded that the poem commemorates, on the surface, the Athenian victory during Cimon's last expedition to Cyprus. This event is praised in such overblown terms, however, that the epigrammatist seems to have viewed it as the victorious conclusion of the whole Persian War.[125] Thus, the poem came to be connected with the Peace, and Isocrates could allude to it as though it were a reference to the Peace. If, as seems likely, Isocrates reflected a genuine popular tradition of the fifth century about the poem, the last distich could have important implications for the present discussion:

... μέγα δ'ἔστενεν Ἀσὶς ὑπ' αὐτῶν
πληγεῖσ' ἀμφοτέραις χερσὶ κράτει πολέμου.

We noted in the earlier chapter that κράτος πολέμου is a poetic term for victory, but what is especially interesting for us is the virtual definition of victory which the lines give: making Asia groan on land and sea. This clearly illustrates one variation of our theme of fear: the tendency to view the last phase of the war as a transfer of war from Europe to Asia, a harming of the King's own territory, and forcing him to fear for his homeland. Whatever the epigrammatist intended to glorify, one can easily see why and how his connection between victory and the humbling of Asia occupied a place in the popular tradition of the Peace in the fifth century.

This chapter should close with a summary of my beliefs about the historiography of the Peace of Callias in order to clarify points that may have become clouded in the details of the preceding arguments. The contention that one tradition of the Peace existed in the fifth century forms the basis of my reconstruction of the historiography. Those who do not accept the literal existence of the Peace would say that this tradition arose, purely in the manner of a popular legend, from the knowledge that the Athenian victories, or more especially the victory at the Eurymedon, led to a transfer of fear to the King and eventually a cessation of hostilities. This 'legend' became what was to remain the heart of the oral version of the tradition; yet beside it there was an Athenian version of certain diplomatic events that implied the existence of the Peace but in no way contradicted the content of the 'legend.' These events are preserved in Herodotus' recollection of Callias' mission to Persia,[126] other stories about Callias,[127] the tradition of the Congress Decree and the results of it including the Athenian monuments, Aristophanes' knowledge of embassies to Persia,[128] Andocides' story of the Peace of Epilycus, and Thucydides' versions of the Spartan treaties with Persia towards the end of the Peloponnesian War. Thucydides was undoubtedly aware of the Peace and other events such as the Congress Decree, but he did not consider them significant in the context and limited scope of his Pentecontaetia. Thucydides' silence, then, does not imply that the Peace never existed, but that the fifth century did not consider it so monumental an event as later ages did.[129]

The early tradition was transmitted primarily through oral media such as the *Epitaphios*, family traditions, scolia and other poetry, and an awareness of the meaning of various monuments. Moreover, although there is no specific, extant evidence for a parallel in a literary medium, one can certainly assume the existence of such a version in the *Atthis*.[130] The fourth century, however, witnessed the appearance of a third medium, a stele that bore a copy of the Peace of Callias. The Athenians seem to have erected this monument beside their copy of the Peace of Antalcidas, in order to prove that their city had made a more glorious peace with Persia than the Spartans had. In this way, the Peace of Callias became a political issue and achieved the proportions of a monumental event only after the year 386.[131] To be sure, the stele does not represent a new infusion of information about the Peace from an independent tradition: we have seen ample evidence to show that the fifth-century form of the 'legend' remained virtually unchanged, and the valuable testimony of Lysias shows that, although the version on the stele may have contained some additional details, the terms of the Peace were essentially the same in the tradition before and after the publication of that document. Either the stele was forged so that specific terms were fourth-century inventions created on the model of the older tradition, or it was a genuine publication of negotiations between Persia and Athens that had been put away in the records chamber after they occurred and only vaguely remembered in the popular mentality.

All sources for the Peace that are to be dated after the publication of the stele can be explained in terms of their reliance on the old, oral tradition, the stele itself, or their own analysis of these forms of the received tradition. The oral version continued to influence many authors, especially the orators, at least until the time of Aristides.[132] I think it possible that Ephorus' account owed much to the *Atthis*, but, barring that, one can see how he constructed it from Isocrates, the stele, and his own chronological investigation. An apparently similar chronological analysis, together with the oral tradition and the stele, explains what we know about Callisthenes' version, and the stele alone seems to have incurred the wrath of Theopompus. Plutarch and the other late sources except Aristides derived their information from the fourth-century literary accounts which we have just noted.[133] Aristides himself, however, has served as the pivotal point of our discussion, and I hope that we have derived at least three worthwhile conclusions from our analysis of his text. The first is that, in spite of his thorough familiarity with all the sources, his accounts do not reveal a knowledge of any contradictions in the various versions that could only be explained by postulating the existence of an alternative tradition. The second point is that Aristides' accounts, particularly the earlier two in the

Panathenaicus, indicate the survival of the oral form of the tradition down to his own day. Finally, and this is his greatest contribution to our understanding of the tradition, Aristides knew that all versions, literary and oral, shared the same essence, the same ethical meaning, that they all proved the same point to the person who examined them μετ'ἀκριβείας. This is evidence for the unity of the tradition that we should not lightly dismiss.

1. For the way in which the other battles against the Persians received short shrift in comparison to Marathon, Salamis, and the Peace, cf. *supra,* Chapter IV, p. 96.
2. For the ancient testimonia, cf. Appendix I. For ancient comments on the popularity of the topic, cf. Demosthenes (T17: συνῦῆκαι... ἃς ἅπαντες ἐγκωμιάζουσι; T18: ὑρυλουμένην...); Plutarch (T35a: περιβόητον εἰρήνην); and possibly Theopompus (T30, T31).
3. T28 and T35, respectively.
4. T35b and T30, T31, respectively; cf. Pausanias (T37).
5. For a history of the scholarship on the question, cf. Meiggs, *Athenian Empire,* pp. 487-503; De Ste. Croix, *Origins,* pp. 310-14; C. Schrader, *La Paz de Calias: Testimonios y Interpretación* (Barcelona: Universidad de Barcelona, Instituto de Estudios Helenicos, 1976). This last work contains the most thorough analysis of ancient testimonia and a full summary of modern scholarship as well as the author's original research. Unfortunately, the present chapter was essentially complete before the book was published. I have taken note of some important points in the book but have not had the opportunity to incorporate the work into my analysis in the manner it deserves. I should mention here, however, that Schrader disagrees with my major premise, that there was never more than one ancient tradition of the Peace. I also tend to believe that our sources reflect a genuine fifth-century peace, whereas Schrader does not. For other recent scholarship which has influenced my thought but was prevented from being added to the notes by the exigencies of publication, see the Bibliography. The most important for my purposes is, J.H. Schreiner, "More Anti-Thukydidean Studies in the Pentekontaetia," *SO* 52 (1977) 19-38.
6. For the Peace of Epilycus, cf. T10. Theopompus (T30) may also refer to this treaty, if we allow Δαρεῖον to stand, *pace* Spengel, Schwartz, and Jacoby, who excise it. A full discussion of the evidence appears in H.T. Wade-Gery, "The Peace of Kallias," *Athenian Studies presented to W.S. Ferguson: Harvard Studies in Classical Philology,* Suppl. vol. I (1940), pp. 127-32, who suggests that this peace was a renewal of that of Callias. However, H.B. Mattingly, "The Peace of Kallias," *Hist.* 14 (1965) 273f., believes that in the fourth century people simply began applying the terms of Epilycus' treaty to a purely fictitious peace of the fifth century. R. Sealey, "The Peace of Callias Once More," *Hist.* 3 (1955) 328f., argues that nobody confused the two treaties, and C.L. Murison, "The Peace of Callias: Its Historical Context," *Phoenix* 25 (1971) 25, 30, denies the existence of the later peace altogether. For the Peace of Antalcidas, cf. Isocrates (T1, T14, T19), Demosthenes (T17), and Diodorus (T29), all of whom illustrate the popularity of contrasting Callias' and Antalcidas' peaces. Cf. also, A.E. Raubitschek, "The Treaties between Persia and Athens," *GRBS* 5 (1964) 151-59.

7. For the possible documentary evidence, cf. T1-T11.

8. Although my approach is different, I would repeat the dictum of E. Schwartz, "Kallisthenes Hellenika," *Hermes* 35 (1900) 111: der Vertrag mit Persien oder der sogenannte Kalliasfrieden ist kein Problem der politischen sondern der litterarischen Geschichte. Cf. A.E. Raubitschek, "Inschriften als Hilfsmittel der Geschichtsforschung," *RSA* 1 (1971) 189.

9. T14. For the date of the *Panegyricus,* cf. R.C. Jebb, *The Attic Orators,* Vol. II (London: Macmillan, 1893), p. 148.

10. For the belief that the Peace was invented for use as propaganda, cf. Sealey, *supra,* n. 6; D. Stockton, "The Peace of Callias," *Hist.* 8 (1959) 61-79; Mattingly, *supra,* n. 6; M. Sordi, "La propaganda del mondo greco," *RSA* 1 (1971) 205-11; Murison, *supra,* n. 6, makes the suggestion that Isocrates invented the Peace; C. Habicht, "Falsche Urkunden zur Geschichte Athens im Zeitalter der Perserkriege," *Hermes* 89 (1961) 25f.

11. Cf., primarily, Raubitschek, *supra,* n. 8, p. 187f. Numerous attempts have been made to explain the silence of the fifth century. A. Andrewes, "Thucydides and the Persians," *Hist.* 10 (1961) 1-18, sees that historian's silence as a result of his ignorance of the importance of relations with Persia in the Peloponnesian War. Others, such as Meyer, *Forschungen,* p. 81, and H. Bengtson, *Griechische Geschichte* (München: Beck, 1969), p. 212, have viewed the Peace as less than an unqualified success for Athenian policy. Their theories would explain much, but they have been strongly challenged by K. Kraft, "Bemerkungen zu den Perserkriegen," *Hermes* 92 (1964) 166f.: cf. also U. Kahrstedt, "Sparta und Persien in der Pentekontaetie," *Hermes* 56 (1921) 324ff.

12. Isocrates (T14); Craterus (T35c). Cf. Murison, *supra,* n. 6, p. 17, and Sealey, *supra,* n. 6, p. 329.

13. The assumption behind the earlier date is that the document was meant to stand in contrast to the Peace of Antalcidas: cf. *supra,* Chapter IV, p. 91 f.; Stockton, *supra,* n. 10, p. 72; Raubitschek, *supra,* n. 8, p. 187f. For the later date, cf. Habicht, *supra,* n.10, p.26; Murison, *supra,* n.6, p.17; Schrader, *supra,* n.5, pp. 29f., 180.

14. One might discern four independent traditions: (1) the tradition of Callisthenes, in which a *de facto* peace is dated to the 460's; Murison, cf. *supra,* n. 6, p. 27f., sees this as the most likely time for an unfruitful series of negotiations between Athens and Persia; (2) the tradition of Diodorus-Ephorus, who place the Peace after the end of the Egyptian affair; (3) Theopompus and Andocides, who refer to a treaty of the 420's; (4) the *Menexenus* (T15) may refer to a truce that belongs after the final Athenian defeat in Egypt and is alluded to by Ctesias (65) and Diodorus (XI. 77. 4f.). For the last possibility, cf. Murison, p. 14. Cf. also W.R. Connor, *Theopompus and Fifth-Century Athens* (Washington: Center for Hellenic Studies and Harvard, 1968), pp. 84f.; 172, nn. 25 and 26. Concerning the identity of the Athenian who was responsible for the Peace, cf. *supra,* Chapter IV, pp. 85ff.

15. Cf. Murison, *supra,* n. 6, p. 20; Sordi, *supra,* n. 10, p. 205f.

16. *Ibid.,* pp. 21, 30f. Murison himself believes that Isocrates invented the Peace and that a forged stele was eventually erected, probably in the 340's. The value of his discussion of the tradition's unity, however, is great even for those who solve the literary problem differently. Cf. Mattingly, *supra,* n. 6, p. 276.

17. The exception is the widespread attention which the rhetorical theme of comparison between the peaces of Callias and Antalcidas has received amongst scholars. Interest has been focused on this topic, however, primarily to support theories about a stele, and the unfortunate result has been an unwillingness to search for hints of rhetorical themes and formulae from the period before the publication of the stele.

18. For Isocrates' initial vagueness, cf. T14. These and Aristides' other opening remarks convinced J. Haury, *Quibus fontibus Aristides usus sit in declamatione quae inscribitur Παναθηναικός* (Diss. Augsburg, 1888), pp. 20ff., that Isocrates was Aristides' source for the Peace.

19. The text reads, εἰς τοῦτο κατῆλθεν, but the Scholion explains (III. 214): ἐταπεινώθη. Forms of ταπεινόω are used in the same context in T14, T27, and T35a.

20. Cf. the Scholion (III. 215): . . . στεφάνου] ὡς ἐπὶ στεφάνου εἶπε, σημαίνων δόξαν καὶ νίκην.

21. The effect of the autonomy clause is noted in B (ἐλευθερίαν) and perhaps hinted at in D, "your dominion is not fixed..."

22. The expression "in all directions" in B probably represents rhetorical exaggeration on the part of Aristides himself: cf. the Scholion (III.215).

23. Diodorus' account is essentially that of Ephorus: cf. *supra*, Chapter IV, p. 77f.

24. *Ibid.*, esp. p. 77, where the passage is cited.

25. *Historischen Angaben*, p. 55f. The similarities cannot be denied:

   1. Land limits:
      a. Aristides, passage B: θαλάττης δ' ἀφέξειν ἴσον πανταχῇ σταδίους πεντακοσίους.
      b. Passage C: τῆς ἵππου δρόμον ἡμέρας τῆς θαλάττης ἀποσχήσεις.
      c. Demosth. (T18): ἵππου μὲν δρόμον ἡμέρας πεζῇ μὴ καταβαίνειν ἐπὶ τὴν θάλατταν.
      d. Plut. (T35a): ἵππου μὲν δρόμον ἀεὶ τῆς Ἑλληνικῆς ἀπέχειν θαλάσσης.
      e. Plut. (T36): οὐδ' ἵππος πρὸς θαλάσσῃ τετρακοσίων σταδίων.

   2. Naval limits:
      a. Aristides, passage B: δυοῖν μὲν ὅροιν εἴσω μηκέτι πλευσεῖσθαι, πρὸς μεσημβρίαν μὲν χελιδονέας, πρὸς δὲ ἄρκτον Κυανέας...
      b. Passage C: οὐ γὰρ ἐᾷ πλεῖν εἴσω Χελιδονέων καὶ Κυανέων.
      c. Demosth. (T18): ἐντὸς δὲ Χελιδονίων καὶ Κυανέων πλοίῳ μακρῷ μὴ πλεῖν.
      d. Plut. (T35a): ἔνδον δὲ Κυανέων καὶ Χελιδονίων μακρᾷ νηὶ καὶ χαλκεμβόλῳ μὴ πλέειν.

   3. Autonomy clause:
      a. Aristides, passages A and B: ἀλλὰ καὶ τοὺς τὴν ἐκείνου χώραν κατοικοῦντας ...δυοῖν μὲν ὅροιν.
      b. Lycurgus (T20): ὅρους τοῖς βαρβάροις πήξαντες... ἀλλὰ καὶ τοὺς τὴν Ἀσίαν κατοικοῦντας.

Beecke's analysis, it should be noted, involves a certain contradiction. He insists that Aristides' divergence from Diodorus (T28) in the matter of naval limits proves that the latter was definitely not a source for the account in the *Panathenaicus*. Diodorus and Lycurgus, however, are remarkably similar: they alone besides the Souda (T43) have a specific autonomy clause, and they alone list Phaselis and the Cyaneans as the sole naval limits. This similarity also extends to these authors' citations of the Oath of Plataea (Diod. XI. 29. 3; *Leoc*. 81; Theopompus may have coupled the Oath with the Peace in his condemnation of the popular tradition: cf. T30, and Connor, *supra*, n.

14, p. 82). A possible conclusion of all this is that Diodorus' source (Ephorus) and Lycurgus employed a common source. In Chapter IV we identified that source as the oral tradition.

26. Cf. *supra*, Chapter IV, p. 85ff.

27. Presumably the Peace followed the battle by no more than five years in this version.

28. Cf. *supra*, Chapter IV, p. 75ff.

29. Aristides' preference is made quite clear when we compare passage C with passage E (*supra*, p. 151).

30. Cf. *art. cit.*, *supra*, n. 6.

31. *Ibid.*, pp. 133-36, where Wade-Gery interprets the tribute clause (Isocrates, T14) as an Athenian agreement to allow Persia to collect tribute in Ionia and connects it with two other clauses that seem to favor Persia: the non-aggression clause (Diodorus, T28: cf. *supra*, p. 148f.) and an agreement on Athens' part to dismantle the fortifications of Ionia (T4). The tribute clause and the matter of the fortifications have been much debated, and Wade-Gery's theses have not been accepted: cf. *ATL* III. 275; Murison, *supra*, n. 6, p. 28, n. 62; Meiggs, *Athenian Empire*, p. 149; Schrader, *supra*, n. 5, pp. 142-45.

32. Passage B: cf. J.H. Oliver, "The Peace of Callias and the Pontic Expedition of Pericles," *Hist.* 6 (1957) 254f.; Meiggs, *Athenian Empire*, p. 492.

33. They were even more commonly known as the Symplegades: cf. Oliver, *ibid.*, p. 255, *pace*, besides Wade-Gery, Sealey, *supra*, n. 6, p. 330. The scholiast on Aristides mentions the Symplegades (T44).

34. Murison, cf. *supra*, n. 6, p. 20f., is the most successful, and the following discussion owes much to him. Schrader, cf. *supra*, n. 5, p. 119f., warns against the dangers of such a process.

35. T14, T19.

36. Wade-Gery interpreted the clause literally and joined it with the other versions to construct a demilitarized zone by land. He was followed by Mattingly, cf. *supra*, n. 6, p. 277, and Andrewes, cf. *supra*, n. 11, pp. 16-18. Sordi, cf. *supra*, n. 10, p. 208, calls attention to Isoc. *Paneg.* (4), 144 (Agesilaus' conquest to the Halys) and 162 (the catchwords, Cnidus to Sinope, which form a concept that is essentially the same as a 'Halys-line').

37. Cf. Thuc. I. 16, for the Halys as the traditional limit of Persian power. Schrader, cf. *supra*, n. 5, pp. 119f., 121, and 177, mentions other examples from the fifth century.

38. Demosthenes (T18, and cited by Schol. Aristid., T44); Plutarch (T35a); Aristides, passages C and D; Himerius (T39); the Souda (T43).

39. Diodorus/Ephorus (T28). Presumably Aristodemus (T38), who speaks of three days' ride by horse, represents a clumsy attempt to reconcile Ephorus with the rest of the tradition. Schrader, cf. *supra*, n. 5, p. 64, mentions the possibility of a textual problem in Aristodemus.

40. Plutarch (T36).

41. Hdt. V. 53f.; the historian contradicts himself slightly by saying, first, that the normal rate was 150 stadia and, second, that the three-day journey from Ephesus to

Sardis comprised 540 stadia. Cf. Xen. *Hell.* III. 2. 11. One should also note that, on the Royal Road from Sardis to Susa, the Persians located stations an average of every 120 stadia.

42. Cf. Oliver, *supra,* n. 32, p. 255. Herodotus himself, in the passage mentioned in the preceding note, is at pains to translate the Persian system of parasangs into stadia or days' walks. I presume that the one day's ride was the 'original' form of the inscribed version of the Peace; it certainly seems to have been used in Craterus' document if we can assume that Plutarch (T35a) and Demosthenes (T18) did not contradict the published version: cf. Schrader, *supra,* n. 5, p. 194.

43. One would certainly like to know whether Aristides' dramatic reading from the treaty in passage C had a literary precedent. Whether or not Aristides invented the passage, however, it demonstrates the orator's knowledge of fifth-century feeling. A limit on the King's navy was one thing, but the Persians were known to be particularly proud of their army and within it the cavalry ranked highest: cf. Aesch. *Pers.* 26, 32, 46f., 95ff., 126f., 598ff., *et passim.*

44. Plutarch's 400 stadia (T36) appears in a context that is too vague to be considered a possible source for Aristides' 500 stadia in passage B. Aristides must have worked from a knowledge of the real distance involved; the use of stadia was no doubt suggested to him by his own exaggerated use of the word a few lines earlier in passage A.

45. After Aristides, it seems, the standard form became frozen, so that the tradition had no existence independent of the form: cf. *supra,* n. 38. Aristodemus is perhaps the exception, although cf. *supra,* n. 39.

46. T18 and T35a, respectively. Cf. *supra,* nn. 38 and 39, for the same dichotomy in the land limits. Schrader, of course, takes this as evidence for the existence of a panegyric tradition which is reflected by Ephorus and independent of the one that influenced the makers of the stele.

47. Isocrates (T14, T16, T19); Ephorus-Diodorus (T28). Perhaps Isocrates gives only the southeastern limit because it would especially thrill the Greeks, who had long feared the Phoenician menace. There does not seem to have been a serious Persian naval threat from the Black Sea. Thus, the northern limit would seem unessential to an author who wished to convey to his audience the unilateral character of the Peace. The northern limit, of course, makes sense only in terms of a bilateral agreement: cf. Wade-Gery, *art. cit., supra,* n. 6.

48. T20.

49. Cf. Sordi, *supra,* n. 10, p. 208. We should not forget that the Chelidonians and Phaselis are, after all, relatively close points: cf. Murison, *supra,* n. 6, p. 20f.

50. T43, T38, and T45, respectively.

51. Cf. *infra,* n. 130.

52. T28, T29.

53. Cf. *supra,* Chapter IV, p. 85.

54. Cf. M. Cary, "The Peace of Callias," *CQ* 39 (1945) 89.

55. T20 and T43, respectively.

56. T18 and T35, respectively.

57. Cf. *supra,* n. 5, pp. 140-46.

58. Cf. *supra*, Chapter IV, p. 91 f. Schrader, *ibid.*, pp. 29f., 180, and Murison, cf. *supra*, n. 6, pp. 21, 30f., date the publication of the stele between Demosthenes' two references, that is, between 352 B.C. (T17) and 343 B.C. (T18).

59. I note that both authors employed Phaselis as a naval limit, and both were familiar with the monuments in the area where the stele stood, i.e., the Peace of Antalcidas and the Cyprus epigram.

60. As Schrader does, cf. *supra*, n. 5, p. 146.

61. I note with interest that the Chelidonians, which are a sure sign of a second tradition for Schrader, appear in the opening section of the highly rhetorical theme of fear which surrounds Plutarch's account of the Battle of Eurymedon. I attribute this frame to Callisthenes, who in turn borrowed it from the panegyric tradition: cf.*supra*, p. 153.

62. T13; cf. Schrader, *supra*, n. 5, p. 54. Stockton, cf. *supra*, n. 10, p. 70, refuses to accept Lysias as a testimonium for the Peace but is refuted by Meiggs, *Athenian Empire*, p. 137.

63. For autonomy, cf. the Peace of Nicias (Thuc. V. 18. 5); the treaty between Sparta and Argos (Thuc. V. 77. 5; 79. 1); Athens' agreement with Selymbria (*IG* I² 116 = *ML* 87); the alliance with Samos (*IG* II² 1 = *ML* 94). For the bilateral nature of Greek treaties in general, cf. Schrader, *supra*, n. 5, p. 104f., and, for a more specific parallel, cf. *IG* I² 57 = *ML* 65: Athens proposes to deal with Perdiccas in a highhanded manner which would recall to some her behavior towards Artaxerxes in the middle of the fifth century. Nevertheless, one subclause in 21f. (καὶ μέτε ἀδικέν μ[έ]τε [ἀ]ὀ[ικέο] - /[ϑαι])confers at least a feeling of reciprocality on the proposed peace.

64. This applies to the first two treaties (T11a and T11b) but not the third (T11c). The Peace of Antalcidas, of course, completely repealed that of Callias by ceding the πόλεις to the King (T11e). Cf. De Ste. Croix, *Origins*, p. 313; Wade-Gery, *supra*, n. 6, p. 146f.

65. For the definition of autonomy in the Peace of Callias, cf. H. Schaefer, "Die Autonomie-Klausel des Kalliasfriedens," in *Probleme der alten Geschichte* (Göttingen: Vandenhöck und Ruprecht, 1963), pp. 253-68. Unfortunately for our discussion, Schaefer's article is primarily concerned with relations between Athens and the Asiatic cities.

66. For autonomy, cf. T28 and T29; for freedom, cf. T27.

67. T20.

68. The same implication probably exists in passage D, "your dominion is not fixed..."

69. Cf. *supra*, n. 6, p. 20.

70. I note with interest the verbal similarity between Plutarch (T35a), ἐταπείνωσε...ὥστε...περιβόητον, and Diodorus (T27), περιβόητον...ἐταπείνωσαν, ὥστε.... If they had a common source (?Ephorus), or if their sources (Callisthenes and Ephorus, respectively) had a common source (?the *Atthis*), then apparently that source was worded in such a way that imitators could cite the territorial limits in various ways and omit the autonomy clause altogether without serious contradiction.

These characteristics, however, are typical of oral, rather than literary tradition. Cf. *infra*, n. 93.

71. T11e.

72. T14.

73. The same implication exists in the *Panathenaicus* (T19), where Antalcidas' treaty

is said to allow the barbarians to sail wherever they wish and to become despots in Greek cities. This passage is, in fact, quite similar to that of Lysias, which was noted above. Cf. also, T16. I should also mention that Isocrates' tribute clause (T14) might have had something to do with the autonomy of the Greek cities: cf. Meiggs, *Athenian Empire*, p. 148, and Cary, *supra*, n. 54, pp. 87-91.

74. The theme continues later in the introduction (I. 244): νῦν δ' ὅτε ἡ ἀρχὴ περιέστηκεν εἰς δικαίου τάξιν, εὖ καὶ καλῶς εἴσεσθε τίνας κεκινήκατε. For the fear inspired by Persia earlier in the war, cf. *supra*, Chapter III, p. 43f.

75. According to Behr, *Sacred Tales*, pp. 87 and 94, the *Panath*. should be dated to A.D. 155 and the *Pro Quatt*. to ca. 161-165. However, Oliver, *Civilizing Power*, p. 34, dates the *Panath*. to 167.

76. I.248.

77. There is an overall similarity here between *Panath.* and *Pro Quatt.*:

Panath.(I. 244): πρὸς δὲ τούτοις καὶ τῶν Ἑλλήνων ἀσφάλειαν εἶναι καὶ σωτηρίαν ὑπελάμβανεν οὐκ εἰ καθείρξασα αὐτοὺς ἐπὶ τῆς ἑστίας τηροίη... ἀλλ' εἰ τοὺς βαρβάρους ὡς ἐπὶ πλεῖστον ὤσαιντο ἀπὸ τῆς Ἑλλάδος.

Pro Quatt. (II. 208): πρὸς δὲ τούτοις καὶ τῆς Ἑλλάδος φυλακὴν ἀληθεστάτην ἡγεῖτο οὐκ εἰ καθείρξας αὐτοὺς οἴκοι παρέχοι... ἀλλ'... εἰ τῆς Ἑλλάδος αὐτοὺς ἀπώσαιτο ὡς δυνατὸν πορρωτάτω.

78. Plutarch (T36) presents a very similar view of Cimon's campaigns in the eastern Mediterranean.

79. *Menex.* 241d, where the Athenians are described as ἀνακαθηράμενοι καὶ ἐξελάσαντες πᾶν τὸ βάρβαρον ἐκ τῆς θαλάττης. Aristides probably had this passage in mind when he wrote, earlier in this part of his narrative, ...ὥσπερ ἄγος καθαίροντες... (I. 245). Himerius (T39) borrows Aristides' very words: ...ὥσπερ ἄγος καθήραντες.... As to the general scheme of these remarks in Plato and Aristides, another late source, the scholiast on Hermogenes, conveys essentially the same idea in T45: Artaxerxes plans to attack Ionia, is deprived of hope, and must accept the terms of the Peace. In his account of the Peace itself and the following passages, though not in his use of this thematic element, the scholiast is nearly identical to Aristodemus. One suspects that they had a common source, probably either Ephorus or the *Atthis*: cf. *supra*, n. 39; *infra*, n. 130.

80. T15. In a sense, the guardian motif is as old as Pindar (fr. 76, Snell): Ἑλλάδος ἔρεισμα, κλειναὶ Ἀθᾶναι. As Aristides makes clear, however, the point of applying the motif to the last phase of the war is not that Athens merely acted as a shield, but that she defended Greece by turning the tables on the King: Athens' defense of Greece became the attack on Asia. This is how the guardian motif can be considered a corollary of the theme of fear in the context of the last phase of the war. Pindar is too early to be glorifying the attack on Asia, but one can see the concept clearly in the last distich of the Cyprus epigram: cf.*supra*,p. 160.

81. Cf. *supra*, Chapter III, p. 52ff.

82. *Ibid.*, p. 44f.

83. T14. Cf. also, T16 and T19.

84. Ephorus seems to have made much of the theme of fear and the King's reversal: cf. Diod. XII. 1. 2f., a passage which precedes T27 by just a few lines. Cf. also, *supra*, n. 79.

85. Cf. *supra*, Chapter IV, p. 76f.

86. The theme of the King's reversal continues between passages A and B: "in fact, the King possessed all the earth up to Attica, until he met the men of Attica on the sea..."

87. The chronology is essentially the same as that of Isocrates (T14): cf. *infra*, n. 108 and Appendix II. For the land limits, cf. ἐδίδου τῶν ἑαυτοῦ. For the naval limit in concrete terms, cf. οὔτε τριήρεις... For an allusion to the autonomy clause, cf. *supra*, p. 149. Cf. Schrader, *supra*, n. 5, p. 54.
88. T14.
89. T45; cf. *supra*, n. 79.
90. T15.
91. For Isocrates, cf. Habicht, *supra*, n. 10, p. 26; Sealey, *supra*, n. 6, p. 332; Murison, *supra*, n. 6, p. 13. For Plato, cf. Murison, p. 14. For Lysias, cf. Stockton, *supra*, n. 10, p. 70.
92. Such, for example, would be the constant attempts to compare the treaties of Callias and Antalcidas or other intrusions of fourth-century propaganda, including the making of the stele. Such also would be Ephorus' and Callisthenes' attempts to organize the chronology of the period.
93. Cf. *supra*, nn. 70 and 79; *infra*, n. 130.
94. Cf. *supra*, p. 145ff.
95. Cf. *supra*, Chapter III, pp. 55ff., and Appendix II.
96. T12.
97. A.E. Raubitschek, "The Speech of the Athenians at Sparta," in *The Speeches in Thucydides: A Collection of Original Studies*, ed. by P. Stadter (Chapel Hill: University of North Carolina, 1973), pp. 41-44.
98. In thus interpreting the 'fear' as fear of Persia, Raubitschek is in agreement with Gomme, *HCT* I. 235, and H.-P. Stahl, *Thukydides: Die Stellung des Menschen im geschichtlichen Prozess* (*Zetemata* 40: Munich, 1966), p. 47. Against such an interpretation is the fact that "fear" immediately below (I. 76. 2) and in the speech of Euphemus (VI. 83. 4) refers to the fear of rebelling allies: cf. also Aristid. *Panath.* I. 288f.
99. Cf. *supra*, Chapter III, p. 62f.
100. This, too, of course, was not mentioned by Thucydides.
101. Cf. Raubitschek, *supra*, n. 97, p. 41.
102. *Ibid.*, pp. 36-42; cf. Appendix II.
103. For the origin of many rhetorical themes in the *Epitaphios*, cf. *infra*, Chapter VII, n. 21.
104. For Herodotus, cf. his famous interpretation of Athens' part in the war at VII. 139. 5, and the Athenian speech before Plataea at IX. 27. For Euphemus' comments, cf. Thuc. VI. 82f. Cf. Raubitschek, *supra*, n. 97, p. 36f.
105. Lys. *Ep.* (2), 57; Isoc. *Paneg.* (4), 99.
106. For the various defenses of the empire, cf. *supra*, Chapter III, p. 61, and n. 117.
107. For a detailed comparison of these three passages, cf. Appendix II.
108. Lysias presents essentially the same structure (cf. Appendix II); thus, we can be reasonably sure that the structure antedates the Peace of Antalcidas, at least.
109. I accept the interpretation of Athens' revision of the League which has been advanced by Raubitschek, cf. *supra*, n. 8, pp. 181-87, and "The Peace Policy of Pericles," *AJA* 70 (1966) 37-41. Cf. K. Dienelt, *Die Friedenspolitik Perikles* (Wien: Rohrer, 1958), pp. 11-23.
110. All three events mark the change from war to peace, all are in technical violation of the Oath and Covenant of Plataea, and all are ignored by Thucydides. These same three statements, of course, can also be applied to the Peace: cf. Diodorus, T26.
111. Cf., however, the opposing analysis of Schrader, *supra*, n. 5, pp. 147-69.
112. Plut. *Per.* 12. 1-3 (= T5).

113. Cf. Stockton, *supra*, n. 10, p. 69f.; Meiggs, *Athenian Empire*, p. 132f.; Schrader, *supra*, n. 5, pp. 166-69. Busolt, *Gr. Gesch.*, III. 349 and n. 1, agrees with the implications of this argument but avoids them by placing the Peace after this debate.

114. Cf. De Ste. Croix, *Origins*, p. 311.

115. Cf. Schrader, *supra*, n. 5, p. 168f., who replies to the suggestion of authorship by Meiggs, *Athenian Empire*, p. 139f.

116. T7.

117. Cf. *supra*, Chapter III, pp. 49ff. For the possible religious significance of Zeus Eleutherios, cf. Raubitschek, *supra*, n. 109, p. 39.

118. Cf. *supra*, Chapter II, pp. 22ff.

119. Just as the allies sent grain to the *Eleusinia* and a phallus to the *Dionysia*, they sent a cow and a panoply to the *Great Panathenaea*: cf. the Cleinias Decree (IG I^2 66 = ML 46) and the reassessment decree of 425/4 (IG I^2 63 = ML 69).

120. T6.

121. For a translation of the text of the decree, cf. T3.

122. Cf. Raubitschek, *supra*, n. 8, p. 184, and n. 109, p. 39.

123. Cf. *supra*, n. 111.

124. Cf. *s.v.* T7.

125. Cf. *supra*, Chapter IV, pp. 83ff.

126. T22.

127. T35, T18, T37, T38, T42, T43.

128. T21.

129. Cf. A.E. Raubitschek, "Herodotus and the Inscriptions," *Bulletin of the Institute of Classical Studies of the University of London* 8 (1961) 61.

130. It is perhaps possible, however, to see the influence of the *Atthis* in Ephorus and those who appear to imitate him. We have seen that Aristodemus (T38) is close to Ephorus in many details about the last phase of the war, and both Aristodemus and the scholiast on Hermogenes (T45) may reflect Ephorus' account of the Peace. Their versions, in turn, are similar to that in the Souda (T43), which adds the autonomy clause in the manner of Ephorus. These late sources, however, had another source (cf. the Chelidonians and the Nessus River), which was apparently fuller than Ephorus but did not contradict him. This source may well have been an *Atthis*. Cf. *supra*, p. 155 and n. 93.

131. Cf. *supra*, p. 149.

132. Of the orators, only Demosthenes (T18) shows any evidence of the influence of an 'alternative' tradition. His version of the Peace itself, however, in no way contradicts our single tradition; it is the biographical details about Callias that are unique.

133. For Aristodemus, the Souda, and the scholiast on Hermogenes, cf. *supra*, n. 130. Himerius (T39), Eusebius (T41), and Ammianus (T40) can be explained in terms of Aristides himself or the oratorical tradition as a whole. Any source that mentions the Chelidonians could account for Polybius (T34) and Livy (T33).

CHAPTER VII

CONCLUSION:

THE TRANSMISSION OF THE TRADITION

In the preceding chapters, our investigation of the last phase of the Persian War has had two goals: to ascertain the content and nature of the fifth-century popular Athenian tradition and to examine the relationship between this tradition and Aristides' *Panathenaicus*. In attempting to achieve the first goal, we have sifted through the sources in search of evidence for fifth-century versions of the myth of Triptolemus, the transfer of the hegemony, the Battle of Eurymedon, the expedition to Egypt, and the Peace of Callias. A popular tradition, the roots of which can be found in fifth-century media, has come to light in each case and has been shown to have enjoyed nearly universal acceptance at Athens outside the circles of scholarly historians. Furthermore, we have seen that the popular versions of the four historical events fit into a larger pattern, a continuous tradition of Athenian history. The survival of this tradition in the *Panathenaicus* has been our main theme, and, I believe, a clear affinity between Aristides and the fifth-century tradition has been demonstrated. In Chapter I, we looked at Aristides' claims of historical accuracy ($\dot{\alpha}\varkappa\varrho\iota\beta\varepsilon\iota\alpha$) and the reliance on popular tradition implied by those claims; now we can report that the orator lived up to his claims with regard to the popular tradition at least.

When once the similarity between Aristides and the old tradition is proved, our chief interest ought to be in tracing the transmission of the tradition over the five hundred years that separate the *Panathenaicus* from the last extant *Epitaphios*, that of Hyperides (322 B.C.). I have not dealt extensively with this topic in the previous chapters, and indeed it must remain beyond the scope of this monograph; yet it is an important issue, which must be considered before we can even begin to complete our picture of the popular tradition. Consequently, I propose to devote the few remaining pages to a brief review of the two alternative methods of solving the problem of Aristides' sources.

The more conventional method, of course, consists in seeking out literary sources for Aristides' remarks. Haury, Beecke, Oliver, and others have employed this sort of *Quellenforschung* with considerable success, and many of our discussions and conclusions in the foregoing pages could lend themselves easily to this method.[1] We noted in Chapter II, for example, that Sophocles, Xenophon, or Philochorus might have inspired Aristides' use of the myth of Triptolemus. Various works of Isocrates, the *Epitaphios* in the *Menexenus*, and other orations in the epitaphic tradition certainly had their effect on Aristides' panegyric interpretation of Athenian history. Common rhetorical topics such as Athens' cultural mission, Athenian panhellenism, the tragic view of Xerxes, and the theme of fear were to be found in any number of authors from Aeschylus and Herodotus to Plutarch and beyond. Historical themes like the popular view of fifth-century chronology and the details of various events could have come from Ephorus or more especially the Atthidographers. What little evidence we have suggests that, in their accounts of the Pentecontaetia, Hellanicus and his successors followed the epitaphic tradition that Thucydides despised, and it is generally believed that Philochorus and the others were quite popular in later antiquity. With very few exceptions, however, the scarcity of extant evidence prevents us from pinpointing Aristides' sources by means of verbal parallels. As a result, the literary method is necessarily inexact and all too often leads the student into insupportable conjecture and fallacious arguments *ex silentio*.[2] Such dangers are unavoidable, but I should like to suggest a less conventional method that may prove to be more fruitful than the literary approach.

Since we have described many of the details and the continuous nature of the tradition that Aristides followed, it should be possible to discover something about this tradition's transmission by induction from its content. For example, in the matters of the political significance of Triptolemus and the sympathetic interpretation of the Egyptian expedition, we have seen that Aristides reproduced a fifth-century tradition that was essentially lost to all intervening literature. This would seem to suggest that the old tradition was transmitted from the fifth century B.C. to the second A.D. through oral or other non-literary media. Again, in the cases of the Battle of Eurymedon and the Peace of Callias, we determined that some sort of pervasive influence upon popular conceptions of these historical events must be posited in order to explain Aristides' detailed similarity to the old tradition and the historical knowledge that that similarity must have assumed on the part of Aristides' audiences. It could, of course, be argued that the tradition of the *Atthis* exerted this kind of influence; yet we have repeatedly seen indications that Aristides wrote the *Panathenaicus* under the influence of a view of history which was more pervasive than that of any literary source could have been and which exhibits many of the hallmarks of oral tradition.

When we attempt to define the pervasive force under which Aristides wrote, we first encounter the very strong feeling of nostalgia for ancient Athens that was sweeping the Roman world in Aristides' time. Aristides' own writings indicate how extensively the classical revival of the second century brought the nostalgic praise of Athens back into vogue.[3] Numerous popular Athenian anecdotes appear in his major works, especially the *Pro Quattuorviris, De Rhetorica, Hymn to Athena, Eleusinus,* and of course the *Panathenaicus.* Aristides' interest in mythical themes such as Athens' primeval gift of grain reflects a contemporary fascination with such topics.[4] Aspects of fifth- and fourth-century Athenian history account for ten of Aristides' eleven declamations, a percentage which Philostratus and Hermogenes confirm for all the declaimers of the period.[5] The immense popularity of these historical declamations caused Plutarch and Lucian to deplore the proliferation of such commonplaces as Marathon, Salamis, the bridging of the Hellespont, and the channelling of Athos, the mere mention of which brought in first prizes at Athens.[6] The high degree of popular appeal in these archaic topics clearly indicates that second-century audiences knew and expected the same topics as their counterparts six centuries before.[7] The nostalgia also affected the historians of Aristides' time. Those who did not Romanize their studies rarely extended them beyond Alexander the Great.[8] Moreover, a resurgence in classical Athenian forms accompanied the increased interest in Attic topics.[9] Atticism became the only acceptable style. Statuary, painting, and even the forms of letters on inscriptions imitated classical models, and the city of Athens itself experienced a remarkable cultural and architectural revival during this period.[10]

If our theory about Aristides' non-literary sources is to have any validity, it will be necessary to maintain that the nostalgia of the second century was not simply an artificial renaissance of a dead tradition; the phenomenon must be viewed rather as a widespread revival of patriotic, local Athenian tradition that survived in some oral or other vital form.[11] There is, for example, some evidence to suggest that the distant descendants of men like Themistocles and Cimon kept alive their ancient family traditions.[12] Furthermore, a living tradition of Athenian history could have survived in the academic circles of the University of Athens. Perhaps, however, a more fruitful source of information for the transmission of a living tradition can be found in the great patriotic festivals of Athens which had a continuous history from at least the fifth century to late Roman times.[13]

It is a well-known fact that Plato's *Menexenus* was read annually at a public ceremony at Athens.[14] Beside this rather artificial survival of the ancient epitaphic tradition, however, one can apparently find a similar, but more vital, form of the transmission of this tradition in the festivals of the *Theseia, Eleutheria, Epitaphia,* and the like. At these festivals, the Athenian ephebes competed in athletic contests for which they had been trained under an official known as a paidotribe or hypopaidotribe.[15] More important for us, however, is the fact that the young men also entered a competition in encomiastic oratory and gave speeches known as διάλογοι or προτρεπτικοὶ λόγοι.[16] After A.D. 136 at the latest, an ephebic official called a διδάσκαλος was put in charge of the ephebes' literary training, which presumably included preparation for the oratorical competitions.[17] A few remains of two ephebic speeches from the *Theseia* survive on several fragments of stone from near the end of the second century after Christ.[18] These fragments exhibit an understandable interest in the mythical exploits of Theseus and, to be sure, in the parallelism between his cultural mission and that of the city of Athens in the person of its ephebes. Another inscription preserves a battered fragment from a narrative of the Persian War in what appears to be an ephebic oration from the *Eleutheria*.[19] Only small portions of the long lines remain, but it is possible to pick out what could be some startling similarities to numerous themes that have been discussed in the preceding chapters (*IG* II² 2788 fin. II a.C.):

1. Athens as the guardian of Greece at Marathon (l.10):

- ἐμ Μαραθῶνι καὶ τὴν Ἑλλάδα διαφυλ[α-

2. The theme of freedom (l. 13):
   - ἐλευθερίας·
3. The Athenian version of the change of hegemony and perhaps the Peace of Callias (ll. 18-21):
   - ψεν· μετὰ δὲ ταῦτα μόνης ἐμοῦ παρ[αμεινάσης? -
   - τετελειῶσθαι τὸν πρὸς τοὺς Πέρσας [πόλεμον -
   - τοὺς] κατὰ τὴν Ἀσίαν Ἕλληνας ἐκβαλλόντων -
   - ἀναγ]κασάντων? συνθήκας ποιήσασθαι τὰς μ -
4. Sending official delegations to Athenian festivals (l. 22):
   - ξέναι δέ με καὶ θεωρίας ἐξαποστέλλον[τας -
5. Zeus Eleutherios:
   a. At Plataea (l. 23):
      - ἀδι]κεῖσθαι? Πλαταιὰς καὶ τὸ ἱερὸν καὶ τὸν βωμὸν [τοῦ Διὸς Ἐλευθερίου -
   b. Possibly at Athens (l. 36):
      - τοῦ Διὸς τοῦ Ἐ[λευθερίου -[20]

There is clearly enough similarity between this inscription and earlier panegyric oratory to warrant the conclusion that these ephebic orations should be considered late representatives of the epitaphic tradition of Athenian history that stretches back through the ages to the early fifth century.[21] Thus, the festivals might well provide an important link in our non-literary transmission of a historical tradition from the fifth century to Aristides.

One can conjecture in a general way that the living historical tradition of the Athenian festivals exerted a considerable influence on anyone writing Athenian history for popular consumption in Aristides' day. It is just possible, however, that we can take the matter one step farther in the case of the *Panathenaicus*. Oliver argues convincingly that Aristides intended this declamation to celebrate a Roman victory over the Parthians.[22] In 161, the Parthians invaded Roman Asia and threw the Greeks into a panic which was not alleviated until Lucius Verus defeated the invaders in 164 and 165. The comparison between the Roman war with the Parthians and the Greek wars with Darius, Xerxes, and Artaxerxes I is an obvious one and was in fact made often enough.[23] Oliver maintains that leitmotifs of war against Persian barbarism and victory for civilized Athens in the *Panathenaicus* attest to the fact that Aristides was reacting to the Roman victory, and he dates the work accordingly. Clearly, then, in the context of the middle 160's, the popular tradition of the Persian War could well have experienced a sudden and meaningful revival, and there is a tenuous bit of evidence that might suggest the way in which the revival could have begun (*IG* II² 2086, ll. 33-38):

> *Out of the Sebastophoric Fund a distribution was made at Plataeae at the dialogue to the ephebes and to those who had been placed in charge of them and for sacrifices to be offered that the emperors might be successful in obtaining (for the empire) the victory as commanders and as pontiffs health, and the expenses of the gymnasiarchy were defrayed from the fund for the time when there was no gymnasiarch, and an urn was dedicated for (the use of) future ephebes.*[24]

Since the inscription belongs to 163/4, after the Parthian invasion but before the Roman victory, the victory to be prayed for is certainly victory over the Parthians. The ceremony in question is the *Eleutheria*, at which the Athenian ephebes had their expenses paid out of the Sebastophoric fund.[25] The διάλογος is surely similar to the one in *IG* II² 2788. It is most interesting that this combination of the theme of victory in the Parthian War and an oration that reproduced the old Athenian tradition of the Persian War should have occurred so shortly before the publication of the *Panathenaicus*. One suspects that the mood exemplified in this inscription, in the *Panathenaicus*, and in the thematically similar *Hymn to Athena*,[26] was exerting a pervasive influence on the Athenian public and indeed throughout the Greek east in the years after the Parthian War. Such a phenomenon would go a long way towards explaining how Aristides could have found and revived a continuous version of the popular Athenian tradition of the fifth century.

1. For the scholars mentioned, cf. *supra*, Introduction, p. 6, n. 18.
2. In the view of Behr, *Loeb Aristides*, Vol. I, p. 4, the traditional method of *Quellenforschung* is not worthwhile: "...it seems most unlikely that the material contained in this work depends on much actual research as such. Aristides' thorough familiarity with the great historians, including Ephorus, as literary objects, and with the orators, poets, and Plato, would provide him with all the background which he required." Behr suggests that, if Aristides did use written sources, they were more likely to be handbooks: cf. "Citations of Porphyry's *Against Aristides* Preserved in Olympiodorus," *AJP* 89 (1968) 195.
3. Tacitus, *Ann.* II. 53, described the Athenians of the late first century as, *vetera suorum facta dictaque praeferentes*. Cf. *supra*, Introduction, p. 1.
4. Cf. *supra*, Chapter II. The theme appears in Pliny, *Epist.* VIII. 24.2; Plut. *Cim.* 10. 7; and Florus, I. 40. 10.
5. For analyses of these declamations, cf. A. Boulanger, *Aelius Aristide et la sophistique dans la province d'Asie au IIe siècle de nôtre ère* (Bibliothèque des Écoles françaises d'Athènes et de Rome, 126: Paris, 1923), pp. 271-99; B. Reardon, *Courants littéraires grecs des IIe-IIIe siècles après J.-C.* (Annales littéraires de l'Université de Nantes, 3: Paris, 1971), pp. 99-119; G. Kennedy, "The Sophists as Declaimers," in *Approaches to the Second Sophistic*, ed. by G. Bowersock (University Park, Penn.: APA, 1974), pp. 19-22; E. Bowie, "Greeks and Their Past in the Second Sophistic," *Past and Present* 46 (1970) 5; G. Kennedy, *The Art of Rhetoric in the Roman World* (Princeton, 1972), pp. 560 and 621.
6. Plut. *Praec. ger. reip.* 17 (= *Mor.* 814c); Luc. *Rh.pr.* 18.
7. Cf. Kennedy, *Art*, *supra*, n. 5, p. 563. For the notion that an oration did not receive official status at the *Greater Panathenaea* until the time of Herodes Atticus, cf. Oliver, *Civilizing Power*, p. 17, and n. 15.
8. Bowie, cf. *supra*, n. 5, pp. 10-27, sees Greek nostalgia resulting from an inferiority complex caused by Roman ascendancy. Aristides, of course, did not extend his historical narrative in the *Panathenaicus* beyond Chaeronea.
9. Bowie, *ibid.*, pp. 29-36.
10. For archaizing art in general, cf. B.S. Ridgway, *Archaic Style in Greek Sculpture* (Princeton, 1977), pp. 303ff., and her many references to earlier scholarship.
11. For the survival of the tradition of Athens' glory in Hellenistic times, cf. W.S. Ferguson, *Hellenistic Athens* (London: Macmillan, 1911), p. 309 and n. 2; Oliver, *Civilizing Power*, p. 18f., who cite several of the following examples: the speech of Nicolaus the Syracusan at Diod. XIII. 21-27, which may go back to Timaeus of Tauromenium; an Amphictyonic decree from ca. 125 B.C. (relevant text cited and translated by Oliver); Cicero, *Verr.* II. 5. 72 (187); *Pro Flac.* 26; *De orat.* I. 4. 13; Aelian, *Var. Hist.* 3. 38; Plut. *Sulla*, 13.5; and the references, *supra*, n. 4, and to some extent those, *infra*, n. 21.
12. For Themistocles, cf. F. Frost, *The Scholarship of Plutarch* (Diss. UCLA, 1961), p. 13. For Cimon, cf. Philostratus, *VS*, *s.v.* Herodes Atticus, sect. 546f.: Herodes claimed descent from Miltiades and Cimon, and he was openly proud of Miltiades' triumph over the Medes and of the way Cimon inflicted punishment upon them for their hybris.
13. For the schools, cf. Ferguson, *supra*, n. 11, pp. 61, 69, 233ff., 257ff., 298ff., 409, 463. In an important sense, the evidence from the schools cannot be separated from

that of the festivals, since many of the students in the universities were ephebes, who were required to take a course of study there. For the festivals themselves, cf. A. Mommsen, *Heortologie antiquarische Untersuchungen über die städtischen Feste der Athener* (Reprint: Amsterdam: Grüner, 1968), p. 410f. (for Artemis Agrotera in honor of Marathon, and for the festival for Salamis), p. 453 (for *Diisoteria*), pp. 278-83 (for *Theseia* and *Epitaphia*); P. Graindor, "Études sur l'Éphébie Attique sous l'Empire," *Musée Belge* 26 (1922) passim, esp. pp. 185-88 (*Antinoeia*), pp. 205-07 (*Theseia*), p. 214f. (*Epitaphia*), p. 219f. (*Eleutheria*); L. Deubner, *Attische Feste* (Berlin: Keller, 1932), p. 174f. (*Diisoteria*), pp. 204-07 (Salamis), p. 209f. (Agrotera), pp. 224-26 (*Theseia*), p. 230f. (*Epitaphia*); J. Day, *An Economic History of Athens under Roman Domination* (Columbia Univ., 1942), pp. 168, 199f., *et passim*; A. E. Raubitschek, "Sylleia," in *Studies in Roman Economic and Social History in Honor of Allen Chester Johnson* (Princeton, 1951), pp. 49-57; C. Pelékidis, *Histoire de l'Éphébie Attique* (Paris: Boccard, 1962), pp. 225-39 (*Theseia, Epitaphia*, and *Sylleia*); H. W. Parke, *Festivals of the Athenians* (London, 1977), p. 55 (Agrotera), p. 81f. (*Theseia*), p. 167f. (*Diisoteria*).

14. Cicero, *Orat.* 44. Graindor, *ibid.*, p. 220, believes that this dialogue was in fact the διάλογος that was recited at the *Eleutheria* (cf. *infra*, n. 24).

15. For a list of such officials and dedications to them, cf. O. W. Reinmuth, "The Ephebic Dedications to Hermes," in D. W. Bradeen and M. F. McGregor (eds.), *Phoros: Tribute to Benjamin Dean Meritt* (Locust Valley, N.Y.: Augustin, 1974), pp. 139-43.

16. For competition in a category called ἐγκώμιον, cf. Graindor, *supra*, n. 13, pp. 179, 188, 207, and 209. For the origin of the ἐγκώμιον category together with funeral games, cf. Diod. XI. 33. 3; Aristot. *Ath. Pol.* 58. 1. For the διάλογος, cf. *IG* II² 2086 and 2113. For the προτρεπτικὸς λόγος, cf. *IG* II² 2291a.

17. For the dedications to the διδάσκαλος, cf. O. W. Reinmuth, "Hoi peri to Diogeneion Again," *TAPA* 93 (1962) 384f.

18. *IG* II² 2291 a and b. For a small fragment of a similar oration, cf. *SEG* XVIII, no. 59.

19. J. H. Oliver, "Roman Emperors and Athenian Ephebes," *Hist.* 26 (1977) 92, n. 11, notes that besides *IG* II² 2086, 2113, and 2788, the famous Acharnae stele also brings together the Ephebes and the commemoration of the Battle of Plataea.

20. Cf. *IG* II² 43, 1.65f.

21. For the commonplaces and major sources of the epitaphic tradition, cf. C. Morawski, *De Athenarum gloria et gloriositate Atheniensium* (Diss. Krakow, 1905; for a different form of the reference, cf. Oliver, *Civilizing Power*, p. 20, n. 6); K. Alewell, *Über das rhetorische Paradeigma* (Diss. Kiel, 1913); O. Schröder, *De laudibus Athenarum a poetis tragicis et ab oratoribus epidicticis excultis* (Diss. Göttingen, 1914); K. Jost, "Das Beispiel und Vorbild der Vorfahren bei den attischen Rednern und Geschichtsschreibern bis Demosthenes," *Rhetorische Studien* 19 (Paderborn: Schöningh, 1936); G. Schmitz-Kahlmann, *Das Beispiel der Geschichte im politischen Denken des Isokrates* (Leipzig: Dieterich, 1939); H. R. Butts, "The Glorification of Athens in Greek Drama," *Iowa Studies in Classical Philology* 11 (= Diss. University of Iowa, 1942); H. Strasburger, "Thukydides und die politische Selbstdarstellung der Athener," *Hermes* 86 (1958) 17-40; H. Herter, "Athen im Bilde der Römerzeit. Zu einem Epigramm Senecas," *Serta Philologica Aenipontana: Innsbrucker Beiträge zur*

Kulturwissenschaft 7-8 (1962) 347-58; W. Kierdorf, *Erlebnis und Darstellung der Perserkriege: Studien zu Simonides, Pindar, Aischylos, und den attischen Rednern: Hypomnemata* 16 (1966); Oliver, *Civilizing Power,* pp. 17-20; C. Collard, "Funeral Oration in Euripides' *Supplices," Bulletin of London University Inst. of Class. Stud.* 19 (1972) 39-53; J. Soffel, *Die Regeln Menanders für die Leichenrede* (Meisenheim am Glan: Hain, 1974). For some ancient lists of epitaphic topics, cf., besides the references in n. 11, *supra,* Aristot. *Rhet. passim* and esp. Darius and Xerxes (1393b1), Marathon and Salamis (1396a13; 1411a32), Miltiades (1411a10), Aristides (1398a10; 1414b36); Plut. *Praec. ger. reip.* 17 (= *Mor.* 814c); *De glor. Ath.* (esp. *Mor.* 345c-350b); Lucian, *Rh. pr.* 14-18; Menander the Rhetorician, *On Epideictic Oratory;* Philostratus, *VS,* 519, 541, 547, and 572.

22. *Civilizing Power,* p. 33f.
23. Oliver, cf. *supra,* n. 19, p. 92.
24. For the translation and interpretation, cf. Oliver, *ibid.* p. 94.
25. *Ibid.*, p. 92, n. 7. Cf. Graindor, *supra,* n. 13, p. 170, n. 3.
26. Cf. F. W. Lenz, "Der Athenahymnos des Aristeides," *Rivista di cultura classica e medioevale* 5 (1963) 329-47.

APPENDIX I

This appendix contains the obvious and possible testimonia for the Peace of Callias, with the exception of the five passages from Aristides which are cited in the text of Chapter VI. The reader is referred to the similar list with commentary in C. Schrader, *La Paz de Calias* (Barcelona: Universidad de Barcelona, 1976), pp. 5-70. I have attempted to arrange the testimonia in a manner that is meaningful in terms of the content of Chapter VI and thus have employed four categories: documentary, primary, secondary, and tertiary. It should be noted at the outset that I will not be using the last three terms in the normal manner of historiographers. I designate as primary those testimonia which rely either fully or in part on oral and possibly also documentary sources, in other words, the living tradition. 'Secondary' applies to literary testimonia which give evidence of personal investigation of the historical facts through examination of documentary, oral, and primary sources, in other words, fifth- and fourth-century historians. Tertiary testimonia are those whose authors copied material from primary or secondary sources.

A. Documentary Sources.

No undoubted documentary sources for the Peace exists, but scholars have noted a number of possible references, several of which I have mentioned and accepted as genuine testimonia for the Peace in the text and notes of Chapter VI.

T1. The Cyprus epigram:
The most recent published text is that of D.L. Page, *Epigrammata Graeca* (Oxford, 1975), p. 26. For a translation, cf. *supra*, Chapter IV, p.78. For an ancient reference to the poem, cf. Isoc. *Paneg.* (4), 179.

T2. The missing tribute list:
It has been deduced from the tribute quota lists that only three lists (*ATL* II, Lists 7, 8, and 9) remain for the four years 449/8-446/5: cf. *ATL* III. 277f. Presumably, the missing list reflects unwillingness on the part of the allies to pay tribute in the year after the Peace was con-

cluded: cf. *ML*, pp. 133-35; D. Kagan, *The Outbreak of the Peloponnesian War* (Ithaca: Cornell, 1969), pp. 113-15, 380f.; R. Sealey, *Phoenix* 24 (1970) 13-28; Meiggs, *Athenian Empire*, p. 154.

T3. The Congress Decree (Plut. *Per.* 17.1):
When the Lacedaemonians began to be annoyed by the increasing power of the Athenians, Pericles, by way of inciting the people to cherish yet loftier thoughts and to deem itself worthy of great achievements, introduced a bill to the effect that all Hellenes wheresoever resident in Europe or in Asia, small and large cities alike, should be invited to send deputies to a council at Athens. This was to deliberate concerning the Hellenic sanctuaries which the Barbarians had burned down, concerning the sacrifices which were due to the gods in the name of Hellas in fulfilment of vows made when they were fighting with the Barbarians, and concerning the sea, that all might sail it fearlessly and keep the peace. (Perrin's Loeb translation)

Cf. *ATL* III. 279; C. Murison, *Phoenix* 25 (1971), n. 63; A.E. Raubitschek, *RSA* 1 (1971) 183-85.

T4. Dismantling the fortifications of Ionia:
H.T. Wade-Gery, *Athenian Studies: HSCP.* Suppl. vol. I (1940), p. 141f., argues that Athens forced the Ionian cities to dismantle their landward fortifications in compliance with the terms of the Peace; cf. S.K. Eddy, *CP* 65 (1970) 10. The idea is rejected by Meiggs, *Athenian Empire*, p. 149f.; cf. Murison, *Phoenix* 25 (1971), n. 62.

T5. The debate on Pericles' building program (Plut. *Per.* 12. 1-3):
But that which brought most delightful adornment to Athens, and the greatest amazement to the rest of mankind; that which alone now testifies for Hellas that her ancient power and splendour, of which so much is told, was no idle fiction, —I mean his construction of sacred edifices, —this, more than all the public measures of Pericles, his enemies maligned and slandered. They cried out in the assemblies: "The people has lost its fair fame and is in ill repute because it has removed the public moneys of the Hellenes from Delos into its own keeping, and that seemliest of all excuses which it had to urge against its accusers, to wit, that out of fear of the Barbarians it took the public funds from that sacred isle and was now guarding them in a stronghold, of this Pericles has robbed it. And surely Hellas is insulted with a dire insult and manifestly subjected to tyranny

when she sees that, with her own enforced contributions for the war, we are gilding and bedizening our city, which, for all the world like a wanton woman, adds to her wardrobe precious stones and costly statues and temples worth their millions."

For his part, **Pericles** would instruct the people that it owed no account of their moneys to the allies provided it carried on the war for them and kept off the Barbarians; "not a horse do they furnish," said he, "not a ship, not a hoplite, but money simply; and this belongs, not to those who give it, but to those who take it, if only they furnish that for which they take it in pay." (Perrin's Loeb translation)

If A.E. Raubitschek, *AJA* 70 (1966) 38-41, is correct, as I believe he is, in his interpretation of the Congress Decree and its aftermath, including the building program, many of the structures that Pericles sponsored (e.g., the Telesterion, Parthenon, and Stoa of Zeus Eleutherios) may mark the end of the war, i.e., the Peace. Two of these, the Temple of Athena Nike and the statue of Athena Promachos, seem to exhibit a special connection with Athens' victorious Peace.

T6. The Temple of Athena Nike:
Despite the late date of this building's construction, a decree (*IG* I^2 24 = *ML* 44) calling for its construction has been dated as early as 450: cf. Meiggs, *Athenian Empire*, pp. 495-503.

T7. The statue of Athena Promachos:
a. Paus. I. 28. 2: In addition to the works I have mentioned, there are two tithes dedicated by the Athenians after wars. There is first a bronze Athena, tithe from the Persians who landed at Marathon. It is the work of Pheidias, but the reliefs upon the shield, including the fight between Centaurs and Lapithae, are said to be from the chisel of Mys, for whom they say Parrhasius, the son of Evenor, designed this and the rest of his works. The point of the spear of this Athena and the crest of her helmet are visible to those sailing to Athens, as soon as Sunium is passed. (Jones' Loeb translation)
b. Demosth. *De fals. leg.* (19), 272: Does anyone say that this inscription has been set up just anywhere? No; although the whole of our citadel is a holy place, and although its area is so large, the inscription stands at the right hand beside the great brazen Athene which was dedicated by the state as a memorial of victory in the Persian war, at the

expense of the Greeks. In those days, therefore, justice was so venerable, and the punishment of these crimes so meritorious, that the retribution of such offenders was honoured with the same position as Pallas Athene's own prize of victory. To-day we have instead—mockery, impunity, dishonour, unless you restrain the licence of these men. (The Vinces' Loeb translation)

Cf. E. Kluwe in *Die Krise der gr. Polis,* (Berlin: Akademie, 1969), pp. 22-28.

T8. The Altar of Peace:
Plutarch (cf. *infra,* T35d) takes this structure as a monument to the Peace. Cf. however, C. Habicht, *Hermes* 89 (1961) 25f.; R.E. Wycherley, *The Athenian Agora,* Vol. III, *Literary and Epigraphical Testimonia* (Princeton: ASCS, 1957), pp. 65-67.

T9. Fourth century stele bearing the Peace of Callias:
The existence of this stele is deduced from various literary testimonia: Isocrates (T14); the contrast between Demosthenes T17 and T18; the supposed reliance of Plutarch and Callisthenes on the same copy of the Peace that Craterus had in his collection (T35c); Theopompus' attack on a peace (T30, T31). Some scholars date the stele between 386 and 380, as I do: cf. *supra,* Chapter IV, p. 91f.; others date it between 352 and 343: cf. Murison, *Phoenix* 25 (1971) 21; Schrader, *La Paz,* p. 180. Habicht, *Hermes* 89 (1961) 25f., argues against the authenticity of such a stele, while A.E. Raubitschek, *Bulletin of the Institute of Classical Studies of the University of London* 8 (1961) 61, argues for its genuineness. Schrader maintains that Demosthenes (T18) and Plutarch (T35a) are closest to the content of the stele; I believe an equal case can be made for Ephorus: cf. *supra,* Chapter VI, p. 149.

T10. The Peace of Epilycus as a renewal of the Peace of Callias (Andoc. *De pace* [3], 29):
Thus—and it is only by calling the past to mind that one can properly determine policy—we began by making a truce with the Great King and establishing a permanent accord with him, thanks to the diplomacy of my mother's brother, Epilycus, the son of Teisander. But later the king's runaway slave, Amorges, induced us to discard the powerful support of his master as worthless. We chose instead what we imagined to be a more advantageous understanding with Amorges himself. The king in his anger replied by allying himself with Sparta, and furnished her with five thousand talents

with which to prosecute the war; nor was he satisfied until he had overthrown our empire. (Maidment's Loeb translation)

Wade-Gery, *Athenian Studies,* pp. 127-32, argues from this and supporting documents that the peace negotiated by Epilycus was a renewal of the Peace of Callias: cf. Meiggs, *Athenian Empire,* p. 134f. Cf., however, Schrader, *La Paz,* pp. 71-103; Murison, *Phoenix* 25 (1971) 24-26. Cf. now A. Blamire, *Phoenix* 29 (1975) 21-26.

T11. Various Spartan treaties with the Persians:
    a. Thuc. VIII. 18.1: The Lacedaemonians and their allies have concluded an alliance with the King and Tissaphernes on the following terms: Whatsoever territory and cities the King holds or the forefathers of the King held, shall belong to the King; and from these cities whatsoever money or anything else came in for the Athenians shall be stopped by the King and the Lacedaemonians and their allies acting in common, to the end that the Athenians shall receive neither money nor anything else. (Forster Smith's Loeb translation)

    b. Thuc. VIII. 37. 1-5: Compact of the Lacedaemonians and their allies with King Darius and the King's sons and Tissaphernes. There shall be a treaty and friendship on the following terms:

"1. Whatsoever territory and cities belong to King Darius or belonged to his father or their ancestors, against these shall neither the Lacedaemonians nor their allies go either for war or to do any harm; nor shall either the Lacedaemonians or their allies exact tribute from these cities. Nor shall King Darius or those over whom the King rules go against the Lacedaemonians or their allies for war or to do any harm.

"2. If the Lacedaemonians or their allies have need of anything from the King or the King from the Lacedaemonians or their allies, whatever they shall persuade one another to do, this shall be right for them to do.

"3. The war against the Athenians and their allies both parties shall wage in common; and if they make peace, both shall make it in common.

"4. Whatsoever forces shall be in the territory of the King, on the summons of the King, shall be maintained at the expense of the King.

"5. If any of the cities that have entered into this compact with the King shall go against the country of the King, the rest shall strive to prevent this and aid the King to the extent of their power; and if any of those who inhabit the King's territory or any territory over which the King has dominion shall go against the territory of the Lacedaemonians or of their allies, the King shall strive to prevent this and give aid to the extent of his power." (Forster Smith Loeb translation)

c. Thuc. VIII. 58.1 (A. Andrewes, *Hist.* 10 [1961] 15): "In the thirteenth year of the reign of Darius, while Alexippidas was ephor at Lacedaemon, an agreement was made in the plain of the Meander by the Lacedaemonians and their allies with Tissaphernes, Hieramenes, and the sons of Pharnaces respecting the King's affairs and those of the Lacedaemonians and their allies.
1. "The King's country, as much of it as is in Asia, shall be the King's; and concerning his own country the King shall determine as he pleases...." (Forster Smith's Loeb translation)

d. Xen. *Hell.* III. 4. 25: After he had done this, Tithraustes sent ambassadors to Agesilaus with this message: "Agesilaus, the man who was responsible for the trouble in your eyes and ours has received his punishment; and the King deems it fitting that you should sail back home, and that the cities in Asia, retaining their independence, should render him the ancient tribute." (Brownson's Loeb translation)

e. Xen. *Hell.* V. 1.31 (= the Peace of Antalcidas): King Artaxerxes thinks it just that the cities in Asia should belong to him, as well as Clazomenae and Cyprus among the islands, and that the other Greek cities, both small and great, should be left independent, except Lemnos, Imbros, and Scyros; and these should belong, as of old, to the Athenians. But whichever of the two parties does not accept this peace, upon them I will make war, in company with those who desire this arrangement, both by land and by sea, with ships and with money. (Brownson's Loeb translation)

Cf. M. Amit, *RSA* 4 (1974) 55-63; M. Goldstein, *CSCA* 7 (1974) 155-64; C. Hamilton, *Sparta's Bitter Victories* (Cornell, 1978), Chapter II.

B. Primary Sources.

Since these testimonia are discussed fully in Chapter VI, I will keep comments to a minimum here. Besides the testimonia given here, I include in this category Callisthenes (T35b) and Aristides (passages A, B, C, and E in Chapter VI).

T12. Thuc. I. 75. 1-3: Considering then, Lacedaemonians, the zeal and sagacity of judgment which we displayed at that time, do we deserve to be regarded with this excessive jealousy by the Hellenes just on account of the empire we possess? And indeed we did not acquire this empire by force, but only after you had refused to continue to oppose what was left of the barbarian forces, and the allies came to us and of their own accord asked us to assume the leadership. It was under the compulsion of circumstances that we were driven at first to advance our empire to its present state, influenced chiefly by fear, then by honour also, and lastly by self-interest as well. (Forster Smith's Loeb translation)

T13. Lys. *Ep.* (2), 56 f. (ca. 390 B.C.): Instead of weakening their allies, they secured their strength along with their own, and displayed their own power to such effect that the Great King no more coveted the possessions of others, but yielded some of his own and was in fear for what remained. In that time no warships sailed from Asia, no despot held sway among the Greeks, no city of Greece was forced into serfdom by the barbarians; so great was the restraint and awe inspired in all mankind by the valour of our people. (Lamb's Loeb translation)

T14. Isoc. *Paneg.* (4), 117f., 120 (ca. 380 B.C.): And so far are the states removed from "freedom" and "autonomy" that some are controlled by alien governors, some have been sacked and razed, and some have become slaves to the barbarians—the same barbarians whom we once so chastened for their temerity in crossing over into Europe, and for their overweening pride, that they not only ceased from making expeditions against us, but even endured to see their own territory laid waste; and we brought their power so low, for all that they had once sailed the sea with twelve hundred ships, that they launched no ship of war this side of Phaselis but remained inactive and waited on more favourable times rather than trust in the forces which they then possessed....

One may best comprehend how great is the reversal in our circumstances if he will read side by side the treaties which were made during our leadership and those which have been published recently; for he will find that in those days we were constantly setting limits to the empire of the King, levying tribute on some of his subjects, and barring him from the sea; now, however,.... (Norlin's Loeb translation)

T15. Pl. *Menex.* 241e: These were the men who fought the sea-fight at the Eurymedon, the men who served in the expedition against Cyprus, the men who voyaged to Egypt and to many another quarter,—men whom we ought to hold in memory and render them thanks, seeing that they put the king in fear and caused him to give his whole mind to his own safety in place of plotting the destruction of Greece.

Now this war was endured to the end by all our citizens who warred against the barbarians in defence of all the other Greek-speaking peoples as well as themselves. But when peace was secured and our city was held in honour,... (Bury's Loeb translation)

T16. Isoc. *Areop.* (7), 80: The barbarians were so far from meddling in the affairs of the Hellenes that they neither sailed their ships-of-war this side of the Phaselis nor marched their armies beyond the Halys River, refraining, on the contrary, from all aggression. (Norlin's Loeb translation)

For a date of ca. 357, cf. W. Jaeger, *Athenian Studies: HSCP* Suppl. vol. I (1940), pp. 433, 439.

T17. Demosth. *De lib. Rhod.* (15), 29: The Greeks have two treaties with the King, one made by our city and commended by all, and the later one made by the Lacedaemonians, which is of course condemned by all. (Vince's Loeb translation)

For a date of ca. 352, cf. W. Jaeger, *Demosthenes* (Cambridge Univ., 1938), p. 230.

T18. Demosth. *De fals. leg.* (19), 273 (343 B.C.): I am sure you have all heard the story of their treatment of Callias, son of Hipponicus, who negotiated the celebrated peace under which the King of Persia was not to approach within a day's ride of the coast, nor sail with a ship of war between the Chelidonian islands and the Blue Rocks. At the inquiry into his conduct they came near to putting him to death, and mulcted him in fifty talents, because he was said to have taken bribes on embassy. Yet no one can cite a more honourable peace made by the city before or since. (The Vinces' Loeb translation)

T19. Isoc. *Panath.* (12), 59-61 (342-339 B.C.): Again, I must set forth how these two cities demeaned themselves toward the barbarians; for this still remains to be done. In the time of our supremacy, the barbarians were prevented from marching with an army beyond the Halys river and from sailing with their ships of war this side of Phaselis, but under the hegemony of the Lacedaemonians not only did they gain the freedom to march and sail wherever they pleased, but they even became masters over many Hellenic states. Well then, does not the city which made the nobler and prouder covenants with the Persian king, which brought to pass the most and the greatest injuries to the barbarians and benefits to the Hellenes, which, furthermore, seized from her foes the sea-coast of Asia and much other territory besides and appropriated it to her allies, which put an end to the insolence of the barbarians and the poverty of the Hellenes....? (Norlin's Loeb translation)

T20. Lycurg. *Leoc.*73: And to crown their victory: not content with erecting the trophy in Salamis, they fixed for the Persian the boundaries necessary for Greek freedom and prevented his overstepping them, making an agreement that he should *not* sail his warships between the Cyaneae and Phaselis and that the Greeks should be free not only if they lived in Europe but in Asia too. (Burtt's Loeb translation)

For a date of 331, cf. F. Durrbach, *Lycurge: Contre Léocrate* (Paris: Budé, 1956), p. 25.

T21. Aristoph. *Ach.* 61-125, may contain a reference to embassies between Athens and Persia under the terms of the Peace: cf. H. Mattingly, *Hist.* 10 (1961) 162, n. 64; Raubitschek, *RSA* 1 (1971) 187; Murison, *Phoenix* 25 (1971) 30. For other embassies, cf. Pl. *Charm.* 158a; Strabo, I. 3. 1.

C. Secondary Sources:

T22. Hdt. VII. 151: It chanced that while Athenian envoys, Callias son of Hipponicus, and the rest who had come up with him, were at Susa, called the Memnonian, about some other business, the Argives also had at this same time sent envoys to Susa,... (Godley's Loeb translation)

Many scholars believe that this refers to Callias' embassy to negotiate the Peace; cf., however, Murison, *Phoenix* 25 (1971) 26f.; D. Stockton, *Hist.* 8 (1959) 69.

T23. Hdt. VI. 42. 2: This he compelled them to do; and he measured their lands by parasangs, which is the Persian name for a distance of thirty furlongs, and appointed that each people should according to this measurement pay a tribute which has remained fixed ever since that time to this day, even as it was ordained by Artaphrenes,... (Godley's Loeb translation)

Wade-Gery, *Athenian Studies.* p. 133f., argues that this passage supports his conception of Isocrates' tribute clause (T14). The interpretation was, however, dismissed in *ATL* III. 275; cf. K. Kraft, *Hermes* 92 (1964) 158-71.

T24. Thuc. VIII. 5. 5: For Tissaphernes was also trying to induce the Peloponnesians to come over to Asia, promis-

ing to furnish them maintenance. For the King, as it
chanced, had lately demanded of him the tribute from his
own province, for which he had fallen into arrears, since
he was not able to exact it from the Hellenic cities because
of the Athenians. (Forster Smith's Loeb translation)
As with T23, the issue is the tribute of Ionia under the
terms of the Peace: cf. Wade-Gery, *Athenian Studies,*
p. 144;A.W.Gomme, *AJP* 65 (1944) 336; M. Cary, *CQ* 39
(1945) 89; Stockton, *Hist.* 8 (1959) 65; Kraft, *Hermes* 92
(1964) 160.

T25. Thuc. VIII. 56. 4: He insisted that all Ionia should be
given up, after that the adjacent islands, and so on. When
the Athenians did not oppose these demands, finally, at
the third conference, fearing that his utter lack of influence would be openly exposed, he insisted that the
King be permitted to build ships and sail along the
Athenian coasts wherever he wished and with as many
ships as he pleased. (Forster Smith's Loeb translation)
The assumption is that this proposal was meant to repeal
the Peace of Callias: cf. T11c; A. Andrewes, *Hist.* 10
(1961) 15; Meiggs, *Athenian Empire,* pp. 141f., 490.

T26. Diod. IX. 10. 5: For they took oath at Plataea that they
would hand down enmity to the Persians as an inheritance
even to their children's children, so long as the rivers run
into the sea, as the race of men endures, and as the earth
brings forth fruit; and yet, despite the binding pledge they
had taken against fickle fortune, after a time they were
sending ambassadors to Artaxerxes, Xerxes' son, to
negotiate a treaty of friendship and alliance. (Oldfather's
Loeb translation)
I place this and the following three testimonia from
Diodorus here, because it is generally accepted that
Diodorus followed the account of Ephorus in the matter
of the Peace as in the rest of the Pentecontaetia. For
Ephorus' date of composition, ca. 345-340, cf. Murison,
Phoenix 25 (1971) 18-20.

T27. Diod. XII. 2. 1: First place belonged to the Athenians,
who had advanced so far in both fame and prowess that
their name was known throughout practically the entire
inhabited world; for they increased their leadership to
such a degree that, by their own resources and without the
aid of Lacedaemonians or Peloponnesians, they overcame
great Persian armaments both on land and on sea, and
humbled the famed leadership of the Persians to such an
extent that they forced them by the terms of a treaty to
liberate all the cities of Asia. (Oldfather's Loeb
translation)

T28. Diod. XII. 4. 4-6: Artaxerxes the king, however, when he learned of the reverses his forces had suffered at Cyprus, took counsel on the war with his friends and decided that it was to his advantage to conclude a peace with the Greeks. Accordingly he dispatched to the generals in Cyprus and to the satraps the written terms on which they were permitted to come to a settlement with the Greeks. Consequently Artabazus and Megabyzus sent ambassadors to Athens to discuss a settlement. The Athenians were favourable and dispatched ambassadors plenipotentiary, the leader of whom was Callias the son of Hipponicus; and so the Athenians and their allies concluded with the Persians a treaty of peace, the principal terms of which run as follows: All the Greek cities of Asia are to live under laws of their own making; the satraps of the Persians are not to come nearer to the sea than a three days' journey and no Persian warship is to sail inside of Phaselis or the Cyanean Rocks; and if these terms are observed by the king and his generals, the Athenians are not to send troops into the territory over which the king is ruler. After the treaty had been solemnly concluded, the Athenians withdrew their armaments from Cyprus, having won a brilliant victory and concluded most noteworthy terms of peace. And it so happened that Cimon died of an illness during his stay in Cyprus. (Oldfather's Loeb translation)

T29. Diod. XII. 26. 2: For the Persians had two treaties with the Greeks, one with the Athenians and their allies according to which the Greek cities of Asia were to live under laws of their own making, and they also concluded one later with the Lacedaemonians, in which exactly the opposite terms had been incorporated, whereby the Greek cities of Asia were to be subject to the Persians. (Oldfather's Loeb translation)

T30. Theopompus, *FGrH* 115 F 153 = Theon, *Progymn.* 2: From Book XXV of Theopompus' *Philippica:* the Hellenic oath, which the Athenians say the Hellenes swore before the battle against the barbarians at Plataea, is falsely reported. So also is the treaty of the Athenians ⟨and⟩ Hellenes with (πρὸς) King [Darius].

This and the following testimonium are frequently understood as elements in Theopompus' attack on the Peace of Callias or at least on the fourth-century stele: cf. Wade-Gery, *Athenian Studies,* p. 125; Murison, *Phoenix* 25 (1971) 22-24, 31. Cf., however, A.E. Raubitschek, *GRBS* 5 (1964) 158; W.R. Connor, *Theopompus and Fifth-Century Athens* (Washington: Center for Hellenic Studies and Harvard, 1968), pp. 4f.; 163, n. 53; 171, n. 120.

T31. Theopompus, *FGrH* 115 F 154 = Harpocr. *s.v.* Ἀττικοῖς γράμμασιν:

In Book XXV of the *Philippica,* Theopompus says that the treaty with the barbarian has been fabricated, since the inscription on the stele was not in Attic lettering but Ionic.

D. Tertiary Sources.

T32. Didymus *in Demosth.,* Col. 7. 71: One could also bring forward many other of the King's benefactions towards the city such as the peace that was promulgated by Callias, the son of Hipponicus.

T33. Livy, XXXIII. 20. 1-3: ...the Chelidonians—a promontory of Cilicia which was included in the ancient Athenian treaty with the Kings of the Persians.

T34. Polybius, fr. 18. 41a. 1 (Souda *s.v.* συνεπισχύσας):
...to hinder Antiochus from sailing near, not for the sake of enmity, but suspecting that he might join forces with Philip and present a hinderence to Greek freedom.

For this and the preceding testimonium, cf. W.E. Thompson, *CP* 66 (1971) 30.

T35. Plut. *Cim.* 13. 4f. (all translations are from Perrin's Loeb):

a. Plutarch himself: This exploit so humbled the purpose of the King that he made the terms of that notorious peace, by which he was to keep away from the Hellenic sea-coast as far as a horse could travel in a day, and was not to sail west of the Cyanean and the Chelidonian isles with armoured ships of war.

The source of the statement is not obvious. Presumably, it is either Callisthenes (or Callisthenes' source: ? the *Atthis*), as I have argued in Chapter VI, or it was a copy of the stele that Craterus put into his collection: cf. Wade-Gery, *Athenian Studies,* p. 125; R. Sealey, *Hist.* 3 (1955) 329; Murison, *Phoenix* 25 (1971) 15-17.

b. Callisthenes (=*FGrH* 124 F 16): And yet Callisthenes denies that the Barbarian made any such terms, but says he really acted as he did through the fear which that victory inspired, and kept so far aloof from Hellas that Pericles with fifty, and Ephialtes with only thirty, ships sailed beyond the Chelidonian isles without encountering any navy of the Barbarians. Cf. Schreiner, *SO* 52 (1977) 19ff.

c. Craterus (= *FGrH* 342 F 13): But in the decrees collected by Craterus there is a copy of the treaty in its due place, as though it had actually been made.
d. The Altar of Peace (= T8): And they say that the Athenians also built the altar of Peace to commemorate this event, and paid distinguished honours to Callias as their ambassador.

T36. Plut. *Cim.* 19. 4: It was not until long afterwards that Agesilaus carried his arms into Asia and prosecuted a brief war against the King's generals along the sea-coast. And even he could perform no great and brilliant deeds, but was overwhelmed in his turn by a flood of Hellenic disorders and seditions and swept away from a second empire. So he withdrew, leaving in the midst of allied and friendly cities the tax-gatherers of the Persians, not one of whose scribes, nay, nor so much as a horse, had been seen within four hundred furlongs of the sea, as long as Cimon was general. (Perrin's Loeb translation)

T37. Paus. I. 8. 2: After the statues of the *eponymoi* come statues of gods, Amphiaraus, and Eirene (*Peace*) carrying the boy Plutus (*Wealth*). Here stands a bronze figure of Lycurgus, son of Lycophron, and of Callias, who, as most of the Athenians say, brought about the peace between the Greeks and Artaxerxes, son of Xerxes. (Jones' Loeb translation)

T38. Aristodemus, *FGrH* 104 F 13: At the same time they carried out an expedition against Cyprus, with Cimon, the son of Miltiades, in command. Then they were afflicted by famine, and Cimon became ill and died in the Cyprian city of Citium. When the Persians noticed that the Athenians were hard pressed, they overconfidently attacked with their fleet. There was a naval battle, and the Athenians were victorious. The Athenians picked Callias, nicknamed 'Laccoploutus,' as their general..., and he negotiated a treaty with Artaxerxes and the rest of the Persians. The treaty consisted of the following terms: 1) Persian warships were not to sail west of the Cyaneans; 2) Persians were not to come any nearer to the coast than a man could reach from the coast on a three day journey—and that is three days' riding on a horse.

T39. Himerius, *Polemarchicus* (6), 29: How shall I praise Plataea? How can I narrate the victories at Mycale, Sestos, Eion, Byzantium, and the victories up and down that coast which the Athenians attacked in their strength? They cut away the remnants of the barbarian empire as though they were cleansing away a ritual pollution. But even if we pass over all this in silence, we shall recall the peace that was made with the King—the peace which bestows more dignity upon the city than any victory in battle.... The King willingly acceded to the city's demand that he stay a day's ride by horse from the coast and not sail a ship beyond the Chelidonians and Cyaneans.

T40. Ammianus Marcellinus, XVII. 11.3: Cimon, the son of Miltiades,...frequently before and then again at the Pamphylian river called Eurymedon defeated the Persian people and compelled that populous race, always so buoyed up with pride, to sue for peace in a most humble manner.

T41. Eusebius:
    a.   Vers.Arm. *Ol.* 79^4: Next to the Eurymedon River, Cimon both conquered the Persians in a naval battle and caused the Persian War to come to an end.
    b.   Jer. *Ol.* 79^4: At the Eurymedon, Cimon beat the Persians in a naval encounter and a fight on land. And the Persian War came to an end. Cf. Sync. 470.7.

T42. The Souda, *s.v.* Callias: Callias, nicknamed 'Laccoploutus,' campaigned against Artaxerxes and confirmed the boundaries set by the treaty in Cimon's time.

T43. The Souda, *s.v.* Cimon: Cimon, the son of Miltiades, campaigned against the barbarians who attacked with Themistocles (sic). He sailed to Cyprus and Pamphylia and fought a campaign; and on the same day he was victorious in both a naval and a land engagement at the Eurymedon. He also drew the boundaries for the barbarians: 1) the Persians could not sail a ship meant for war within the Cyaneans, Chelidonians, and Phaselis (a city of Pamphylia); 2) the Kings were not allowed to march any nearer to the coast than a day's ride by horse; 3) the Greeks and those in Asia were to be autonomous. Cimon died in Cyprian Citium.

T44. Schol. Aristid. III. 213f.:
    a. BD on Passage A in Chapter VI, *supra:* Thus Demosthenes, a ride by horse...(T18). Callias was the ambassador who arranged this peace after the Persian War, and the King could not go beyond the Cyaneans by sea.

    b. AC on Passage B: Aristides uses the term "weakened" well, since he shows that it was weakened from a great empire and power to a small one.

    c. C calls the Chelidonians 'Rocks,' and the Cyaneans 'Symplegades.'

d. BD on Passage B, "crowning act:" The meaning is glory and victory.

T45. Schol. Hermog. (= C. Walz, *Rhetores Graeci*, Vol. V, p. 388): After the Persian War and the death of Xerxes, his son Artaxerxes turned again to the affairs of Asiatic Greece, but he found himself deprived of hope. Thus, the Greeks and barbarians concluded a treaty, in which the stipulated boundaries were, the Cyanean Rocks, the Nessus River, Phaselis of Pamphylia, and the promontory of the Chelidonians.

APPENDIX II

The accounts of the Peace found in Lysias (T13, in Appendix I) and Isocrates (T14, T16, and T19) do not appear in continuous narratives of the Pentecontaetia; they contribute rather to those authors' apologies for the Athenian Empire. The sequence of topics in the *Panegyricus* is as follows: (1) the wars of freedom (to 99); (2) a defense of the empire (to 109); (3) a comparison with the empire of Lysander (to 117); (4) a contrast between the treaties of Callias and Antalcidas (to 121). Lysias follows a similar pattern: (1) the wars of freedom (to 47); (2) the Greek wars of the Pentecontaetia (to 53); (3) a brief account of the empire, which includes an apology and the reference to the Peace (to 57). In defending the empire, both authors point to the longevity of the Athenian rule (seventy years) and Athens' encouragement of democracy and tranquility. Isocrates addresses the question of judicial administration and stresses Athens' superiority to Sparta in this respect (*Paneg*. (4), 113; *Panath*. (12), 66). These apologies bear a remarkable resemblance to the defense of the empire given by the Athenian speakers at Sparta as recorded in the first book of Thucydides.

The Athenians begin by praising their city's achievements during the wars of freedom, a topic that is bound to grate on the minds of the audience (Thuc. I. 73. 2: cf. Hdt. VII. 139). The Athenians note that their fathers fought alone at Marathon (I. 73. 4: cf. Isoc. *Paneg*. (4), 86), and that at Salamis they supplied the true commander (74. 1: cf. Isoc. *Panath*. (12), 51; Lys. *Ep*. (2), 42), the greatest number of ships (74.1: cf. Isoc. *Paneg*.(4), 98; Lys. *Ep*. (2),42),and the most enthusiastic morale (74. 1: cf. Isoc. *Paneg*. (4), 96, 99; Lys. *Ep*. (2), 33). From the foregoing account of the war, the Athenians derive the justification of their empire (75. 1: cf. 73. 1): ἆρ' ἄξιοί ἐσμεν, ὦ Λακεδαιμόνιοι, καὶ προθυμίας ἕνεκα τῆς τότε καὶ γνώμης ξυνέσεως ἀρχῆς γε ἧς ἔχομεν τοῖς Ἕλλησι μὴ οὕτως ἄγαν ἐπιφθόνως διακεῖσθαι; After this statement, the Athenians begin their defense of the empire. They point out that Athens received the hegemony at the behest of the Greeks and without Spartan opposition. This topic also passed into the fourth-century orators. Furthermore, to prove that the empire was honorably administered, the Athenians insist that their city ruled with more moderation than the Spartans or anyone else in such a position of power would have:

1. (76. 1): καὶ εἰ τότε ὑπομείναντες διὰ παντὸς ἀπήχθεσθε ἐν τῇ ἡγεμονίᾳ, ὥσπερ ἡμεῖς, εὖ ἴσμεν μὴ ἂν ἧσσον ὑμᾶς λυπηροὺς γενομένους τοῖς ξυμμάχοις καὶ ἀναγκασθέντας ἂν ἢ ἄρχειν ἐγκρατῶς ἢ αὐτοὺς κινδυνεύειν.

2. (76. 3-4): ἐπαινεῖσθαί τε ἄξιοι οἵτινες χρησάμενοι τῇ ἀνθρωπείᾳ φύσει ὥστε ἑτέρων ἄρχειν δικαιότεροι ἢ κατὰ τὴν ὑπάρχουσαν δύναμιν γένωνται. ἄλλους γ᾽ ἂν οὖν οἰόμεθα τὰ ἡμέτερα λαβόντας δεῖξαι ἂν μάλιστα εἴ τι μετριάζομεν· ἡμῖν δὲ καὶ ἐκ τοῦ ἐπιεικοῦς ἀδοξία τὸ πλέον ἢ ἔπαινος οὐκ εἰκότως περιέστη.

As if to illustrate the second passage (cf. G. de Ste. Croix, *CQ* 55, n.s. 11 (1961) 95-100), the Athenians claim that, although Athens was called litigious in her administration of justice, she actually treated the allies with far more generosity than would have been employed by any other imperial power (77. 2): καὶ οὐδεὶς σκοπεῖ αὐτῶν τοῖς καὶ ἄλλοθί που ἀρχὴν ἔχουσι καὶ ἧσσον ἡμῶν πρὸς τοὺς ὑπηκόους μετρίοις οὖσι διότι τοῦτο οὐκ ὀνειδίζεται. The Athenians close this section of their speech with a challenge to Sparta's pretensions of justice (77. 6):

Ὑμεῖς γ᾽ ἂν οὖν εἰ καθελόντες ἡμᾶς ἄρξαιτε, τάχα ἂν τὴν εὔνοιαν ἣν διὰ τὸ ἡμέτερον δέος εἰλήφατε μεταβάλοιτε, εἴπερ οἷα καὶ τότε πρὸς τὸν Μῆδον δι᾽ ὀλίγου ἡγησάμενοι ὑπεδείξατε, ὁμοῖα καὶ νῦν γνώσεσθε. ἄμεικτα γὰρ τά τε καθ᾽ ὑμᾶς αὐτοὺς νόμιμα τοῖς ἄλλοις ἔχετε καὶ προσέτι εἷς ἕκαστος ἐξιὼν οὔτε τούτοις χρῆται οὔθ᾽ οἷς ἡ ἄλλη Ἑλλὰς νομίζει.

Isocrates clearly reflects the Athenians' defense of their empire. He made a comparison between the empires of Athens and Sparta axiomatic for his defense of the Athenian empire (*Panath*. (12), 66): ἐπειδὰν γὰρ τὰ τοιαῦτα κατηγορῶσιν, οἷς ἔνοχοι Λακεδαιμόνιοι μᾶλλον τυγχάνουσιν ὄντες, οὐκ ἀποροῦμεν τοῦ περὶ ἡμῶν ῥηθέντος μεῖζον ἁμάρτημα κατ᾽ ἐκείνων εἰπεῖν. Adversaries of Athens might cast in her teeth the episodes of Melos and Scione, but they fail to consider the city's true moderation (*Paneg*. (4), 102):

ἔπειτ᾽ εἰ μὲν ἄλλοι τινὲς τῶν αὐτῶν πραγμάτων πραότερον ἐπεμελήθησαν, εἰκότως ἂν ἡμῖν ἐπιτιμῷεν· εἰ δὲ μήτε τοῦτο γέγονε μήθ᾽ οἷόν τ᾽ ἐστὶ τοσούτων πόλεων τὸ πλῆθος κρατεῖν, ἢν μή τις κολάζῃ τοὺς ἐξαμαρτάνοντας, πῶς οὐκ ἤδη δίκαιόν ἐστιν ἡμᾶς ἐπαινεῖν, οἵτινες ἐλαχίστοις χαλεπήναντες πλεῖστον χρόνον τὴν ἀρχὴν κατασχεῖν ἠδυνήθημεν;

Melos and Scione were nothing compared to the atrocities of Lysander and his decarchies (*Paneg.* (4), 110f.; *Panath.* (12), 68). Although Athens had the power to brutalize her subjects, she actually ignored her power and treated them as equals (*Paneg.* (4), 109): μόνοι δὴ τῶν μεγάλην δύναμιν λαβόντων περιείδομεν ἡμᾶς αὐτοὺς ἀπορωτέρως ζῶντας τῶν δουλεύειν αἰτίαν ἐχόντων. One must compare this passage with Thucydides, I. 77. 1: καὶ ἐλασσούμενοι γὰρ ἐν ταῖς ξυμβολαίαις πρὸς τοὺς ξυμμάχους δίκαις καὶ παρ' ἡμῖν αὐτοῖς ἐν τοῖς ὁμοίοις νόμοις ποιήσαντες τὰς κρίσεις ... Isocrates also took up the matter of judicial administration (*Paneg.* (4), 113: cf. *Panath.* (12), 66): ἀλλὰ πρὸς τοῖς ἄλλοις καὶ περὶ τῶν δικῶν καὶ τῶν γραφῶν τῶν ποτε παρ' ἡμῖν γενομένων λέγειν τολμῶσιν, αὐτοὶ πλείους ἐν τρισὶ μησὶν ἀκρίτους ἀποκτείναντες ὧν ἡ πόλις ἐπὶ τῆς ἀρχῆς ἀπάσης ἔκρινεν.

Aristides fully understood the rhetorical need for a conventional defense of the empire. Even though the scope of the *Panathenaicus* enabled the orator to present a continuous narrative of the Pentecontaetia, into which he placed his main account of the Peace of Callias (passages A and B, in Chapter VI), he later returned to the Peace (passage C) in an apologetic context which is very similar to that of Thucydides and Isocrates in the passages noted above. Aristides implemented Isocrates' design of defending the Athenian empire by comparing it with the Spartan. He condemned Lysander's administration (I. 275); he contrasted the treaties of Callias and Antalcidas (I. 277); he compared Athens' seventy years in power with Sparta's brief reign (I. 280); and he mitigated the affairs of Melos and Scione by suggesting greater atrocities by others (I. 286f.). Nevertheless, Aristides knew that a defense by comparison was inadequate and he voiced his distaste for such a procedure (I. 265): ἀεὶ μὲν οὖν ἔγωγ' ἐμεμψάμην τοῖς ἐπιτιμῶσι τῇ τῶν Λακεδαιμονίων πόλει καὶ τοῦθ' ὑπὲρ τῆς ὑμετέρας ἀξιοῦσι ποιεῖν· ἐκείνοις μὲν γὰρ ἀπεχθάνονται, ὑμᾶς δ' οὐ κοσμοῦσιν, ὡς οἴονται.

The taunt was clearly aimed at Isocrates, and Aristides repeats it later (I. 287; cf. Oliver, *Civilizing Power,* p. 138f.). To correct Isocrates, Aristides has recourse to a more realistic apology which closely follows the argument of the speech of the Athenians in Thucydides. The main points of similarity between Aristides and Thucydides are as follows:

1. The opponents fail to consider the true nature of politics.
   a. Thuc. I. 76. 2: οὕτως οὐδ' ἡμεῖς θαυμαστὸν οὐδὲν

πεποιήκαμεν οὐδ' ἀπὸ τοῦ ἀνθρωπείου τρόπου, εἰ ἀρχήν τε διδομένην ἐδεξάμεθα.

  b. *Panath.* I. 287: ἀλλά μοι δοκοῦσιν ὅλως ἠγνοηκέναι τὴν τῶν πραγμάτων φύσιν . . . κτλ.

2. That nature consists of the rule of the stronger over the weaker.

  a. Thuc. I. 76. 2: αἰεὶ καθεστῶτος τὸν ἥσσω ὑπὸ τοῦ δυνατωτέρου κατείργεσθαι.

  b. *Panath.* I. 288: ἅπασα γὰρ δήπουθεν ἀρχὴ τῶν κρειττόνων ἐστὶ καὶ παρ' αὐτὸν τὸν τῆς ἰσότητος νόμον.

3. Although Athens had such strength, she used it more justly than anyone else.

  a. Thuc. I. 76. 3: ἐπαινεῖσθαί τε ἄξιοι οἵτινες χρησάμενοι τῇ ἀνθρωπείᾳ φύσει ὥστε ἑτέρων ἄρχειν δικαιότεροι . . . κτλ.

  b. *Panath.* I. 288: . . . ὅταν δείξῃ τῶν ἄλλων εἴτε Ἑλληνικῶν δυνάμεων εἴτε καὶ βαρβαρικῶν βασιλειῶν ἡντινοῦν ἐλάττονι τῷ τῆς πλεονεξίας γιγνομένῳ χρησαμένην ἢ τὸν τῶν Ἀθηναίων ἔστι δῆμον εὑρεῖν.

4. Instead of praise Athens received blame for her efforts.

  a. Thuc. I. 76. 4: ἡμῖν δὲ καὶ ἐκ τοῦ ἐπιεικοῦς ἀδοξία τὸ πλέον ἢ ἔπαινος οὐκ εἰκότως περιέστη.

  b. *Panath.* I. 289: οὐ γὰρ διὰ τὴν ἄλλην ἐπιείκειαν χάριτος παρ' ἐνίων ἔτυχεν, ἀλλ' εἴ τι προσηνάγκασεν, ἐπιφανῶς ἔδοξε βιάζεσθαι.

As a result of all these similarities, we can probably be safe in saying that Aristides was aware of the affinity between Thucydides' and Isocrates' defenses of the empire. Since the late author was unencumbered with Isocrates' scruples about appearing to be a politician of the Thrasymachean brand, he could return to a more original justification of the empire, one that more clearly reflects popular thinking of the Athenian imperial period. Cf. J. Chambers, *PP* 30 (1975) 177-91.

SELECTED BIBLIOGRAPHY

(1) EDITIONS OF GREEK AND LATIN TEXTS

For Aelius Aristides the following texts have been employed by the author:

1. For the *Panath., Rhet.,* and *Pro Quatt.*: Lenz, F.W., and Behr, C.A., edd. *Aristidis Opera Omnia.* Vol. I. Leiden: Brill. Fasc. 1, 1976; fascs. 2 and 3, 1978.

2. For the *Rom., Eleus.,* and *Athena*: Keil, B., ed. *Aristidis quae supersunt omnia.* Vol. II. Berlin: Weidmann, 1898.

3. For other works and the Scholia: Dindorf, W., ed. *Aristides.* 3 vols. Leipzig: Weidmann, 1829.

For the sake of consistency, all references are identified by the volume and page number in Dindorf's edition. All translations of Aristides are the author's own.

As for other ancient works, the author has consulted the most recent Teubner edition, with the following exceptions. (1) The most recent Oxford Classical Texts were used for Aeschylus, Aristophanes, Aristotle's *Poetics,* Nepos, Demosthenes, Herodotus, Lysias, Thucydides, and Xenophon. (2) The most recent Budé editions were employed for Aeschines and the Greek Anthology. (3) For Himerius and certain other late evidence, the author used:

(a) Colonna, A., ed. *Himerii Declamationes et Orationes.* Rome: Typis Publicae Officinae Polygraphicae, 1951.

(b) Walz, C., ed. *Rhetores Graeci.* 9 vols. Tübingen: Cotta, 1832-1836.

Unless otherwise mentioned in the notes, citations of fragments were taken from Jacoby, *FGrH.* Translations taken from the Loeb Classical Library have been so designated in the text. Standard American abbreviations have been employed for the more common journals; for the others, I have either used a rather full form of abbreviation or the abbreviations in *L'Année philologique.*

(2) GENERAL REFERENCES

ALLROGGEN, D. "Herodot als literarisches und politisches Vorbild des Demosthenes." *Hermes* 103 (1975) 423-33.

BAUMGART, H. *Aelius Aristides als Repräsentant der sophistischen Rhetorik.* Leipzig: Teubner, 1874.

BAYER, E., and HEIDEKING, J. *Die Chronologie des Perikleischen Zeitalters.* Darmstadt: Wiss. Buchges., 1975.

BELOCH, K.J. *Griechische Geschichte* 4 vols. 2nd edition. Strassburg: Trübner, 1912-1927.

BENGTSON, H. *Griechische Geschichte.*4 Vol. III.4, *Handbuch der Altertumswissenschaft.* Munich: Beck, 1969.

BLASS, F. *Die attische Beredsamkeit.* 3 vols. Leipzig: Teubner, 1887-1898.

BOULANGER, A. *Aelius Aristide et la sophistique dans la province d'Asie au IIe siècle de notre ère.* Paris: Bibliothèque des Écoles françaises d'Athènes et de Rome, 1923.

BOWERSOCK, G., ed. *Approaches to the Second Sophistic.* University Park, Pa.: American Philological Association, 1974.

BOWIE, E. "Greeks and their Past in the Second Sophistic." *Past and Present* 46 (1970) 3-41.

BROADHEAD, H.D. *The Persae of Aeschylus.* Cambridge University, 1960.

BUTTS, H.R. *The Glorification of Athens in Greek Drama. Iowa Studies in Classical Philology.* Vol. XI (= Diss. University of Iowa, 1942).

CONNOR, W.R. *The New Politicians of Fifth-Century Athens.* Princeton, 1971.

--------. *Theopompus and Fifth-Century Athens.* Washington: Center for Hellenic Studies and Harvard, 1968.

DAY, JOHN. *An Economic History of Athens under Roman Domination.* Columbia University, 1942.

DEANE, P. *Thucydides' Dates, 465-431 B.C.* Don Mills, Ontario: Longman, 1972.

DE ROMILLY, J. *Thucydide et l'impérialisme athénien.* Paris: Société d'édition "Les Belles Lettres," 1947.

DEUBNER, L. *Attische Feste.* Berlin: Keller, 1932.

EGERMANN, F. "Thukydides über die Art seiner Reden und über seine Darstellung der Kriegsgeschehnisse." *Hist.* 21 (1972) 575-602.

FINLEY, M.I. *The Use and Abuse of History.* New York: Viking, 1975.

GOMME, A.W. *The Greek Attitude to Poetry and History.* Sather Classical Lectures, Vol. XXVII. University of California, 1954.

GRAINDOR, P. "Études sur l'éphébie attique sous l'empire." *Musée Belge* 26 (1922) 165-228.

GRUNDY, G.B. *Thucydides and the History of his Age.* Vol. II. Oxford, 1948.

GUELKE, C. *Mythos und Zeitgeschichte bei Aischylos: Das Verhältnis von Mythos und Historie in Eumeniden und Hiketiden. Beitr. zur klass. Philol.* Vol. 31. Meisenheim: Hain, 1969.

HAAS, A. *Quibus fontibus Aristides in componenda declamatione, quae inscribitur* πρὸς Πλάτωνα ὑπὲρ τῶν τεττάρων, *usus sit.* Diss. Greifswald, 1884.

HABICHT, C. "Falsche Urkunden zur Geschichte Athens im Zeitalter der Perserkriege." *Hermes* 89 (1961) 1-35.

HAURY, J. *Quibus fontibus Aristides usus sit in declamatione quae inscribitur* Παναθηναικός. Diss. Augsburg, 1888.

HENDERSON, M. "Plato's *Menexenus* and the Distortion of History." *A Class* 18 (1975) 25-46.
HERTER, H. "Athen im Bilde der Römerzeit. Zu einem Epigramm Senecas." *Serta Philologica Aenipontana: Innsbrucker Beitr. zur Kultur.* 7-8 (1962) 347-58.
HOOKER, G., ed. *Parthenos and Parthenon. Greece and Rome,* Suppl. to Vol. 10. Oxford, 1963.
HOW, W., and WELLS, J. *Commentary on Herodotus.* 2 vols. Oxford, 1912.
JACOBY, F. *Atthis.* Oxford, 1949.
---------.*s.v.* Herodotus, *RE,* Suppl. 2, cols. 205-520.
---------.*s.v.* Ktesias, *RE,* cols. 2032-2073.
JEBB, R.C. *The Attic Orators.* 2 vols. London: Macmillan, 1876.
JOHNSON, J. *Plutarch on the Glory of the Athenians: A Reassessment.* Diss. Univ. of So. Calif., 1972.
JONES, C. "Aelius Aristides,Εἰς βασιλέα."*JRS* 62 (1972) 134-52.
JOST, K. *Das Beispiel und Vorbild der Vorfahren bei den attischen Rednern und Geschichtschreibern bis Demosthenes.* Paderborn: Schöningh, 1936. (= *Rhetorische Studien* 19).
KAGAN, D. *The Archidamian War.* Cornell, 1974.
---------. *The Outbreak of the Peloponnesian War.* Cornell, 1969.
KENNEDY, G. *The Art of Persuasion in Greece.* Princeton, 1963.
--------. *The Art of Rhetoric in the Roman World.* Princeton, 1972.
KIERDORF, W. *Erlebnis und Darstellung der Perserkriege: Studien zu Simonides, Pindar, Aischylos, und den attischen Rednern.*Göttingen: Vandenhöck and Ruprecht, 1966. (= *Hypomnemata* 16).
LENZ, F.W. "Der Athenahymnos des Aristeides." *Rivista di Cultura classica e medioevale* 5 (1963) 329-47.
LORAUX, N. "Marathon ou l'histoire idéologique. A propos des paragraphes XX à XXVI de l'Oraison funèbre en l'honneur des soldats qui allèrent au secours des Corinthiens, attribuée à Lysias." *REA* 75 (1973) 13-42.
MACAN, R.W. *Herodotus, the Seventh, Eighth and Ninth Books.* 2 vols. London: Macmillan, 1908.
MOMMSEN, A. *Heortologie.Antiquarische Untersuchungen über die städtischen Feste der Athener.* Reprint. Amsterdam: Grüner, 1968.
PARKE, H.W. *Festivals of the Athenians.* London: Thames and Hudson, 1977.
OLIVER, J.H. "Roman Emperors and Athenian Ephebes." *Hist.* 26 (1977) 89-94.
PEARSON, L. "Historical Allusions in the Attic Orators." *CP* 36 (1941) 209-29.
---------. *The Local Historians of Attica.* Philadelphia: American Philological Association, 1942.
PÉLÉKIDIS, C.*Histoire de l'éphébie attique.* Paris: Boccard, 1962.
PODLECKI, A.J. *The Life of Themistocles: A Critical Survey of the Literary and Archaeological Evidence.* Montreal: McGill—Queens, 1975.
---------. *The Political Background of Aeschylean Tragedy.* University of Michigan, 1966.
---------. "Simonides: 480." *Hist.* 17 (1968) 257-75.
RAUBITSCHEK, A.E. *Dedications from the Athenian Akropolis.* Cambridge, Mass.: Archaeological Institute of America, 1949.
---------. "Herodotus and the Inscriptions." *Bulletin of the Institute of Classical Studies of the University of London* 8 (1961) 59-61.

---------. "Inschriften als Hilfsmittel der Geschichtsforschung." *RSA* 1 (1971) 177-95.
---------. "The Peace Policy of Pericles." *AJA* 70 (1966) 37-41.
---------. "The Speech of the Athenians at Sparta." *The Speeches in Thucydides: A Collection of Original Studies.* Edited by P. Stadter. University of North Carolina, 1973.
---------. "Theophrastus on Ostracism." *ClMed* 19 (1958) 73-109.
REARDON, B. "The Anxious Pagan." *EMC* 17 (1973) 81-93.
REINMUTH, O.W. *"Hoi peri to Diogeneion* Again." *TAPA* 93 (1962) 374-88.
---------. "The Spirit of Athens after Chaeronea." *Acta of the Vth Internat. Congr. of Greek and Latin Epigraphy* (1967). Oxford: Blackwell, 1971. Pp. 47-51.
SCHACHERMEYER, F. *Perikles.* Stuttgart: Kohlhammer, 1969.
SCHLATTER, F.W., S.J. *Salamis and Plataea in the Tradition of the Attic Orators.* Diss. Princeton, 1960.
SCHMID, W., and STÄHLIN, O. *Geschichte der griechischen Literatur.* Vol. II/1, *Handbuch der Altertumswissenschaft.* Munich: Beck, 1934.
SCHMITZ-KAHLMANN, G. *Das Beispiel der Geschichte im politischen Denken des Isokrates.* Leipzig: Dieterich, 1939.
SCHRÖDER, O. *De laudibus Athenarum a poetis tragicis et ab oratoribus epidicticis excultis.* Diss. Göttingen, 1914.
SCHWARTZ, E. "Kallisthenes Hellenika." *Hermes* 35 (1900) 106-30.
SOHLBERG, D. "Aelius Aristides und Diogenes von Babylon: Zur Geschichte des rednerischen Ideals." *MH* 29 (1972) 177-200; 256-77.
SORDI, M. "La propaganda del mondo greco." *RSA* 1 (1971) 197-211.
STRASBURGER, H. "Thukydides und die politische Selbstdarstellung der Athener." *Hermes* 86 (1958) 17-40.
TRAVLOS, J. *Pictorial Dictionary of Ancient Athens.* New York: Praeger, 1971.
ULLMAN, B.L. "History and Tragedy." *TAPA* 73 (1942) 25-53.
UXKULL-GYLLENBAND, W., GRAF. *Plutarch und die griechische Biographie.* Stuttgart: Kohlhammer, 1927.
WALBANK, F. "History and Tragedy." *Hist.* 9 (1960) 216-34.
WELLES, C.B. "Isocrates' View of History." *The Classical Tradition: Studies in Honor of Harry Caplan.* Edited by L. Wallach. Cornell University, 1966.
WILAMOWITZ-MOELLENDORFF, U. VON. *Aristoteles und Athen.* Reprint. Dublin: Weidmann, 1966.
WYCHERLEY, R.E. *Literary and Epigraphical Testimonia.* Vol. III of *The Athenian Agora.* Princeton: American School of Classical Studies, 1957.

(3) TRIPTOLEMUS

COOK, A.B. *Zeus.* Vol. I. Cambridge University, 1914.
DUGAS, C. "La mission de Triptolème." *Mélanges d'Archéologie et d'Histoire* (École française de Rome) 62 (1950) 7-31 and plates.
FRAZER, SIR J.G. *Apollodorus: The Library.* New York: Putnam, 1921.
FURTWÄNGLER, A., and REICHHOLD, K. *Griechische Vasenmalerei.* Ser. III. Munich: Bruckmann, 1932.

GROSSMAN, B. *The Eleusinian Gods and Heroes in Greek Art.* Unpubl. Diss. Washington University, 1959.
KERÉNYI, C. *Eleusis: Archetypal Image of Mother and Daughter.* Translated by R. Manheim. New York: Schocken Books, 1977.
MATTINGLY, H.B. "Athens and Eleusis: Some New Ideas." *Phoros: Tribute to Benjamin Dean Meritt.* Edited by D.W. Bradeen and M.F. McGregor. Locust Valley, N.Y.: Augustin, 1974.
MONTANARI, F. "L'episodio eleusino delle peregrinazioni di Demetra: A proposito delle fonti di Ovidio, *Fast.* IV, 502-62 e *Metam.* V, 446-61." *ASNP* 4 (1974) 109-37.
MYLONAS, G.E. *Eleusis and the Eleusinian Mysteries.* Princeton, 1961.
OVERBECK, J. *Griechische Kunstmythologie.* Reprint. Osnabrück: Biblio, 1968.
RICHARDSON, N.J. *The Homeric Hymn to Demeter.* Oxford, 1974.
SCHWENN, F. *s.v.* Triptolemus, *RE.* VII A, cols. 213-230.
SIMMS, R. "The Eleusinia in the Sixth to Fourth Centuries." *GRBS* 16 (1975) 269-79.

(4) DEPARTURE OF THE SPARTANS

BRUNT, P.A. "The Hellenic League against Persia." *Hist.* 2 (1953) 135-63.
HAMMOND, N.G.L. "The Origins and Nature of the Athenian Alliance of 478/7 B.C." *JHS* 87 (1967) 41-61.
JACKSON, A.H. "The Original Purpose of the Delian League." *Hist.* 18 (1969) 12-16.
LARSON, J.A.O. "The Constitution and Original Purpose of the Delian League." *HSCP* 51 (1940) 175-213.
----------. "Federation for Peace in Ancient Greece." *CP* 39 (1944) 145-62.
LEWIS, D.M. "Themistocles' Archonship." *Hist.* 22 (1973) 757f.
MEYER, H.D. "Vorgeschichte und Begründung des delisch-attischen Seebundes." *Hist.* 12 (1963) 406-46.
NESSELHAUF, H. *Untersuchungen zur Geschichte der delisch-attischen Symmachie. Klio.* Beiheft 30 (Neue Folge, Heft 17), 1933.
RAUBITSCHEK, A.E. "The Covenant of Plataea." *TAPA* 91 (1960) 178-83.
SCHULLER, W. *Die Herrschaft der Athener im ersten attischen Seebund.* Berlin: De Gruyter, 1974.
SEALEY, R. "The Origin of the Delian League."*Ancient Society and Institutions: Studies Presented to Victor Ehrenberg on his 75th Birthday.* Oxford: Blackwell, 1966.
SIEWERT, P. *Der Eid von Plataiai.* Munich: Beck, 1972.
----------. "The Ephebic Oath in Fifth-Century Athens." *JHS* 97 (1977) 102-11.
STAHL, H.-P. "Learning through Suffering? Croesus' Conversations in the History of Herodotus." *YCS* 24 (1975) 1-36.
THOMPSON, H.A., and WYCHERLEY, R.E. *The Agora of Athens.* Vol. XIV of *The Athenian Agora.* Princeton: American School of Classical Studies, 1972.
WICKERSHAM, J. *Hegemony and Greek Historians.* Diss. Princeton, 1972.

(5) THE BATTLE OF EURYMEDON

BADIAN, E., and BUCKLER, J. "The Wrong Salamis?" *RhM* 118 (1975) 226-39.

BARNS, J. "Cimon and the First Athenian Expedition to Cyprus." *Hist.* 2 (1953) 163-76.

FRIEDLÄNDER, P. *Epigrammata: Greek Inscriptions in Verse: From the Beginnings to the Persian Wars.* University of California, 1948.

----------. "Geschichtswende im Gedicht." *Stud. ital. d. filol. cl.* N.S. 15 (1938) 89-120.

GRENFELL, B., and HUNT, A. *The Oxyrhynchus Papyri.* London: Egypt Exploration Fund, 1898-1927.

HAMMOND, N.G.L. "The Campaign and Battle of Marathon." *JHS* 88 (1968) 13-57.

KAIBEL, G. *Epigrammata Graeca.* Reprint. Hildesheim: Olms, 1965.

MERITT, B.D. "Epigrams from the Battle of Marathon." *The Aegean and the Near East.* Edited by S. Weinberg. Locust Valley, N.Y.: Augustin, 1956.

MOSLEY, D. "Callias' Fine." *Mnemosyne* 26 (1973) 57f.

PAGE, D.L. *Epigrammata Graeca.* Oxford, 1975.

PARKER, S.T. "The Objectives of Cimon's Expedition to Cyprus." *AJP* 97 (1976) 30-38.

PEEK, W. "Die Kämpfe am Eurymedon." *Athenian Studies Presented to W.S. Ferguson. HSCP,* suppl. vol. I (1940) 97-120.

----------. *Griechische Vers-Inschriften.* Vol. I. Berlin: Akademie, 1955.

PREGER, T. *Inscriptiones Graecae Metricae.* Reprint. Chicago: Ares, 1977.

PRITCHETT, W.K. "Marathon." *University of California Publications in Classical Archaeology* 4 (1960) 137-90.

RAUBITSCHEK, A.E. "Two Monuments Erected after the Victory of Marathon." *AJA* 44 (1940) 53-59.

RUBINCAM, C. "A Note on Oxyrhynchus Papyrus 1610." *Phoenix* 30 (1976) 357-66.

SCHREINER, J.H. "Anti-Thukydidean Studies in the Pentekontaetia." *SO* 51 (1976) 19-63.

SORDI, M. "La vittoria dell'Eurimedonte e le due spedizioni di Cimone a Cipro." *RSA* 1 (1971) 33-48.

WADE-GERY, H.T. "Classical Epigrams and Epitaphs." *JHS* 53 (1933) 71-104.

(6) THE EXPEDITION TO EGYPT

BIGWOOD, J.M. "Ctesias' Account of the Revolt of Inaros." *Phoenix* 30 (1976) 1-25.

BURIAN, P. "Pelasgus and Politics in Aeschylus' Danaid Trilogy." *WS* N.F. 8 (1974) 5-14.

GARVIE, A.F. *Aeschylus' Supplices: Play and Trilogy.* Cambridge University, 1969.

KIENITZ, F.K. *Die politische Geschichte Aegyptens vom 7. bis zum 4. Jahrhundert vor der Zeitwende.* Berlin: Akademie, 1953.

LIBOUREL, J. "The Athenian Disaster in Egypt." *AJP* 92 (1971) 605-15.

LUPPINO, E. "L'intervento ateniese in Egitto nelle tragedie eschilee." *Aegyptus* 47 (1967) 197-212.
PEARSON, L. "Thucydides as Reporter and Critic." *TAPA* 78 (1947) 37-60.
PEEK, W. "Ein Seegefecht aus den Perserkriegen." *Klio* 32 (1939) 289-306.
PODLECKI, A.J. "Politics in Aeschylus' *Supplices*." *Class. Folia* 26 (1972) 64-71.
RAUBITSCHEK, A.E. "Kimons Zurückberufung." *Hist.* 3 (1955) 379-80.
----------. "Theopompus on Thucydides the Son of Melesias." *Phoenix* 14 (1960) 81-95.
SALANITRO, G. "La data e il significato politico delle *Supplici* di Eschilo." *Helikon* 8 (1968) 311-40.
SALMON, P. *La politique égyptienne d'Athènes.* Brussels: Académie Royale de Belgique, 1965.
SCHARF, J. "Die erste ägyptische Expedition der Athener." *Hist.* 3 (1954) 308-25.
WESTLAKE, H.D. "Thucydides and the Athenian Disaster in Egypt." *CP* 45 (1950) 209-16.

(7) THE PEACE OF CALLIAS

AMIT, M. "A Peace Treaty between Sparta and Persia." *RSA* 4 (1974) 55-63.
ANDREWES, A. "Thucydides and the Persians." *Hist.* 10 (1961) 1-18.
BOSWORTH, A. "The Congress Decree: Another Hypothesis." *Hist.* 20 (1971) 600-16.
CARY, M. "The Peace of Callias." *CQ* 39 (1945) 87-91.
EDDY, S.K. "The Cold War between Athens and Persia, ca. 448-412 B.C." *CP* 68 (1973) 241-58.
----------. "On the Peace of Callias." *CP* 65 (1970) 8-14.
GOMME, A.W. "Athenian Notes." *AJP* 65 (1944) 321-39.
GRIFFITH, G. "A Note on Plutarch, *Pericles.* 17. 1." *Hist.* 27 (1978) 218f.
HANDS, A. "In Favor of a Peace of Kallias." *Mnemosyne* 28 (1975) 193-95.
KRAFT, K. "Bemerkungen zu den Perserkriegen." *Hermes* 92 (1964) 144-71.
MATTINGLY, H.B. "The Peace of Kallias."*Hist.* 14 (1965) 273-81.
MERITT, B.D. "Perikles, the Athenian Mint, and the Hephaisteion."*PAPhS* 119 (1975) 267-74.
MURISON, C.L. "The Peace of Callias: Its Historical Context." *Phoenix* 25 (1971) 12-31.
OLIVER, J.H. "The Peace of Callias and the Pontic Expedition of Pericles." *Hist.* 6 (1957) 254-55.
RAUBITSCHEK, A.E. "The Treaties between Persia and Athens." *GRBS* 5 (1964) 151-59.
SCHAEFER, H. "Die Autonomie-Klausel des Kalliasfriedens." *Probleme der alten Geschichte.* Göttingen: Vandenhoeck und Ruprecht, 1963.
SCHRADER, C. "El decreto del Congreso y el fragmento 153 de Theopompo." Cuad. de Investigación-Filol.(Logroño Servicio Publicaciones Col. Univ.). I, 1, 1975, pp. 77-101.

———. *La Paz de Calias: Testimonios y Interpretación*. Barcelona: Universidad de Barcelona, Instituto de Estudios Helenicos, 1976.
SCHREINER, J.H. "More Anti-Thukydidean Studies in the Pentekontaetia." *SO* 52 (1977) 19-38.
SEAGER, R. "The Congress Decree: Some Doubts and a Hypothesis." *Hist.* 18 (1969) 129-41.
SEALEY, R. "The Peace of Callias Once More." *Hist.* 3 (1955) 325-33.
STOCKTON, D. "The Peace of Callias." *Hist.* 8 (1959) 61-79.
WADE-GERY, H.T. "The Peace of Kallias." *Athenian Studies Presented to W.S. Ferguson. HSCP.* suppl. vol. I (1940) 121-56.

(8) SUPPLEMENTARY BIBLIOGRAPHY

In this section of the bibliography, I include works which have come to my attention after the manuscript was complete and works which I have not been able to obtain.

BARATTE, F. "Le sarcophage de Triptolème au Musée du Louvre." *RA* (1974) 271-90.
BOFFO, L. "Cimone e gli alleati di Atene." *RIL* 109 (1976) 442-50.
DELVOYE, C. "Art et politique à Athènes à l'époque de Cimon." *Le monde grec: Pensée, littérature, histoire, documents. Hommages à C. Préaux.* Univ. libre de Bruxelles—Fac. de Philos. & Lettres, 52. Brussels, 1975. Pp. 801-807.
FLACH, D. *Antike Grabreden als Geschichtsquelle: Leichenpredigten als Quelle historischer Wissenschaften.* Cologne: Böhlau, 1975. Pp. 1-35.
FREIJEIRO, A. BLANCO. "El Nilo de Igabrum."*Habis* 2 (1971) 251-56. Apropos of Triptolemus.
KRISCHER, T. "Die enkomiastische Topik im *Epitaphios* des Perikles." *Mnemosyne* 30 (1977) 122-35.
KUMANIEKI, M. "Quelques remarques sur les sources orales chez Thucydide." *Assoc. G. Budé: Actes IXe Congres.* Paris: Les Belles Lettres, 1975. Pp. 152-65.
MERENTITIS, K.I. "Ἐπιγράμματα τοῦ Σιμωνίδου ἀναφερόμενα εἰς τοὺς Περσικοὺς Πολέμους." *EEAth* 24 (1973-74) 729-75.
MOGGI, M. "Autori greci di Persika, I: Dionisio di Mileto." *ASNP* 2 (1972) 433-68.
———. "Le guerre persiane nella tradizione letteraria romana." *CS* 9 (1972) 5-49.
PARSIKOV, A.Y. "On the Chronology of the Athenian Campaign in Egypt." *Vestnik Drevnej Istorii* 111 (1970) 107-12. (In Russian with a summary in English.)
PELEKIDIS, C. "Συμβολὴ στὴν ἱστορία τῆς Πεντηκονταετίας." *Dodone* 3 (1974) 407-39.
PERLMAN, S. "Panhellenism, the Polis, and Imperialism." *Hist.* 25 (1976) 1-30.
PIÉRART, M. "Thucydide et la chronologie des cinquante ans." *LEC* 45 (1976) 109-23.
PRANDI, L. "La liberazione della Grecia nella propaganda spartana durante la guerra del Peloponneso." *CISA* 4 (1976) 72-83.

SCHAUENBURG, K. "Εὐρυμέδων εἰμι." *MDAI(A)* 90 (1975) 91-121.

SCHWARZ, G. "Eine Hydria des Berliner Malers in Graz." *JOEAI* 50 (1972-75) 125-33. Apropos of Triptolemus.

----------. "Zwei eleusinische Szenen auf einem Kelchkrater des Berliner Malers in Athen." *Arch. Anz.* (1971)178-82. Apropos of Triptolemus.

SORDI, M. "Atene e Sparta dalle guerre persiane al 462-1 a. C." *Aevum* 50 (1976) 25-41.

INDEX LOCORUM

(References are to pages; notes appear as decimals after page numbers.)

Aelius Aristides (ed. Dindorf)		
Ad Ath.	I. 18	16
Panath.	I. 152	9
	167	15f.
	194	1
	195	43,45
	204	69.56
	206	44
	209	44
	211	57
	212	44
	217	58
	223	45
	223f.	56,59, 67.34
	231	66.24
	243	43f.,151
	244	43,66.10, 121,169.77
	245	15,44
	246	39,66.11,94
	246f.	75
	247	107,129
	248	111,152
	248f.	154
	249f.	142f.,150, 165.25
	250	42,105.73
	260	1
	265	198
	276	42,77
	277	143,165.25
	287-89	199
Rom.	I. 325f.	144
	336	16
Eleus.	I. 416f.	16,30,32.4
	421	32.9
Pro Quatt.	II.208	95f., 106.85,151f., 169.77
	209	75,93
	210	79
	212	119f.

Aeschines
Ctes. (3),	183	106.81

Aeschylus
Pers.	233f.	56
	548-53	122
	584-94	123
	714	123
Suppl.	605ff.	126

Ammianus Marcellinus
XVII. 11.3	93,194

Andocides
De pace (3),29	184f.

Aristodemus
FGrH 104 F 13	193

Aristotle
Poetics. 1451b	2

Callimachus
Ad Dem. 21	27

Callisthenes, Hellenica
FGrH 124 F 15	76
F 16	77

Cicero
De or. II.62	xvi, 5

Claudian
De rapt. Per. I.12-14	33.22

Craterus
FGrH 342 F 13	86

Demosthenes
De lib. Rhod. (15), 29	188
De fals. leg. (19), 272	183f.
273	165.25,188

Didymus
On Stoa of Zeus	50
In Dem., col. 7. 71	192

Diodorus, Bibliotheca historica
I. 2. 2			12.24
I. 29.3f.			36.59
IX. 10.5			190
XI. 41.4			47
60.3ff.			77f.,81
61.7			102.32
71.3			124
71.4			138.100
XII. 2.1			153,190
3.2ff.			81
4.4ff.			85,191
26.2			191

Dionysius of Halicarnassus
   Antiq. Rom. I. 12. 2   34.28
Ephorus
   FGrH 70 F 192   76
Epigrams
   Cyprus expedition   78,93, 122,160
   Eurymedon   102.37
   Marathon   55,71.80&81
   Salamis(?)   72.87
Eusebius
   Vers. Arm. Ol. 79.4
   (Syn. 470. 7)   93,194
Hecataeus
   FGrH 1 F 1a   11.11
Herodotus
   VI. 42.2   189
   VII. 10.2   123
        139.5   47
        151   189
Himerius
   Pol. (6), 29   193f.
Hyperides
   Ep. (6), 5   69.62
IG
   I^2 57   168.63
        76   23f.
   II^2 140   36.65
        2086   177
        2788   175f.
Isocrates
   Paneg. (4), 9   8
               28   17,32.9
               30   8,17
               72   55
               83   47
               89   69.62
               99   60
               102   197
               109   198
               113   198
               117   153
               117ff.   91,187
               179   90f.
   Philip. (5), 59   10.7
   Areop. (7), 80   188

   Panath. (12), 66   197
                   149   7
                   150   7f.
                   271   2
Justin (Trogus)
   II. 15.20   93
   III. 6.6.   132.12
Livy
   XXXIII. 20. 1-3   192
Lycurgus
   In Leoc. 72f.   89
               73   165.25,189
Lysias
   Ep. (2), 55   149f.
             56f.   149,154,187
             57   73.113
Marmor Parium
   Ep. A 12, Jacoby   35.45
      A 13   35.46
Ovid
   Metam. V. 652   28
Panyassis
   Fr. 24, K (= Apollod.
     I. 5. 2)   34.26
Pausanias
   I. 8.2   193
     28.2   183
Philochorus
   FGrH 328 F 104   26
              F 117   63f.
Pindar
   Fr. 77, Snell   47
Plato
   Menex. 240e   56
           241d,e   88,109,188
           242a   63
   Leg. 782b   36.61
Plutarch
   Cim. 6.2   115
          11.3   115
          12.1ff.   76,95,153
          13.4   77,95, 153,192
          13.5   86,192
          15.2   118
          18.1   113,121

	18.5ff.	113f.,124	70.6	111
	19.4	165.25,	70.9	112
		193	73.1	196
Per.	12.1ff.	182f.	74.1	58
	17.1	182	75.1-3	61,69.60,
	20.3	116,119,		88,187
		121	76.1-4	88,197,199
Them.	31.4ff.	116,	77.1f.	197f.
		165.25	77.6	197

Polybius

I. 1. 2.		12.25	
Fr. XVIII. 41a. 1		192	

96.1 — 43,48
100.1 — 75f.
104.1f. — 110f.,127f., 131.5
110.2 — 132.17, 135.58

Scholia

in Aristid. (ed. Dindorf)

III.	54	37.73	
	55	36.59	
	210	101.25,120,	
		136.71,151f.	
	211	131.2	
	213f.	194	
	215	165.20	

in Hermog. Walz
    V.388   194f.

Sophocles, *Triptolemus*

Fr.	596f., Pearson	20
	611	34.30

Suda

s.v. Cimon, Callias   93,194

Theopompus, *Philippica*

FGrH 115	F	153	191
	F	154	192

Thucydides

I.	14.3	70.68
	20.1	7
	20.3	7
	22.2	3
	22.4	4

II.	36.4	63
	41.1	57
	41.3	61
III.	10.2	88
	10.3	68.49
VI.	54.1	7
	76.3	88
VII.	87.6	135.58
VIII.	5.5	189
	18.1	185
	37.1-5	185f.
	56.4	190
	58.1	186

Virgil

Georg. I. 19   28

Xenophon

Ath. Pol. 2. 7		135.59
Hell. III. 4. 25		186
IV. 8.1		11.19
V. 1.31		186
VI. 3.6		25

INDEX NOMINUM ET RERUM

AELIUS ARISTIDES, *passim:* historiography, Chapter I, 29ff., 39ff., 59ff., 94ff., 110ff.; *Panath.*, Introduction, 9, 15, 59, 75, 79ff., 92, 152ff., 158, 172ff., 176f., 199; *Pro Quatt.* 75, 79f., 82, 92, 151ff., 174; the Scholia, 24, 119f. Cf. the Index Locorum

AESCHYLUS: *Persae, xvii,* 52ff., 83, 122f., 125, 153; *Suppl.,* 126ff. Cf. the Index Locorum

ANTALCIDAS, PEACE OF, 63, 91f., 140, 144, 149ff., 158, 161, 186, 197

APOLLODORUS, 20

ARISTODEMUS, 108f., 148, 193. Cf. the Index Locorum

ARISTOGITON, cf. Tyrannicides

ARISTOTLE, *xiii,* 2ff.

ARTAXERXES I, 54, 107, 110, 123, 176. Cf. Hybris

ARTEMISIUM, BATTLE OF, 44f., 93

ATHENS, *passim:* Delian League, 23, Chapter III; Athenian Empire, imperialism, 24f., 61, 157f., Appendix II; Athenian festivals, 22ff., 27, 30, 175ff.; Athens in the 2nd century A.D., *xiii, xvi,* 1&2, 30f., 175ff.; Athenian monuments, *ix,* 6 (Tyrannicides), 20 (Eleusinium), 22f., 159f., (Telesterion), 23, 160 (Parthenon), 50f., 91f., 159 (Zeus Eleutherios), 125 (Lechtheid casualty list), 159, 183f. (Athena Promachos), 160, 183 (Athena Nike), 184 (Altar of Peace); Athenian philanthropy, cf. Triptolemus

Atthis, Atthidographers, *xiv*ff., 6, 26f., 63f., 155f., 161f., 174.

CALLIAS, SON OF HIPPONICUS, 85ff., 140, 161

CALLIAS, PEACE OF, Chapter VI, 174, 197, Appendix I; terms, 76f., 146ff.; chronology, 41ff., 47, 62ff., Chapter IV, 107f.; stele, 91f., 141, 149, 184; as a rhetorical topos, 44, 47, 91, 95f., 108. Cf. Hybris

CALLISTHENES, 76ff., 86, 95, 140, 145f., 149, 153f., 162

CHELIDONIANS, cf. Callias, Peace of

CHRONOLOGY, *passim:* Cyprus expedition, 117f.; the Eurymedon and the Peace of Callias, Chapter IV, 107f., 141f., 145f., 161; unity of Persian War, Chapter III, 156ff.

CICERO, *xvi,* 5.

CIMON, 22, 29, 52, Chapter IV, 112ff., 151ff., 175

CONGRESS DECREE, 158, 160f., 182f.

CRATERUS, 86, 141, 148f.

CTESIAS, 77, 82, 108f., 123, 128

CYANEANS, cf. Callias, Peace of

CYPRUS, ATHENIAN EXPEDITION TO, 42, 77ff., 110, 113ff., 152; epigram, 78, 82ff., 89ff., 95, 122, 160f., 181

CYRUS THE GREAT, 52. Cf. Hybris

DARIUS I, 44f., 176. Cf. Hybris

DEMETER, cf. Triptolemus

DEMOSTHENES, 63, 145, 148ff., 160, 188. Cf. the Index Locorum

DIDYMUS, 50, 192

DIODORUS, *passim:* 27, 77f., 81, 108f., 117ff., 124f., 128, 140, 148ff., 190f. Cf. the Index Locorum

EGYPT, ATHENIAN EXPEDITION TO, 79, 85, Chapter V, 152, 173

ELEUSIS, ELEUSINIAN RELIGION, cf. Triptolemus

EPHEBES, cf. Athens, festivals

EPHORUS, *passim: xiv,* 4, 47, 76ff., 89f., 109f., 117, 144ff., 148ff., 162. Cf. Diodorus
EPIGRAMS, 6, 55, 82ff., 89ff., 95f., 122, 160f.
EPILYCUS, PEACE OF, 140, 184
EPITAPHIOS, EPITAPHIC TRADITION, 8, 10, 17, 52ff., 130, 149, 156ff., 161, 172ff.
EURYMEDON, BATTLE OF, 42 (Pamphylia), Chapter IV, 107ff., 125, 142ff., 151ff., 174
FEAR (φόβος, δέος), THEME OF, 42ff., 52, 77, 95f., 124, 151ff., 159. Cf. Callias, Peace of, rhetorical topic; Hybris
FIRST FRUITS (ἀπαρχαί), 16f., 23f., 28
FREEDOM (ἐλευθερία, σωτηρία), 42f., 46ff., 125ff., 176; autonomy clause of Peace of Callias, 144, 148ff.; Zeus Eleutherios, 50f., 126, 159, 176
HADRIAN, *xiii,* 30.
HARMODIUS, cf. Tyrannicides
HEGEMONY, Chapter III, 197ff.
HELLANICUS, 77, 82, 155, 173
HERODOTUS, *passim: xiii,* 3, 47, 52f., 60, 123, 128f., 140, 147, 153, 161, 173. Cf. the Index Locorum
HISTORIOGRAPHY, cf. Aelius Aristides, Rhetoric
Homeric Hymn to Demeter, 18, 20f.
HYBRIS, OF THE PERSIAN KING(S), PUNISHED BY ATHENS, 42, 44, 52ff., 75, 79, 108, 122f., 151ff. Cf. Callias, Peace of, rhetorical topic; Fear
INAROS, 108ff., 120, 124ff. Cf. Egypt, Libyans
Io, cf. Libyans
ISOCRATES, *passim: xiv, xvi,* 2ff., 17, 24f., 52, 58, 90ff., 109, 117f., 141, 146ff., 158, 173, 187ff., 197ff. Cf. the Index Locorum
JUSTIN (EPITOME OF TROGUS), 93, 109
LIBYANS, 107f., 112, 126ff. Cf. Egypt
LIVY, 5, 192
LUCIAN, 6f., 52, 174
LYCURGUS, ORATOR, 47, 58, 63, 88ff., 145, 148ff., 189. Cf. the Index Locorum
LYSIAS, 47, 88, 149, 154, 162, 187, 197. Cf. the Index Locorum
MARATHON, BATTLE OF, 42f., 45f., 55, 96, 140, 157, 174
Marmor Parium, 20, 26, 52
MYTHOLOGY, POLITICAL USE OF, cf. Triptolemus
PANYASSIS, 25
PAUSANIAS, 20, 183, 193
PENTECONTAETIA, *xv,* 3f., 8f., 18, 29, 40, 62ff., 156f., 173, 197.
PERICLES, 52ff., 85, 87, 115f., 158ff.; building policy, 22f., 29, 158ff., 182f. Cf. Congress Decree
PHASELIS, cf. Callias, Peace of
PHILOCHORUS, 26f., 29, 173
PHRYNICHUS, 53f.
PLATAEA, BATTLE OF, 45, 47, 56f., 60, 96; speech of Athenians before battle, *xiv,* 60, 152; Covenant of, 23, 47, 50, 158; Oath of, 23, 47, 158, 160

PLATO, *Menexenus*, xvii, 8, 17, 47, 57, 88, 117, 125, 128, 152ff., 173, 175, 188. Cf. the Index Locorum
PLUTARCH, 4, 52, 76ff., 95, 112ff., 120, 140, 145, 148ff., 158ff., 173f. Cf. the Index Locorum
POLYBIUS, 4, 192
RHETORIC (AND ORATORY), *passim:* historical truth ($ἀκρίβεια$, $ἀλήϑεια$), Introduction, Chapter I, 16ff., 46ff., 155f., 163, 172ff.; historical topoi, 46ff., 107f., 151ff., 174
SAITES, SAIS, cf. Libyans
SALAMIS, BATTLE OF, 43ff., 54, 56ff., 89, 96, 122, 140, 157, 174
SALLUST, 5
SOPHOCLES, 20ff., 29, 173
SUDA, 148
SPARTA, SPARTANS, *passim:* 39ff., 45, 143
TACITUS, 5
TANAGRA, BATTLE OF, 62ff., 118
THEMISTOCLES, 52f., 87, 114, 116f., 175
THEOPOMPUS, *xiv,* 4, 7, 76, 86f., 112ff., 130, 140, 162, 191f.
THERMOPYLAE, BATTLE OF, 44ff., 93
THUCYDIDES, *passim:* Introduction, 7, 40, 48ff., 62ff., 75ff., 86ff., 108ff., 140, 145, 161, 185f.; Epitaphios, *xiv,* 57, 61, 653; in opposition to the popular tradition, 7f., 48ff., 87f., 110ff., 128ff., 173.; Athenian speech at Sparta in Book I, *xiv,* 55, 58ff., 88, 156f., 187, 197ff. Cf. the Index Locorum
TRADITION(s), *passim:* oral, *xv,* 5ff., 30f., 80, 88, 94ff., 130f., 142, 151, 155f., Chapter VII; popular, Introduction, Chapter I, 17f., 25, 30, 42, 46f., 80, 84, 90ff., 94ff., 107f., 110, 117, 121, 124ff., 128ff., 140f., 145ff., 161f., Chapter VII
TRIPTOLEMUS, Chapter II, 39, 173
TYRANNICIDES, 5ff.
XENOPHON, *xiii,* 25, 29f., 173, 186.
XERXES, 39, 44f., 122ff., 152f., 176. Cf. Hybris
ZEUS ELEUTHERIOS, cf. Freedom